THE LEGACY OF VATICAN II

THE
LEGACY OF
VATICAN II

EDITED BY
Massimo Faggioli and
Andrea Vicini, SJ

Paulist Press
New York / Mahwah, NJ

Cover image by SWEviL/Shutterstock.com
Cover and book design by Lynn Else

Library of Congress Cataloging-in-Publication Data

The legacy of Vatican II / edited by Massimo Faggioli and Andrea Vicini, SJ.
    pages cm
    ISBN 978-0-8091-4922-3 (pbk. : alk. paper) — ISBN 978-1-58768-486-9 (ebook)
    1. Vatican Council (2nd : 1962-1965 : Basilica di San Pietro in Vaticano)
I. Faggioli, Massimo, editor.
    BX8301962 .L425 2015
    262`.52—dc23

                                                                    2014035569

ISBN 978-0-8091-4922-3 (paperback)
ISBN 978-1-58768-486-9 (e-book)

Published by Paulist Press
997 Macarthur Boulevard
Mahwah, New Jersey 07430

www.paulistpress.com

Printed and bound in the
United States of America

Contents

CONTENTS

Foreword

2013 was an important year at Boston College, where I serve as dean of the School of Theology and Ministry: it marked both the fiftieth anniversary of the opening of the Second Vatican Council, as well as the sesquicentennial of Boston College itself. After a series of conversations with two nationally respected scholars—Massimo Faggioli of the University of St. Thomas in St. Paul, Minnesota, and Andrea Vicini, SJ, of Boston College—about how best to mark these two epochal anniversaries, we agreed on a series of conversations among scholars who have studied both Vatican II and its long-term effects in the United States and internationally. Those conversations took place at Boston College on September 26, 2013, under the title "The Legacy of Vatican II."

Thanks largely to the careful planning and superb selection of participants by Massimo and Andrea, that September 26, 2013, conference was an embarrassment of riches for the invited guests who attended the discussions. Organized into three separate sessions, time was balanced in each session between the panelists and the discussions that followed between the panelists and the doctoral students and scholars from Boston and much further afield who were the invited guests for the event.

Papers presented by the first panel focused on the issue of "Jesuits and the Second Vatican Council." Dennis Doyle, David Hollenbach, Jared Wicks, and Susan Wood offered a rich array of stories, as well as in-depth analyses of scholarly work by a number of Jesuits who had, in one sense, been preparing for the Council decades before it was called: an American Jesuit like

John Courtney Murray as well as other key Jesuits at Vatican II like Augustin Bea, Henri de Lubac, and Otto Semmelroth. I served as moderator of this session, coordinating a lively conversation between panelists and the members of the audience that followed the panelist's presentations.

The second panel was organized around the topic of "Continuity and Change at the Second Vatican Council," and included scholars of the stature of Peter Hünermann, John O'Malley, Leslie Woodcock Tentler, and Christoph Theobald. Hünermann and Theobald addressed complex questions like the relationship of Vatican II to previous ecumenical councils—especially those of Trent and Vatican I—as well as the influence of the theological schools that had developed in Europe in the half century before 1963 to contextualize the theological work that was done at the Council, while Leslie Tentler cast further light on the history of the debate on contraception—a debate that took place during and after Vatican II but not on the floor of the conciliar debates. Andrea Vicini did an excellent job eliciting the back and forth among the four presenters and questions posed by audience members. The quality of questions generated by theology doctoral students in the audience was especially impressive, and augured well for the future of our craft.

The third session of the day addressed the broadest range of topics of panel presentations: John Baldovin talked about how the liturgies celebrated during the Council were themselves emblematic of the theological changes taking place during the conciliar sessions. Lisa Sowle Cahill discussed how the language and arguments of the Council shaped a new trajectory in moral theology and social ethics in the decades that followed. Richard Gaillardetz adumbrated the ecclesiological implications of the documents being produced, while Brad Hinze highlighted the relations between Vatican II and new Catholic communities promoting grassroots democracy. Massimo Faggioli masterfully guided a wide-ranging conversation that served as a perfect capstone of our day.

My thanks go to all who made possible the celebration of that wonderful event of the conference and the publication of its proceedings. I am delighted that the superb presentations offered during that day are now available to an even wider audience, thanks to our friends at Paulist Press who have generously agreed to publish this volume, especially Chris Bellitto, Bob Byrns, and Mark-David Janus, who have done impressive work before and during the fiftieth anniversary of Vatican II not only to keep alive the memory of the Council, but also to resume a much-needed conversation in the Church, in the academia, and in the public square.

Mark S. Massa, SJ
Dean, Boston College School of
Theology and Ministry

Massimo Faggioli

Introduction

Studies on Vatican II and the Future of Catholicism

The studies on Vatican II have shaped, in these last fifty years after the conclusion of the Council, a debate that has become an integral part of the history of modern Catholicism. The vast amount of books, articles, essays, and papers published on Vatican II is due to the fact that now in every corner of the world, theologians and historians analyze Vatican II as a theological and historical event, trying to understand its meaning in light of the "signs of the times." The very fact that theologians of the Catholic Church have been talking about the meaning of Vatican II for fifty years is one of the signs of the times of our Church.[1]

This volume is part of this vast debate, but the very *status quaestionis* about Vatican II has changed during the period of time between the moment Boston College School of Theology and Ministry decided to organize the conference in 2011 and the event of the conference, held in September 2013. When the Boston College conference on Vatican II was taking shape at the School of Theology and Ministry, in the spring of 2011, the original intent was to reexamine the contribution and the legacy of some of the most important Jesuits at Vatican II and to reflect on the value of Vatican II in the Church and the world of today. But between the first planning phase and the celebration of the conference in September 2013, the Catholic Church went through a historic moment of passage—with the resignation of Benedict XVI and the election of Pope Francis—that has directly to do with the history of Vatican II and of post–Vatican II: the resignation of the last pope who was a participant of Vatican II (as a *peritus*) and the election of the first pope who had no part in Vatican II, having been ordained priest in the Society of Jesus in 1969.

The conference of September 2013 took place in an extraordinary moment in the life of the Church and confirmed some of the intuitions articulated—either unconsciously or prospectively—in the spring of 2011 by the steering committee of the conference. The first intuition was about the role of Vatican II in the life of the Church: for anyone who has paid attention to the pontificate of Pope Francis, there is no doubt on the role (largely unstated, but impossible to miss) of Vatican II in his theological identity. The second intuition was about the role of the Society of Jesus in the post–Vatican II Church. The third element was related to the public relevance of Vatican II for the contemporary debate on major social issues.

This volume has no ambition to replace studies on the history of the Jesuits in the twentieth century, nor to replace the fundamental works on the history by Vatican II that have shaped our understanding of the Council in these last twenty years.[2] But it does have the ambition to invite to a dialogue on different issues that so far have been addressed separately: the contribution of a particular theological tradition and religious order at Vatican II; a specific set of theological issues (ecclesiology, liturgy, moral theology, ecumenism) related to a particular national and cultural landscape (the United States); the theological and historical relevance of the crossing of these elements for a Catholic Church that is more and more undeniably global.

At the beginning of a new pontificate—the first of a Jesuit, post–Vatican II priest who was elected pope in 2013—it is clear that the debate on the hermeneutic of Vatican II needs to be grounded in a solid historical appreciation of the Council. This necessity is more evident today when we have a separation (if not sometimes an opposition) between the *historical hermeneu-*

tic of the Council (what historians know and say about Vatican II), the *theological hermeneutic* (what use theologians make of Vatican II), and the *institutional hermeneutic* (what use the Church as an institution makes of Vatican II in its bureaucratic and governmental aspects). If it is true that the interpretation of Vatican II is not unavoidably linked with the interpretation of its aftermath, it is also true that most narratives of Vatican II (especially those against Vatican II) are linked with a nostalgic interpretation of the pre–Vatican II era and of its culture. In this, the scholarly debate cannot pretend to be detached from a big cultural and pedagogical issue in the Church of today, that is, communicating Vatican II to a new generation of Catholics (of seminarians, priests, and lay ministers especially) when the fathers (the council fathers and other fathers and mothers) are not there anymore to tell that story. It is not enough to read the texts of Vatican II, and not even to read them well, and it is not enough to read the *History of Vatican II* well: we must question those texts in light of these last fifty years of Church history.

In other words, without the event of Vatican II and the events of these last fifty years of Church history, the texts of the Council are silent—especially for the young generations of Catholics. Vatican II is not a text: it is an "event," a *gesto* (in Italian) with a "style," an "act" that begins with John XXIII and with *Gaudet Mater Ecclesia*. In this, the debate on Vatican II raises a serious methodological issue for Catholic culture and Catholic theology in postmodernity: that is, the issue of the compatibility between understanding Vatican II (and Catholicism in the twentieth century, for that matter) and the tendency to *deconstruct* Church history in a series of narrower fields of "Catholic studies" defined by gender, ethnic-national culture, local versus global, and so on.

The research on Vatican II has made huge steps forward in these last twenty-five years also thanks to the variety of methodologies and approaches: theological history of Vatican II (history of ideas); biographical approach (prosopography of Vatican II); social history of Vatican II (groups of influence, think tanks); history of canon law; history of bureaucracy (of the Roman Curia and of the elites of the Church); history of the mass media perception and transmission of the event; history of the "outsiders" (women of Vatican II, laypeople, ecumenical observers, etc.). The volume of the proceedings of the 2013 Vatican II conference at Boston College is part of this methodological debate, and demonstrates that it is possible to merge new methodological insights (such as the study of post–Vatican II liturgies and the research on the reception of the moral theology of the Council) and a classical "church history" approach (such as the contribution of individual theologians at Vatican II).

The authors of this volume play a significant role in the next step in the effort of the studies on the history and theology of Vatican II to engage various methodologies and issues related to Vatican II that have been so far neglected or "subcontracted" to different addressees (laity, religious orders, priests, liturgists, moral theologians, etc.) of a particular document or moment of Vatican II. Understanding the Church in the public arena needs a renewed understanding of the theology of Vatican II in the public arena. In this sense, this volume is part not only of the large literature on Vatican II, but of a larger conversation on the future of Catholicism in the modern world.

Notes

1. See Massimo Faggioli, *Vatican II: The Battle for Meaning* (Mahwah, NJ: Paulist Press, 2012) and the overview of the literature on Vatican II published in the journal *Cristianesimo nella Storia* starting in 2002.

2. Especially Giuseppe Alberigo, ed., *History of Vatican II*, English-language trans. ed. Joseph A. Komonchak, 5 vols. (Maryknoll, NY: Orbis, 1995– 2006). Second Italian edition with a new preface by Alberto Melloni (Bologna: Il Mulino, 2012–14); John W. O'Malley, *What Happened at Vatican II* (Cambridge, MA: Belknap Press of Harvard University Press, 2008).

Part I
THEMES
Continuity and Change
in Vatican II

1
_____

John W. O'Malley, SJ

Vatican II Revisited as Reconciliation
THE FRANCIS FACTOR

Vatican Council II opened over fifty years ago. This stark fact means that between then and now the Council has inexorably moved from experience, to memory, and finally, to history. For people in the world today under sixty, the Council is nothing more than an item in a history book or perhaps something they have heard their grandparents talk about. Pope Francis is the first pope in fifty years not to have participated in the Council. He marks the end of an era—and perhaps the beginning of a new one.

For us who study the Council, this situation offers an occasion to step back to take a bigger look at it. Instead of our usual practice of considering the Council's documents one by one without regard for the whole corpus, we can take a deep breath and ask ourselves what happened. We can in that way revisit the Council and then take account of the event that took place on March 13, 2013, the election as pope of Jorge Mario Bergoglio. That is what I will try to do in the pages that follow.

To provide the full perspective on the Council, we need even to step back from the sixteen-document corpus to take into consideration other official documents pertinent to Vatican II. Among them, for instance, is the "Message to the World" that the

Council issued on October 20, 1962, less than two weeks after it opened. The document spelled out clearly the basic framework within which the Council wanted to work:

> We urgently turn our thoughts to the problems by which human beings are afflicted today....Like Christ, we would have pity on the multitude heavily burdened by hunger, misery, and lack of education....As we understand our work, therefore, we would emphasize whatever concerns the dignity of the human person, whatever contributes to a genuine community of peoples.[1]

The "Message" did not come out of nowhere. When Pope John XXIII convoked the Council, he in gentle but firm ways gave it a direction. He had had an experience of "the world" wider and more direct than any pope for centuries. As a young priest, he served as medical orderly and chaplain in the Italian army during World War I. He afterward spent decades as papal diplomat among either predominantly Orthodox or Muslim populations. While stationed in Istanbul during World War II, he at firsthand experienced the plight of refugees from Nazi persecution and did his best to help them. He later performed well as nuncio in Paris at a most delicate moment for the Church in the immediate postwar years. Then before his election as pope, he served with distinction as bishop (technically, patriarch) of Venice.

We should not be surprised, therefore, that at the day of the Council's opening, October 11, 1962, he introduced the theme of reconciliation. In his address *Gaudet Mater Ecclesia* ("Mother Church Rejoices"), the pope indicated to the Council his hopes for it. We now know that Pope John wrote the address entirely on his own, revising it again and again. Every word was carefully chosen.[2] The "Message to the World" two weeks later is in fact best interpreted as the Council's first response to the pope's address.

When the address is looked at as a whole and put into the context of papal pronouncements of the previous century and a half, its force and distinctive character clearly emerge. To begin with, the pope distanced himself, and therefore the Council, from a scolding and suspicious approach toward "the world."[3] He expressed the hope that the Council would "face the future without fear." The Church should deal with both what was right and what was wrong in today's society in a positive way, "making use of the medicine of mercy rather than severity...demonstrating the validity of [the Church's] teaching rather than by condemnations." He thus raised the crucial question of the Council's style of discourse and specified it as "predominantly pastoral in character" because the Church, through the Council, "desires to show herself to be the loving mother of all, benign, patient, full of mercy and goodness."

People heard what they wanted to hear in the address, as the headlines the next day showed. Nonetheless, the majority in the Council, by which I mean at least 85 percent of the bishops, got the central point: the Council was to take a positive stance on issues as far as possible and to show the Church as a "benign and patient" institution. Although John did not use the word *reconciliation*, that is what he was talking about.

But the Council fathers did not have to wait until the Council opened to know what the pope wanted to accomplish. On January 25, 1959, when he announced his intention to convoke the Council, he specified two general goals for it. The first was to promote "the enlightenment, edification, and joy of the entire Christian people," and the second was to extend "a renewed cordial invitation to the faithful of the separated communities to participate with us in this quest for unity and grace, for which so many souls long in all parts of the world."[4] From the very first moment, therefore, he placed reconciliation squarely on the agenda.

John then established the Secretariat for Christian Unity. At first he seems to have intended that the Secretariat serve as not much more than a coordinating body for the so-called observers sent to the Council by the Protestant and Orthodox churches, but he soon began to expand its remit. Finally, shortly after the Council opened, he constituted it a full-fledged Commission of the Council, with the right to create and submit documents for action by the Council, just as the other Commissions did. By word and deed, therefore, Pope John made reconciliation a goal of the Council.

Vatican II was an enormously complex event. It cannot be reduced to simplistic formulas. Nonetheless, we must never forget that the documents of Vatican II are not a grab bag of discreet elements. Unlike the documents of previous Councils, those of Vatican II form a coherent unit. That is, certain themes and orientations run through them as common threads. These themes and orientations transcend the individual documents, even though they are derived from them. The documents of Vatican II deliver messages bigger than those of the documents considered in isolation from one another.

Given the Council's complexity, different approaches are needed to grasp its meaning. A fruitful approach, I believe, is to focus on two special characteristics of the Council. The first is to examine the crisis in Catholicism that the Council was forced to confront, and the second, as I have already intimated, is to examine the literary genre the Council employed to formulate its decrees. In the ways the Council developed these two characteristics, it coordinated them, which resulted in a message of reconciliation, the Council's ultimate finality. In what follows I will analyze these two characteristics, demonstrate their affinity with each other, and describe the significance of the result. In the brief, final section, I will suggest how Pope Francis early in his pontificate began to carry the result forward.

THE CRISIS OF MODERNITY

It is often said of Vatican II that, unlike previous ecumenical councils, it met without being faced with a crisis that demanded action. Pope Paul III, for instance, convoked the Council of Trent (1545–63) to deal with the crisis of the Reformation and the long-standing and insistent cry for the reform of the Church. Over a millennium earlier the Emperor Constantine convoked the first ecumenical council, Nicaea (325) to deal with the problem of Arianism that was causing widespread and heated controversy in the Church, dividing it especially in the East into two seemingly irreconcilable parties.

This assertion about Vatican II, however, is false on two counts. First, at least a few councils, such as Lateran I and II, met without an immediate crisis (or just after the crisis had been resolved). Second and most important, Vatican II did in fact face a crisis, even though that crisis did not explicitly figure in the generally adduced reasons for its convocation. The Council met in a period of a profound crisis not only for Catholicism but for all Christian churches. It was a crisis all the more serious for not being clearly perceived as such at the time—or at least not clearly named. Yet, the crisis was real, pervasive, and far-reaching in its ramifications—perhaps the most serious and radical in the history of Christianity. We can call it the crisis of modernity.

This is not to say that the fathers of the Council did not have some awareness of what was happening. They tended to speak of it in positive terms as "the new era" that was opening up for the Church and for humanity at large. Moreover, the documents they forged were meant to meet some of the challenges of the new era, as I will attempt to show. When we view the documents with this perspective, we see how the Council, both wittingly and unwittingly, tried to respond to the challenge.

The crisis had roots deep in history. It was early propelled on its way by the Scientific and Industrial Revolutions but took on its sharpest characteristics after the French Revolution, during the century and a half leading up to Vatican II. That is the period I have called "the long nineteenth century."[5] The Church in its official pronouncements during this era almost invariably assumed a sharply negative stance toward every aspect of "the modern world." True, as the twentieth century moved along, the Church (and here I mean principally the papacy) modified its stance in certain important instances, particularly during the pontificate of Pope Pius XII, but it never officially distanced itself from it. That changed with Vatican II. A stance of reconciliation replaced a stance of alienation.

"The modern world"—a phenomenon so complex as to be almost intractable! To try to deal with it I will limit myself to five aspects that are particularly pertinent to the Council. They are, in the order in which I will discuss them, (1) multiculturalism; (2) religious pluralism; (3) radical political and social shifts provoking a crisis of authority; (4) the emergence of a newly sharp historical consciousness, now applied even to sacred subjects; and (5) the social, economic, and cultural situations of "the men and women of today."

MULTICULTURALISM

The world has of course always been multicultural, but air travel, television, and forced migrations made it a fact of daily life that has only increased in intensity in the years since the Council. Moreover, in the 1960s and 1970s the violent end of colonialism and the resulting animus against Western cultural imperialism hit the Church's missionaries hard and raised profound questions about the degree they had acted as unofficial agents for their respective governments. The situation raised the symptomatic question of the role of Latin liturgy at the moment when the newly decolonized countries demanded recognition of the dignity of the usages of their cultures.

The Church had of course consistently presented itself as catholic in the sense of embracing all peoples. Although there was considerable truth in the claim, Catholicism was so strongly imprinted with the culture of the West as to seem identical with it. There had been important efforts to mitigate the problem, as with the Jesuits in China in the seventeenth century led by Matteo Ricci. The Jesuits even won permission to celebrate mass in Chinese, and they published a Chinese missal. In the eighteenth century, however, the Holy See condemned such experiments. During the nineteenth and early twentieth centuries, both Catholic and Protestant missionaries saw themselves as bearing "the white man's burden" of bringing "civilization," that is, Western ways, to their flocks. It was this approach that the Council gently but firmly repudiated.

The very first document of the Council, the constitution "On the Sacred Liturgy," *Sacrosanctum Concilium*, in effect directed the Church to break out of its Eurocentrism and to admit other cultures as partners. *Sacrosanctum* is crucially important for significant issues beyond what it prescribes for liturgy. Among those issues was the crisis of multiculturalism, to which it responded in unmistakably clear terms. It set the Council on its course when it affirmed, "The church cultivates and fosters the qualities and talents of different races and nations," and it admits their customs "into the liturgy itself, provided they harmonize with its true and authentic spirit" (no. 37).[6] The idea recurs in the decree "On the Church's Missionary Activity," *Ad Gentes,* as when it stipulates, "The faith should be imparted by means of a well adapted catechesis and celebrated in a liturgy that is in harmony with the character of the people" (no. 19).[7]

RELIGIOUS PLURALISM

The most obvious and direct acts of reconciliation of the Council were the decrees "On Ecumenism," *Unitatis Redintegratio,* and "On Non-Christian Religions," *Nostra Aetate.* The former opens, "The restoration of unity among Christians is one of the principle concerns of the Second Vatican Council" (no. 1).[8] It goes on to tell Catholics to respect the beliefs of those not in communion with the Church, and it prescribes a process of dialogue with them. Such steps might seem cautious and minimal, but they amounted to a dramatic reversal of the policy of belittling and condemning other Christian bodies and of counseling Catholics to avoid as far as possible all contact with them. The Code of Canon Law (1917) forbade Catholic participation in any non-Catholic religious service, even weddings and funerals. As canon 1258 categorically stated, "In no way is it permitted for the faithful to take part in any way in non-Catholic services" (no. 1258).[9]

In the middle of the seventeenth century, the conclusion of the catastrophic Thirty Years' War brought to a close a century of bloody conflicts between different Christian churches waged in the name of the God of love. From that point forward the Catholic Church generally eschewed violence as a means of settling religious differences, but until the eve of the Council,

Catholic theologians and apologists routinely denigrated other churches and cast them in the worst possible light. On a higher and less contemptuous level but still insisting upon quarantine, Pope Pius XI in 1928 in the encyclical *Mortalium Animos* forbade Catholic participation in the ecumenical movement that had been gaining in importance since the beginning of the century and wanted to enlist Catholics in its cause.

The decree of Vatican II on ecumenism signaled a change of 180 degrees, so much so that a small minority during and after the Council denounced it as heretical. However, as the result of decades of study and conversation carried on semi-officially and behind the scenes in the 1940s and 1950s, the Council accepted the decree with unexpected ease. After centuries of alienation, which seemed only to exasperate an already-bad situation, the time had arrived for seeking common ground.

Nostra Aetate did not enjoy the same easy course in the Council as did *Unitatis Redintegratio.* The opposition to it was so fierce that it was almost withdrawn from the agenda.[10] John XXIII himself had been responsible for putting it there. Out of his deep concern about anti-Semitism and Christian responsibility regarding the Holocaust, he mandated that the Council consider a document "On the Jews." No doubt, it was the growing awareness of the horror of the Holocaust that for many prelates at the Council made a statement imperative.

In its early drafts, therefore, *Nostra Aetate* dealt exclusively with the Jews. Objections were raised to it on theological grounds but also on political. The prospect of the document stirred up fear in Arab countries that this was a step toward Vatican recognition of the state of Israel, which up to that point the Vatican had not done. The Council was finally able to convince them that *Nostra Aetate* had nothing to do with politics, and meanwhile exegetes and theologians were able to convince an overwhelming majority of bishops of the theological acceptability of the document; the Jews were not an accursed people. With such problems resolved, *Nostra Aetate* won approval, but only after it was expanded to include other non-Christian religions, most notably the Muslims. The small minority in the

Council that rejected *Unitatis Redintegratio* rejected this document even more fiercely.

The decree finally and categorically marked the official end of Catholic-inspired pogroms against the Jews and holy crusades against the Muslims. Few decrees of the Council seem more timely today in our post-9/11 era. *Nostra Aetate* sounds a note of reason and compassion. It is the diametrical opposite of hate-inspired polemics, and it invests the Catholic Church and individual Catholics with a newly minted role as agents of reconciliation in the present tense international situation. The Catholic way is not to respond to violence with more violence but to wash the feet of those perceived to be one's enemies.

RADICAL POLITICAL
AND SOCIAL SHIFTS

With its cry of "Liberty! Equality! Fraternity!" the French Revolution upset the hierarchical paradigm that had undergirded Western society until that moment, and it especially challenged even mitigated versions of the divine right of kings. It toppled rulers from their thrones. If those rulers returned, it was often for a limited time and surely with rights and duties drastically trimmed. In mid-century, furthermore, Marx and Engels issued their rallying cry in the *Communist Manifesto*, "Workers of the world, unite! You have nothing to lose but your chains!" Thus took place a series of social, economic, and political revolutions massive in their implications and without parallel in the history of the world. It provoked a profound crisis of authority. Who is in charge here? Whence is authority to govern derived? What are the limits of even legitimate authority?

The papacy had stock answers to these questions, and it viewed the changes that were taking place as inversions of the divinely ordered structure of the universe. Authority flowed from the highest to the middlemost, from the middlemost to the lowest. *Liberty* was a bad word. But bit by bit, especially beginning with Leo XIII, the popes' attitude began to soften. When Leo, in his encyclical *Rerum Novarum* (1891), conceded that workers had the right to organize to secure their rights, he shocked and scandalized the Catholic social elite. Pius XII's Christmas address (1944) broadcast worldwide, marked the first time a pope ever positively praised democracy as a political form, which he described as particularly "compatible with the dignity and liberty of citizens."[11]

By the end of World War II, liberty had begun to work its way into standard Catholic vocabulary. But did liberty extend to the choice of one's religion? The Holy Office adamantly denied that it did. It still clung firmly to the ideal of the confessional state, in which the state supported the Church, even to the point of enforcing civil disabilities against members of other churches and religions.

The Council's declaration "On Religious Liberty," *Dignitatis Humanae*, responded to this situation and in so doing reconciled the Church to the issue of freedom of conscience that had become so paramount in modern discussions of the role of the state in religious matters. Like *Nostra Aetate*, this document had an especially troubled history in the Council, and like *Nostra Aetate*, its future at one point seemed in such danger that its sponsors considered withdrawing it from the agenda.

Discussions about religious liberty often seemed to assume that democracy was the form of government most likely to promote and ensure it. Implicit in such an assumption was that authority to govern did not descend from on high but was the result of consent freely given. The question was inevitable: What did this mean for the structures of authority in the Church? Of course, the Church was divinely founded on the rock of Peter, whose successors held the primacy among all bishops. That much was unquestioned and unquestionable. But in what fashion was the primacy to be exercised? That was the question the Council undertook to answer.

For several decades before the Council, scholars had begun to question the strongly ultramontane interpretations of Church history that predominated through most of "the long nineteenth century." They had begun to show that through the first millennium and beyond the Church had for the most part functioned in a synodal fashion, with the papacy generally intervening in that process only as the final arbiter in disputes. Moreover, in a remarkable study published in 1955, Brian Tierney rescued "conciliarism" from the categorical rejection of it in vogue after the rise of ultramontanism.[12] He showed that medieval canonists assumed that responsibility for the good of the Church was distributed among various offices and corporations in which the episcopal office reigned above all others. Each of these offices had its own intrinsic (not delegated) authority. Tierney implicitly showed that the conciliarism operative at the Council of Constance (1414–18), which deposed two popes and forced the resignation of a third, was an instrument the bishops used not against the papacy but to save it from its own folly.

By the time of the Council, the stage had been set for the constitution "On the Church," *Lumen Gentium*, to propose to the Council the doctrine of episcopal collegiality. That doctrine, solidly based on the Tradition of the Church, was not an attempt to democratize the Church in order to make it more amenable to modern sensibilities. Nonetheless, those sensibilities acted as a catalyst to bring the teaching to the fore, and in fact, the teaching helped make the authority structure of the Church seem less like a vestige of the most extreme forms of divine-right monarchy of the seventeenth century.

HISTORICAL CONSCIOUSNESS

The recovery of the doctrine of collegiality in the decades before the Council points to a sharpened sense of historical consciousness, of discrepancy between the past and the present, as one of the most salient intellectual characteristics of the long nineteenth century. During this period a historical approach to virtually every subject, including sacred subjects, took deep hold. This development challenged with seemingly devastating force the boast that "the Catholic Church does not change." Historians showed how the Church had in fact changed. In 1932, for instance, the Austrian Jesuit Josef Andreas Jungmann published a book confirming that the form of the sacrament of penance requiring private confession of sins as practiced in the medieval and modern Church was unknown in the apostolic and patristic eras.[13] Although Pope Pius IX defined the dogma of the Immaculate Conception of the Virgin Mary in 1854, an act that required Catholics to accept it as an article of apostolic faith, historians convincingly showed that the dogma was unknown as such until the high Middle Ages. How was the Church to deal with such phenomena?

Perhaps even more troubling was the increasingly widespread acceptance of Darwin's *Origin of the Species* (1859). What did this do to the story of Adam and Eve and the biblical account of the origin of the human race? How was it possible to save the authority of the sacred text in the face of such criticisms? How was it possible to assert continuity with the apostolic past in the face of ever-mounting evidence of discontinuity with it?

Awareness of historical change in its acute modern form developed in the years before the Council as a pervasive and constitutive element in the "crisis of modernity" that faced the Council. Pope John had himself implicitly introduced the issue when he sounded *aggiornamento*, a form of change, as one of the Council's principal tasks, and, to the Council's credit, it did not dodge the issue. The word *change* itself (*mutatio*) and other words indicating change appear prominently in the very first sentence of the very first document of the Council, *Sacrosanctum Concilium*: "It is the intention of this holy council to *improve* (*augere*) the standard of daily Christian living among Catholics, to *adapt* (*accommodare*) those structures that are subject to *change* (*mutationes*) so as better to meet the needs of our time."

Change became a theme of the Council and a fundamental issue under the issues that reached a climax in the constitution "On the Church in the Modern World," *Gaudium et Spes*. In that document words like *progress, development,* and even *evolution* appear frequently, characteristically, and in a positive sense. John Henry Newman's *Essay on the Development of Christian Doctrine* (1845) provided the Council with its greatest help in this regard. Newman used different analogies to show how teachings could evolve while remaining fundamentally true to their origin.

Vatican II did not solve the relationship between continuity and discontinuity in the Tradition of the Church, but it took heed of the problem and recognized that change is just as important in trying to understand the Tradition as is continuity. Providing a theoretical solution to the problem of change within continuity fell outside the Council's agenda and even outside its competence. For the Church, as for many other organizations, this problem does not easily yield to theoretical solutions, even though theologians and other scholars need to analyze it as best they can. The merit of the Council is that it reconciled the Church to the problem in the sense of recognizing its existence, taking account of its importance, and providing a few examples of where it has operated in the long Tradition of the Church.

"THE MEN AND WOMEN OF TODAY"

Although this reconciliation pervades the Council's documents from beginning to end, it most clearly emerges in *Gaudium et Spes*. About that document we need to note two important facts. First, the title of the document is "The Church *in* the Modern World," not the Church for the modern world, nor the Church against the modern world. In other words, the Council recognizes as a fact of life that each and every one of us, even Church members, constitute the modern world. We cannot in any way step out of that reality, even if we want to. Therefore, neither can the Church step out of it.

Second, for the first time ever in the history of the Church, a Council document addresses not Church members but "all humanity." As it says, "The second Vatican council now immediately addresses itself not just to the church's own daughters and sons and all who call upon the name of Christ but to people everywhere....It sees this world as the world of men and women, the whole human family in its total environment; the stage of human history notable for its toil, its tragedies, and triumphs, the world that Christians believe has been established and kept in being by the creator's love,...liberated [from sin] by Christ...so that it could be transformed according to God's purpose and come to its fulfillment" (no. 2).[14]

Although the Church-world relationship was not on the agenda when the Council opened, it had clearly emerged by the end of the Council's first year. No wonder, for it took up in an explicit way the theme of reconciliation with the modern world that Pope John proposed in his opening address. Beyond recognizing that the Church is now and ever has been "in the world," the document takes the further step of recognizing the consequences of that fact: the Church and world are reciprocally dependent: "The church, as at the same time an identifiable group and a spiritual community, proceeds on its way with the whole of humanity and shares the world's earthly lot, while also being a leaven and sort of soul of human society" (no. 40).[15] *Gaudium et Spes* then elaborates on how the Church contributes to the well-being of the world but, most remarkably, then elaborates on what the Church receives from the world (no. 44).

When the Council directed *Gaudium et Spes* to all persons of good will, whether believers or not, it extended reconciliation to its ultimate limits. It is therefore a fitting way to conclude our examination of five ways in which the Council tried to respond to "the crisis of modernity." John XXIII's opening address sounded the theme of reconciliation but in an understated and altogether generic way. The Council took up reconciliation as a fundamental orientation and imbued it with remarkable scope. It extended it to the Church's relationship to non-Western cultures; to non-Catholic Christians; to non-Christian believers; to the new economic, social, and political situation of the modern world; to the problem of change; and in its final document, to "all humanity."

THE STYLE OF DISCOURSE ADOPTED BY THE COUNCIL

I have written extensively on this topic, and therefore I can be relatively brief here.[16] To understand the turn the Council took concerning the style of its documents, we must return again to Pope John's opening address. In it, as I mentioned, he told the Council to make "use of the medicine of mercy rather than of severity...demonstrating the validity of [the Church's] teaching rather than by condemnations,"[17] and he thus raised the question of the style the Council should use in formulating its decisions.

It is understandable that interpreters have generally been content to designate the Council's style as pastoral and leave it at that. Yes, indeed, the style was pastoral, but that does not tell us much. We can and need to be more specific. I argue that the dominant and most characteristic style is a form of what is technically known as epideictic or demonstrative rhetoric, in other words, panegyric. The choice of that form fosters the emergence of a distinctive vocabulary, which after form is the second element that determines the style of Vatican II. The third is the intertextual character of the documents; that is, they build upon one another, paraphrase one another, and qualify one another, and in so doing bind them together into a thematic unity. To summarize: the three constitutive elements of the style of Vatican II are form, vocabulary, and intertextuality, each of which helps determine the other two to create a coherent corpus.

It was the ancient theorists of rhetoric, among whom the better known today are Cicero and Quintilian, who isolated and described the epideictic category.[18] For these theorists, rhetoric means first and foremost the art of oratory. It was the art of persuasion—that is, *the art of winning consensus*, the art of inducing an audience to work together in a common cause or share appreciation for certain ideals and values. It was the art of persuading audiences to reconcile their differences so that they might contribute to something greater. To that extent, rhetoric was the art of reconciliation.

Epideictic was one of the several instantiations of rhetoric, one of its genres. It was generally exercised in a ceremonial situation where the purpose was to win appreciation for persons or institutions or to denigrate them so as to make them repugnant.

Epideictic is a fancy name for something we experience in daily life, even though its practitioners may not recognize that they are conforming to ancient theory. We experience it, for instance, sometimes in homilies but certainly in every funeral eulogy and in every patriotic speech. The most sublime instance

17

of it in American history is Lincoln's *Gettysburg Address*.[19] Lincoln was not trying to accuse the Confederacy of perfidy, nor was he arguing that the war was just. He was trying simply to raise appreciation for what was at stake in the war and present it as a noble enterprise, worthy of the great cost.

Like the man who did not know he had been speaking prose all his life, the prelates at Vatican II did not know they were writing epideictic. But that is not a problem if we pay heed to the ancient theorists on rhetoric. Those theorists maintained that their categories were simply a codification of life as they observed it. In other words, epideictic existed before the theorists named and classified it. I would even venture to say that every society and culture throughout history has practiced it in some form or other. We human beings want to praise good and noble things.

How did the Council come to adopt that form? On the very first working day of the Council, October 22, 1962, Cardinal Josef Frings of Cologne explicitly brought the question to the floor when he commended *Sacrosanctum* "for its modest and truly pastoral style, full of Holy Scripture and the Fathers of the Church."[20] The prelates at the Council wanted therefore to take a positive approach, and they knew that that meant abandoning, or at least radically modifying, the way most of the draft documents prepared for them had been formulated.

To understand the problem we need to look at how previous councils conceived of themselves. Even though there were important councils before Nicaea, we can take Nicaea as our paradigm. It is fair to say that when Emperor Constantine convoked it, he saw it as in some measure the ecclesiastical equivalent of the Roman Senate. What the Senate did was make laws and render verdicts in high-level criminal cases. It was concerned with public order in the empire. Nicaea was concerned with public order within the Church, whether regarding proper teaching or proper discipline, especially discipline of the clergy. It therefore issued laws prescribing or proscribing certain behaviors, and it heard the criminal case against Arius. Laws invariably carry penalties for nonobservance, and negative verdicts in criminal cases carry even heavier penalties.

With Nicaea the pattern was set. Although in pursuing the

goal of public order, later councils adopted a number of literary forms, the most prevalent was the canon, a short ordinance prescribing or proscribing some action. Canons commonly ended with an anathema, that is, a sentence of excommunication. When Vatican II opened, the canon was far from being an irrelevant relic of the past. The Roman synod that Pope John convoked in 1960, often considered at the time as a "dress rehearsal" for Vatican II, issued 755 canons. This language-tradition was precisely what the Council wanted to avoid. But what to put in its place? The question continued to be raised through the whole of the first period, October to December 1962. At that point, however, the Council was clearer about what it did not want than about what it wanted to replace it.

Nonetheless, by the opening of the second period in September 1963, Vatican II had begun to find its voice, as expressed especially in the first chapter of *Lumen Gentium*, the first document on the agenda for that period. In witting or unwitting homage to Henri de Lubac's *Méditation sur l'Église* (in English, *Splendor of the Church*), the first chapter of the document bore the same title as the first chapter of de Lubac's book, "The Mystery of the Church." Just as important, in a general way, that chapter, plus most of the rest of the text, adopted the literary style of de Lubac's book, which was really a book on ecclesiology. The chapter, for instance, almost overflows with images of the Church and its members that suggest fecundity, dignity, abundance, goodness, safe haven, welcome, communion, tenderness, and warmth. It was thus a dramatic break with the legalistic and even polemical style of ecclesiological textbooks. De Lubac was inspired by the fathers of the Church. We must recall that the system of education in which the fathers were trained from their earliest days was rhetorical.[21] Rhetoric was the culmination of the education that almost universally prevailed in the early Christian centuries. For de Lubac and others like him, this rhetorical style provided a welcome alternative to the dry, cerebral, dialectical style prevalent in theology at the time, which was a run-down form of neo-Scholasticism. To that extent, epideictic was also an alternative to the Scholastic underpinnings of the theological enterprise of the times.

Consonant with the new style was *Lumen Gentium*'s adoption of *dialogue* as one of its most characteristic words, a word no previous Council had ever uttered and a striking indication of the new vocabulary the new form would introduce into the documents of the Council from this point forward. The vocabulary consisted in words of friendship, partnership, reciprocity, mutual esteem, human dignity, and a Christian optimism about the possibilities of the contemporary situation.

The vocabulary was further propelled forward by two concepts *Lumen Gentium* introduced into the Council that henceforth became Council themes, even though they were at times hotly contested. The first was the description of the Church as "the people of God," an important qualification of the then-prevalent image of the Church as a monarchy, a strictly top-down institution. The second, clearly consonant with the first, was episcopal collegiality, that is, the doctrine that bishops share responsibility with the pope for the governance of the universal Church.

Meanwhile, the decrees "On Ecumenism" and "On Non-Christian Religions" abandoned, as mentioned, the faultfinding attitude and vocabulary of previous ecclesiastical documents and theological textbooks. In the declaration "On Religious Liberty," *Dignitatis Humanae*, the primacy of conscience in moral decision making emerged with a clarity new in the history of ecumenical councils. As a striking instance of the intertextual character of the Council's documents, *Gaudium et Spes* carried the theme of conscience further. It described it as "the secret core and sanctuary of the human person" and as "the interior law inscribed on our hearts" (no. 16).[22]

The adoption of epideictic rhetoric had an important theological repercussion. It implicitly inclined the Council to favor a theology more incarnational than eschatological, a theology more inclined to emphasize the goodness of creation and the incarnation than the fall and the atonement, a theology closer to Thomas Aquinas than Martin Luther, more reminiscent of the fathers of the Eastern Church than Saint Augustine—more inclined to reconciliation with human culture than alienation from it. In that theology, grace is not alien to nature but perfects it. It is reconciled with nature.

The adoption of epideictic meant that the documents of the Council, when viewed as a single, coherent corpus, called for a significant attitude shift and, consequently, a behavior shift—on the part of all Catholics and especially on the part of leaders of the Church. It wanted to forge a certain personality for the Church, a personality that radiated benignity, patience, and a limitless abundance of mercy and goodness, to paraphrase the words of Pope John. Aspects of the attitudinal and behavioral shifts characteristic of that personality can be expressed as follows:

from commands to invitations
from threats to persuasion
from coercion to conscience
from monologue to dialogue
from sin obsession to recognition of dignity
from top down to shared
from ruling to serving
from exclusion to inclusion
from hostility to friendship
from rivalry to partnership
from faultfinding to search for common ground
from contempt to appreciation
from behavior modification to inner appropriation
    of values.

In summary,

from alienation to reconciliation.

THE FRANCIS FACTOR

With the election to the papacy of Jorge Mario Bergoglio, reconciliation overnight assumed a prominence in papal agenda that it had not had since the pontificate of John XXIII. Although the popes in the intervening decades kept the ideal alive in certain ways and in varying degrees, none made it as central to their agenda as Pope Francis did in the early months after his election.

While Vatican II was in session, Bergoglio was a young Jesuit in far-away Argentina. Everything he knew or learned about the Council was at best secondhand. Nonetheless, his words and deeds as pope have indicated that he fully interiorized the Council's basic orientation. Perhaps his nonparticipation has in fact been an advantage. It can be argued that his predecessors could never fully extricate themselves from the battles they fought in the Council. Francis is free of those battles and those memories. He now seems implicitly to be asking us to step back, to put behind us the memories of liturgical wars, doctrinal wars, and other wars in which we have been engaged in the past fifty years, and now to turn our gaze outward. He invites us to revisit the Council and to see it with fresh eyes.

Just how Jorge Mario Bergoglio developed into the kind of person he is has already been the subject of a number of studies.[23] He has himself spoken frankly about how much he has changed and developed over the course of the years. Fascinating though we might find the unfolding of his life story, it is less important than the kind of person he has turned out to be and the kind of Church of which he hopes to be the living exemplar.

He set the pattern while archbishop of Buenos Aires, most notably in the dialogue he conducted with Rabbi Abraham Skorka.[24] In the history of the Church no other pope has ever in his life sat down with a non-Christian to have a one-on-one conversation about each other's religious beliefs. The conversation with Rabbi Skorka was not a single encounter but went on for months and covered a range of issues. It was carried on as a genuine dialogue, that is, not an attempt to convert the other but simply to understand him and to appreciate why he believed as he did.

When, shortly after his election, he created the commission of eight cardinals from around the world to advise him about a wide range of Church matters, especially the reform of the Roman Curia, he seemed to suggest that dialogue within the Church would be as prominent a feature of his pontificate as dialogue with those outside the Church. As strictly advisory, the commission does not quite fulfill what the Council intended by ratifying the doctrine of episcopal collegiality, but it seems to be a first step in furthering the teaching of the Council.

Pope Francis's deeds thus speak even louder than his words. When, just a few weeks after he was elected, he on Holy Thursday washed the feet of the Muslim woman, a convicted criminal, he sent a powerful message. Even more powerful was his trip on July 8, 2013, to the island of Lampedusa. It was the first time since his election that he ventured outside Rome. He went there to comfort the African refugees in their despair and in their grief over the tragic loss of life of others seeking haven there. In words unusually harsh for him, the pope afterward excoriated the "globalization of indifference" of which the world's indifference to the Lampedusa tragedy was but an instance.

The pope is showing us how we must revisit Vatican II. In a world wracked by discord, war, threat of nuclear proliferation, hate-spewing blogs, and a "globalization of indifference" toward the suffering of others, even when it is on a massive scale, he takes seriously the new mission of reconciliation the Council gave the Church. He takes seriously the Church's oldest and most fundamental mission, which the Council, following the lead given by Pope John XXIII, tried simply to update: the mission to show the Church to be "the loving mother of all, benign, patient, full of mercy and goodness."

Notes

1. The official text is to be found in *Acta Synodalia Sacrosancti Concilii Vaticani II*, 52 vols. (Vatican City: Typis Polyglottis Vaticanis, 1970–99), I/1, 230–32, my translation.

2. See Alberto Melloni, *Papa Giovanni: Un cristiano e il suo concilio* (Turin: Giulio Einaudi, 2009), 258–71.

3. The official text is to be found in *Acta Synodalia*, I/1, 166–75.

4. See Angelo Giuseppe Roncalli–Giovanni XXIII, *Pater amabilis: Agenda del pontefice, 1958–63*, ed. Mauro Velati, Edizione nazionale dei diari di Angelo Giuseppe Roncalli–Giovanni XXIII, 7 (Bologna: Istituto per le scienze religiose, 2007), 25.

5. See John W. O'Malley, *What Happened at Vatican II* (Cambridge, MA: Harvard University Press, 2008), 53–92.

6. Norman P. Tanner, ed., *Decrees of the Ecumenical Councils*, 2 vols. (Washington, DC: Georgetown University Press, 1990), 2:828. On the broader significance of the document, see Massimo Faggioli, *True Reform: Liturgy and Ecclesiology in "Sacrosanctum Concilium"* (Collegeville, MN: Liturgical Press, 2012).

7. Tanner, *Decrees*, 2:1027–28.

8. Ibid., 2:908.

9. *Codex Iuris Canonici* (Vatican City: Typis Polyglottis Vaticanis, [c. 1918]), 423.

10. See, e.g., Giovanni Miccoli, "Two Sensitive Issues: Religious Freedom and the Jews," in Giuseppe Alberigo, ed., *History of Vatican II*, trans. Joseph A. Komonchak, 5 vols. (Maryknoll, NY: Orbis, 1995–2006), 4:135–93. On the general background, see now John Connelly, *From Enemy to Brother: The Revolution in Catholic Teaching on the Jews, 1933–1965* (Cambridge, MA: Harvard University Press, 2012).

11. See *Acta Apostolicae Sedis*, 37 (1945): 10–12.

12. See Brian Tierney, *Foundations of the Conciliar Theory: The Contribution of the Medieval Canonists from Gratian to the Great Schism* (Cambridge: Cambridge University Press, 1955).

13. See Josef Andreas Jungmann, *Die lateinischen Bussriten in ihrer geschichtlichen Entwicklung* (Innsbruck: Rauch, 1932).

14. Tanner, *Decrees*, 2:1069.

15. Ibid., 2:1093.

16. See, e.g., O'Malley, *What Happened*, 43–52, 305–13. For important background, see John W. O'Malley, *Praise and Blame in Renaissance Rome: Rhetoric, Doctrine, and Reform in the Sacred Orators of the Papal Court, c. 1450–1521* (Durham, NC: Duke University Press, 1979), 36–76; and John W. O'Malley, *Four Cultures of the West* (Cambridge, MA: Harvard University Press, 2004), 127–77.

17. Roncalli, *Pater Amabilis*, 25.

18. Still basic is Theodore C. Burgess, "Epideictic Literature," *Studies in Classical Philology* 5 (1922): 89–261. See also, e.g., George A. Kennedy, *The Art of Persuasion in Greece* (London: Routledge and Kegan Paul, 1965), especially 152–205.

19. See Garry Wills, *Lincoln at Gettysburg: The Words That Remade America* (New York: Simon and Schuster, c1992).

20. *Acta Synodalia*, I/1, 309–10.

21. See, e.g., Henri I. Marrou, *A History of Education in Antiquity*, trans. George Lamb (New York: Sheed & Ward, 1956); Henri I. Marrou, *Saint Augustin et la fin de la culture antique* (Paris: E. de Boccard, 1958); and O'Malley, *Four Cultures*, 127–77.

22. Tanner, *Decrees*, 2:1077.

23. See, e.g., Sergio Rubin and Francesca Ambrogetti, *Pope Francis: Conversations with Jorge Bergoglio* (New York: G. P. Putnam's Sons, 2013); Paul Vallely, *Pope Francis: Untying the Knots* (New York: Continuum, 2013); and Alberto Melloni, *Il Conclave di Papa Francesco*, (Rome: Istituto della Enciclopedia Italiana, 2013), 64–95; and Austen Ivereigh, *The Great Reformer: Francis and the Making of a Radical Pope* (New York: Henry Holt and Company, 2014).

24. Jorge Mario Bergoglio and Abraham Skorka, *On Heaven and Earth: Pope Francis on Faith, Family, and the Church in the Twenty-first Century*, trans. Diego F. Rosemberg (New York: Image, 2013).

2

_____

Christoph Theobald, SJ

The Principle of
Pastorality at Vatican II

CHALLENGES OF A
PROSPECTIVE INTERPRETATION
OF THE COUNCIL[1]

Today, a "prospective" interpretation of the conciliar event and of the work of Vatican II is demanded because of the cultural changes, sometimes called "second revolution,"[2] that separate us from the Council's time and force us to change our relationship with the Council. The main task is not anymore to read the documents, which are marked by the context of those years, in order to draw from them a fairly complete *teaching* that, then, we would need to *apply*. Today's main challenge is to enter more deeply into the "ways of proceeding" *or* "the way of proceeding" that the Council was able to invent and that may be designated by the term *pastorality*. The emphasis on this "way," or on this *modus*, allows us to avoid any confusion between different cultural situations. At the same time, it allows us to address our own confusions in light of the Council's achievements. This is possible because we become aware that our own confusions are situated within a long time frame, which, by letting aside the modernist's crisis, dates back to the way in which Catholicism was shaped during the modern era.

26

I will briefly return to this historic change after explaining the term *pastorality* and after having showed how, through a genetic vision of the Church in history and society, at least sketched in the last conciliar texts, a kind of "generative grammar"[3] for addressing the challenges that are ours was in the making.

THE EXPLANATION OF "PASTORAL STYLE" BY THE COUNCIL

If we want to understand the principle of pastorality of Vatican II, we should not limit ourselves to the few statements of the famous opening speech of John XXIII that invited the Council's fathers to *"measure everything according to the forms and proportions of a Magisterium with a mainly pastoral character."*[4] It is also necessary to analyze—historically—the process of *conciliar* reception of this principle and show how it becomes the magnet that attracts various texts and textual groups of the Council to form a real *corpus*, "open," as we shall see. Three aspects gradually imposed themselves on the self-understanding of Vatican II:[5]

1. During the first period (1962–63), the Council's assembly understands that it is necessary to abandon the juxtaposition between "doctrinal" and "pastoral" and to aim at presenting the Catholic truth in a style that makes *possible* its "reception" by our contemporaries.
2. In the second and third period (1963–64), the Council realizes even more forcefully that introspection. It also understands which type of "reform" the Church must accept to propose and to present the gospel in a credible and an acceptable manner. We find this perspective of a permanent self-reform in the "Constitution on the Church" (*Lumen Gentium*) and the "Decree on Ecumenism" (*Unitatis Redintegratio* 6).

   Thus if, in various times and circumstances, there have been deficiencies in moral conduct or in church discipline, or even in the way that Church teaching has been formulated—*to be carefully distinguished from the deposit of faith itself*—these can and should be set right at the opportune moment (*UR* 6).

3. It was not until 1965 that appeared a third aspect of the principle of pastorality: a new attention to the historical and cultural roots of the *recipients* of the gospel and the discovery that revelation is entirely historical and therefore subject to continual reinterpretation *according to the situation* of those to whom it is transmitted. The Pastoral Constitution *Gaudium et Spes* (no. 44) talks about a "proper way to proclaim the revealed word (*accommodata praedicatio*) which must remain the law of all evangelization (*lex omnis evangelizationis*)," and number 22 of the "Decree on Missionary Activity" *Ad Gentes* makes explicit this "law":

To achieve this goal, it is necessary that in each major socio-cultural area, such theological speculation should be encouraged, in the light of the universal Church's Tradition, as may *submit to a new scrutiny the words and deeds which God has revealed*, and which have been set down in Sacred Scripture and explained by the Fathers and by the magisterium. (*AG* 22).

The intrinsic and reversible relationship between the gospel and context that appears here is the real reason why the process of "*measuring everything according to the forms and proportions* of a Magisterium mainly pastoral" is not completed at the end of the Council and should, instead, be claimed once again and continued locally and globally, every time a new historical context requires it. The Council's corpus is "suspended" because of the *effective* process of contextual interpretation of the gospel.

Moreover, the Council codifies the fundamental structure, the *lex* of this process of contextual interpretation of the gospel. Hence, we can affirm that this process is "open" (remaining at the same time in relation to its matrix that is the biblical corpus). The inevitable and felicitous contextual pluralization of the figures of Christianity, which depends on this historical and cultural "openness" of the corpus, could be obscured by a Catholic legitimate concern for unity. However, the global *vision* that the Council effectively proposes to those who will receive the Council has a "genetic side" that is discretely present in its last documents. This genetic side provides the foundation for a "generative grammar." Today, this generative grammar allows the believers to articulate their being Christian and ecclesial in *multiple* ways.

A GENETIC VISION OF THE CHRISTIAN AND ECCLESIAL EXISTENCE

In recent years, the theological research has highlighted the phenomenon of intertextuality and the idea of a "textual *corpus*" that, despite its internal complexity and multiple forms of compromise, offers a *coherent vision*. The idea of a textual *corpus* articulates the threefold ultimate referent, that is, the gospel of God or revelation, modern society, and the Church—where the latter is doubly *decentered* by our listening to God's word *and* by the presence of the other. The idea of "genesis," of a genetic vision, is dispersed in the Council's documents. Moreover, this idea is not limited to just *one* aspect of the coherent vision of the Council's *corpus,* but it concerns, at the same time, the gospel of God or revelation, modern society, and the Church—*specifically in their mutual articulation.* Finally, our perception of this genetic vision depends on a dual interpretive decision:

1. A diagnostic assessment of our situation invites us to relativize the classical distinction between already Christianized countries and mission countries. This relativization leads, first, to *going beyond the juxtaposition* of conciliar texts on the Church by placing, on one side, *Lumen Gentium* and *Gaudium et Spes,* and on another side, *Ad Gentes.* Second, this

relativization also leads to reinterpret the overall vision of *Lumen Gentium* in light of the "Decree on Mission," *Ad Gentes*. However, the "Decree on the Missionary Activity of the Church" is the only document that provides us with a *genetic vision* of faith and of the Church in society. Hence, it allows us to reinterpret the overall vision of *Lumen Gentium* in this perspective.

Our second interpretive decision requires the following:

2. To identify the biblical background of these texts and give to it—"in the footsteps" of *Dei Verbum*—the status of *matrix* of *our* way of considering the birth of faith and of *today's* Church.

This two-track operation is based in particular on the scriptural indications, particularly from Luke's Gospel, and on the pneumatological indications (*AG* 4).[6] In particular, *Ad Gentes* 4, which focuses on the mission of the Holy Spirit, is a real rewriting of *Lumen Gentium* 4. We mention only the last sentence, which refers to seventeen passages of the Acts of Apostles, which are spread throughout the whole document, and that, with the "etc." at the end of this quote, it appears to be an invitation to read again the whole book of the Acts of Apostles: "Sometimes [the Holy Spirit] even visibly anticipates the Apostolic action, just as the Holy Spirit unceasingly accompanies and directs it in different ways" (*AG* 4).

We do not have the time to fully develop this two-track operation—biblical and ecclesiological. We can remember, however, what chapter 2 of *Ad Gentes* says about the three stages of an *ecclesiological genesis* within society. The starting point is provided by the "testimony" of Christians in their non-Christian environment.

The purpose of this "presence" is, first, "that others consider their good works and glorify the Father (Matt 5:16)." This is a decisive addition of the decree *Ad Gentes* that reaffirms in a new way the "sacramentality" of the Church that has been expressed in *Lumen Gentium* 1.

The second purpose of this presence is that the non-Christians "can perceive more fully the real meaning of human life and the universal bond of the community of mankind" (*AG* 11.1). Moreover, the second article of the decree *Ad Gentes* focuses on the preaching of the gospel, with an analysis of the process of conversion and of its spiritual and sacramental structure, where the process of conversion is aimed at gathering the people of God (*AG* 13–14). We mention once again only the first sentence that, as with the rest of *Ad Gentes*, is filled with scriptural references, particularly from the Acts of the Apostles: "Wherever God opens *a* door of speech for proclaiming the mystery of Christ, there is announced to all men with confidence and constancy, the living God" (*AG* 13.1).

It is only in the third article of the decree *Ad Gentes* that the "formation" of the Christian community is traced—we could say, from the bottom up. The ministries that are needed for the genesis of the Christian community are first of all mentioned to their fullest extent: "In order to plant the Church and to make the Christian community grow, various ministries are needed, which are raised up by divine calling from the midst of the faithful congregation, and are to be carefully fostered and tended to by all" (*AG* 15.7). It is only afterward that *Ad Gentes* addresses the priestly ministry and other specific vocations (*AG* 16–18).

Of course, these different steps have an *ideal and typical* character that must be understood from the scriptural thread of the text, especially from the ecclesiological-genetic vision of the Acts of the Apostles that begins to surface in *Ad Gentes* 4, but also in a series of paragraphs of *Lumen Gentium*. If we want to encourage the missionary *creativity* that is integral to this "foundational" perspective (*LG* 5), we must help the faithful to insert themselves *actively* (*participatio actuosa*) in the life of the Church and, accordingly, we should transmit to them a "way of proceeding," by placing the future of Christian life and of the ecclesial community in the hands of the *whole* people of God.

Definitely, this is the main aim of the Council. At this crucial juncture the idea of a generative grammar of our faith is presented. This idea underlies both the event of the Council and the corpus of Vatican II. Today, because of the current contextual changes, mentioned at the beginning of my essay, we should make explicit this idea of a generative grammar.

A WAY OF PROCEEDING: THE CORE OF A GENERATIVE GRAMMAR OF THE FAITH

This way of proceeding was prepared well before the Council by the multiple movements of renewal and by their pastoral and spiritual pedagogies, which are evoked in the decree on ecumenism *Unitatis Redintegratio* (no. 6). This way of proceeding has two inseparable sides: first, it is a way to hear God speak to us; second, it is a way to get along among humans.[7]

1. As to the first side, there is a textual line that needs to be identified. This line goes from chapter 6 of *Dei Verbum*—on the Holy Scripture in the life of the Church, to the numbers 9 and 10 of *Sacrosanctum Concilium*—on the liturgy as the summit and the source at the heart of all other ecclesial activities, going through the numbers 4 and 11 of *Gaudium et Spes*—on discerning the signs of the times.

   In these passages, the Council describes three different practices whose *articulation* is the first challenge of the grammar that should be conveyed to the faithful. These three practices are, first the reading of the Scriptures; second, the discernment of the signs of the times; third, the access to one's interiority and to the "colloquium" with God in solitude and in the liturgy.

   Both the interpretation of the Bible and the interpretation of the present moment cannot be separated, just as it is impossible to hear God's voice *today* without discovering God's voice already at work in those we encounter daily and in their culture. But to discuss further the interpretation of the Bible and the interpretation of the present moment, we affirm that they are both based on our listening ability and learning capability; moreover, they both aim at an ongoing conversion. Finally, we should consent to receive the spiritual initiation that is outlined in *Sacrosanctum Concilium* 9 and that is not theologically far from the chapter 2 of the decree *Ad Gentes*. This spiritual initiation recalls that the first steps are listening to the gospel, before the journey continues (in number 10 of *Sacrosanctum Concilium*) by experiencing the liturgy as the "source" and "summit" of the journey, and then returning to one's everyday life.

2. As to the other side of this way of proceeding, which can be called communicative, it is closely related to the first side that I just described, while at the same time it is the context where we verify it, because it is impossible to hear God speak without wanting to understand each other. Again, the "collegial" practice of the Conciliar fathers precedes the texts that testify their collegial practice, especially when we consider some indications of the decree *Unitatis Redintegratio* 11 and of the declaration *Dignitatis Humanae* 3 on "the *common* search for the truth."

Two aspects are highlighted: first, the importance of *reasoning and arguing*, in the "Declaration on Religious Freedom" (*Dignitatis Humanae*); second, the criterion of *concordance* between *what* is sought by the research partners—the truth of the gospel—and *how to search it* "with love of the truth, charity and humility," as the "Decree on Ecumenism," (*Unitatis Redintegratio*) affirms. The criterion of concordance is crucial because it leads all members and partners of a specific group or community, independently of any authoritarian strategy, to the *original experience* of a victory over violence and to the spiritual understanding of their own *becoming*.

Finally, the generative grammar of the Council is rooted in the *modus agendi* of Christ himself (*DH* 11), its *modus conversationis*

33

(*DV* 7)—that is, how Jesus relates to and lives with others—or even Jesus' way of being poor and humble (*LG* 8). We mention at least the beginning of the *Vita Christi*, as found in the "Declaration on Religious Freedom," which highlights the paradoxical nature of Christ's "way":

> God calls men to serve Him in spirit and in truth, hence they are bound in conscience but they stand under no compulsion....This truth appears at its height in Christ Jesus, in whom God manifested Himself and His *ways* with men. Christ is at once our Master and our Lord and also meek and humble of heart. In attracting and inviting His disciples He used patience. He wrought miracles to illuminate His teaching and to establish its truth, but His intention was to rouse faith in His hearers and to confirm them in faith, not to exert coercion upon them...the apostles followed the same *way*....This is the *way* along which the martyrs and other faithful have walked through all ages and over all the earth. (*DH* 11)

Hence, the christological side is inseparable from the pneumatological side; for whatever the language, *any* grammar is waiting for a word actually uttered by one person or another, here and now, where the listening and the understanding always reveal an *unpredictable* surprise. And this is especially true when, at the same time, in listening and in winning over violence, the voice of God is heard—without confusion, without separation.

In conclusion, the novelty of this approach to the common faith in its "expressive" (*GS* 44)[8] plurality is confirmed by the conciliar conflict that it provoked and that appears to be a "paradigmatic conflict." Here it is enough to mention as a proof of this conflict the corrections made by the curia to the opening speech of John XXIII.

The pope had actually written his opening speech in Italian. He mentioned this version several times before his death and it is included in the *Decree on Ecumenism* 6 (*UR*, cited previously). On the day of the opening of the Council, however, he read the official Latin version, crafted by his translator.[9] The Italian version takes distance from Vatican I when it distinguishes the "substance of the deposit of faith," taken as *a whole* and without making reference to an internal plurality that is already part of such an expression. However, without considering the historical form that such an expression already had at that time, the Latin translation replaces the more *historical* distinction with the more *dogmatic* distinction between "the deposit, that is, *the truths contained in our venerable doctrine*" and "the form in which *these truths* are enounced" (while these truths keep the same meaning and the same scope; this is an explicit reference to the canon of Vincent of Lérins that appears in Vatican I).[10]

Hence, the hermeneutic conception of the faith that is involved in the distinctions of John XXIII disappears. Moreover, the self-reform of the Church is reduced to secondary elements and it concerns only the pastoral application of a teaching that is acquired once and for all. These changes are not without consequences. They indicate a fundamentalist and uncompromising relationship that such a type of magisterium would want to maintain with the Tradition and with Scripture, on the one hand, and with the recipients of the gospel on the other hand.

We find here a conflict that runs through all the modern era, including the modernist crisis. The insistence on the *modus* or "style" of the expression of the faith implies a rationality that is historical and "procedural" or "communicative," as we find in Kant and in other modern thinkers. This rationality emerges forcefully in the conciliar assembly when it faces an uncertain future, if this future is simply considered collectively according to some basic rules. In this essay, we explained this rationality in terms of generative grammar. This concept aims at thinking, *at the same time*, the collective "formation" of the conciliar corpus *and* what today allows us to shape the Christian and ecclesial existence in our contemporary context, while allowing an ecclesial agreement due to a similar way of proceeding that is based on the same christological and pneumatological reference.

Notes

1. Translated from the French by Andrea Vicini, SJ.

2. Henri Mendras, *La Seconde Révolution française 1965–1984* (Paris: Gallimard, 1988).

3. The idea of "generative grammar" was developed by the American linguist Noam Chomsky, *grosso modo* at the time of the Council. Without endorsing all of Chomsky's search results that, in many respects, are dated, we keep the main idea, namely that a grammar generates all the statements of a language and that such a grammar represents the intuitive knowledge that speaking subjects have on the formation of their statements. I believe that this idea could be applied by analogy to the *mode of generation* (*mode d'engendrement*) of the conciliar texts and especially on what concerns the way of *training* (*former*) today's Christian and ecclesial existence in our own cultural situation.

4. *Acta Synodalia Sacrosancti Concilii Oecumenici Vaticani II,* Cura et studio Archivi Concilii Oecumenici Vaticani, vols. 1–6 in 33 books (Città del Vaticano: Typis Polyglottis Vaticanis, 1970–99), I/1, 172 and the critical edition (original version in Italian) of Alberto Melloni, in Giuseppe Alberigo et al., *Fede, tradizione, profezia: Studi su Giovanni XXIII e sul Vaticano II* (Brescia: Paideia, 1984), 239–83.

5. See Christoph Theobald, *La réception du concile Vatican II.* Vol. I. *Accéder à la source,* Unam sanctam. Nouvelle série 1 (Paris: Cerf, 2009), 290–363.

6. For a first insight, see *As grandes intuições de futuro de Concílio Vaticano II: A favor de uma "gramática gerativa" das relações entre Evangelho, sociedade et Igreja,* Cadernos Teologia Pública, ano X/77 (São Leopoldo RS, Brazil: Universidade do Vale do Rio dos Sinos, 2013).

7. For more details, see Theobald, *La réception du concile Vatican II,* 894–900.

8. *Gaudium et Spes* 44 evokes the *facultas exprimendi* of the faith, thus providing a valuable indication to reflect on its inherent creativity.

9. See above note 3 (the critical edition of the text) and "L'apologétique historique d'Alfred Loisy: Enjeux historiques et théologiques d'un livre inédit," in Alfred Loisy, *La crise de la foi dans le temps présent,* unedited text published by François

Laplanche, with studies by Rosanna Ciappa, François Laplanche, and Christoph Theobald. Foreword by Claude Langlois. Bibliothèque de l'École des Hautes Études–Sciences religieuses 144 (Turnhout: Brepols, 2010), 687–93.

10. Henricus Denzinger and Adolfus Schönmetzer, SJ, eds., *Enchiridion symbolorum, definitionum et declarationum de rebus fidei et morum*, 34th ed. (Barcinone: Herder, 1967), no. 3020.

3

Peter Hünermann

Continuity and Discontinuity in an Epochal Transition of Faith

THE HERMENEUTICS OF VATICAN II

My contribution refers to Vatican II as legacy, but even more it refers to Vatican II as seed and task. The title "Continuity and Discontinuity in an Epochal Transition of Faith: The Hermeneutics of Vatican II" indicates the structure of the following essay:

1) Vatican II happened in an epoch-making transition in humankind.
2) An epochal transformation of faith?
3) The constitutive fundamental change in Vatican II.
4) The consequences of this change:
   a) The change of *ratio fidei* and the style of Christian life;
   b) the "pastoral" texts as "constitutional" texts.

VATICAN II HAPPENED IN AN EPOCH-MAKING TRANSITION OF HUMANKIND

In this introductory section, I want to underscore first of all that John XXIII as well as Paul VI and the fathers of the Council were aware of the fact that humankind was beginning to live in a new global era. Therefore faith needs to be proclaimed in a new way, but "in fullness and purity to the people of our times, so that they can understand and accept it with alacrity."[1] Over and over again the documents of the Council speak of "modern times,"[2] and they refer to "the circumstances and needs of our time" as to the Holy Spirit and the changes he brought about in "these times."[3] The short and somewhat rough description in the introductory chapter of *Gaudium et Spes* (nos. 4–10) demonstrates that the bishops are fixing the moment in which the industrialized "western world" of the late nineteenth and the beginning of the twentieth century with its economic, cultural, social, and political achievements, and its dangerous, even death-bringing tendencies, are spreading into global dimensions and intensifying in its endeavors (*GS* 4–5). The bishops speak of "this immense undertaking, in which the whole human race is already engaged."[4] They do not see the full range of consequences, which will appear only in the last decades of the twentieth century. But they are aware of some of the most remarkable changes, produced by the epoch that follows the epoch of industrialization: the deep transformation of social structures and the breakdown of the traditional system of values, an abandonment of religion, not just as individual decision but as cultural movement of big crowds connected with a modern view of the world, and so on.[5]

Karl Polanyi coined the term *great transformation* to classify this epoch-making transition.[6] The term *great transformation* is used in contemporary research literature to characterize the three megatransitions transforming the life of humankind in the totality of its dimensions: in this view, the first epoch-making change takes place in the Neolithic age with the development of sedentary life, the foundation of the first cities, agriculture, specialized handcraft, new social forms, and lifestyle. The second great transformation occurs in the nineteenth and the first half of the twentieth centuries with industrialization, and the third great transformation, generally called "radical" or "global modernization," started in the second half of the twentieth century, continuing and accelerating in our days.[7] The term *anthropocene* to characterize this age of the earth has become common in the last years, because humankind within this third epoch is the most effective actor to determine the future of the globe. Human responsibility extends to the whole globe and sphere of life. Humankind has obtained the competences to decompose and reconstruct reality in new forms and in the different dimensions including life. The extension of scientific research represents as well the vast field of extended liberty to form reality, our own personal and social life.

The immense growth of power is based on methodological research in strictly functional forms with their specific logic, their long and controlled action chains, generating a polycentric reality. "The basic experience of post-modernity—in contrast to enlightenment—consists in the fact that one cannot any more understand reality from a central perspective."[8] This general approach marks social life as well: it is split up in functional dimensions, which stay in themselves as systematic unities, endowed with their own goals, logics, and methods. Human beings get their specific identity through integration in them and have to struggle, to find a certain coherence between these different identities and ambiances.[9] All these changes are not simply factual substitutes. They are based on the philosophical insight that there *is* no central perspective.

As a matter of fact, the second and third of the great transformations are accompanied and enabled by changes in philosophical reflections and discoveries of new ways to think and argue. Philosophers speak of the "Copernican turn" to characterize this shift of thinking. From Kant on, the main question is not anymore, "What are the objects of thinking?," "What is this?," "What is the object of acting?," "What am I going to do?"

The philosophical question now is, "What are the conditions of possibility to experience this or that object?" The reason to put the fundamental question that way is the *constitutive* character of the possibility of experience for the objects themselves. The *modus quo*, in which we perform our encounter with reality, is *constitutive* for the *id quod*, for the objects, we encounter. And, on the other hand, the "given reality" implies a certain *modus quo* to get access to it. This mutual relationship is not conceived in the traditional manner, expressed in the medieval phrase, "*Quidquid recipitur ad modum recipientis recipitur*" (Whatever is received into something is received according to the condition of the receiver). Ancient and medieval philosophers thought only of accidental differences, which occur if two persons look at the same object and everybody sees it in a slightly different way because of his or her personal interests, taste, and so on. Since Kant, modern philosophy treats relationships in a quite different way, just as scientists (e.g., biologists and physicists) treat other things, or other objects, by regarding and analyzing them as material substance.

This transcendental insight qualifies as well post-Kantianism, Husserl's and Heidegger's phenomenology, Wittgenstein's reflections, and analytical and linguistic philosophy. And that is valid as well for the methodical presuppositions of sciences and modern humanities. As transcendental reflections and statements are not to be understood in a categorical way, they cannot be summarized in a unique categorical manner of speaking. The experience of the modern world is and remains pluralistic.[10] There is no "central perspective." But the autonomy, the proper logic or structure of the different entities or systems does not mean that they are cut off from the others in self-sufficiency or autarchy. Autonomy does not mean autarchy. The different dimensions need each other; they can be brought into a certain convergence only by wisdom. From here the question arises, If Vatican II happened within this epoch-making change, how do these transformations affect faith, which is to be proclaimed "in purity and fullness to the people of our time"?

41

AN EPOCHAL
TRANSFORMATION OF FAITH?

An epochal transformation of faith seems to be theologically contradictory. Is faith not the answer to divine revelation, to be witnessed and transmitted through the ages, unaltered in its truth? Faith is profoundly human. Did Jesus not proclaim faith in ordinary language? Did the prophets, did the apostles not confess the word of God?

Theological tradition considers faith as *habitus infusus,* God-given virtue. St. Thomas differentiates faith from other acquired competences, or *habitus* in general as Aristotle describes them. Faith concerns the fundamental attitude, in which humanity "has" itself, "has" the world, "has" the others, in a God-given way.[11] "In the virtue of faith human beings recognize and long out for the only good, which can fulfill their striving for truth and perfection."[12] The formal object of faith is God as *prima veritas,* which means God in so far as God founds all cognoscibility and all cognition of things. All material objects of faith are recognized in faith only if considered under this formal objective. So faith characterizes all acts of the faithful, all acts of recognition and knowing, as acts of will. Therefore faith cannot be understood as affirmation of any particular truth as such. Particular truth can be affirmed in faith only insofar as this particular truth belongs to and is integrated in *ipsius veritatis rationem.*

Ipsa veritas, quae manifestabilis est et manifestativa omnium is the light of faith, to which humanity commits itself.[13] And what about the confession of faith, the enunciation of articles of faith in ordinary language? Here follows the answer of Thomas: "The act of the faithful does not intend (aim) at the word as such (the word as 'what can be said') but at the matter."[14] This means that all explicit acts of faith—the personal decision for faith as well as all the acts motivated by faith—include and are marked fundamentally by thanksgiving and praise on the one hand and commitment and devotion to the mystery of God on the other hand. If we want to describe these acts formally, faith as personal act always has a categorical, concrete form that is a finite expression of all comprehensive performances of thanksgiving and commitment to God.

In perfect correspondence to this characteristic of faith, Thomas describes how God can be thought. His axiom reads, *Ad cognitionem Dei oportet uti via remotionis*—to know God, one has to use the way of removal.[15] Following exactly this principle, Thomas starts from sense-based experience: there must be something ultimate moving in this mobile and moving universe, some ultimate sense and aim of all, and so on. The famous five arguments are nothing else than the statement of radical contingency of the world. Generally people call that item *God*, but nobody knows, what it or he or she is. The first removal or the first exclusion starts from here: God cannot be something that is in itself marked by quantity, as occurs in all sensory-based experience, because all that is qualified by quantity can be divided, split up in parts. This cannot be an ultimate reason in any sense whatsoever. Therefore to confess *one* God cannot mean to characterize God by a numeric term (*terminus numeralis*).[16]

The ongoing logic of exclusion or removal in Thomas's great chapter on God in the *Summa theologiae* I, q. 4–26 can be summarized as follows: God cannot be an *ens* (entity). An entity can be (exist) or not be (not exist); it is an *aliud quid*, that means an *aliquid* having a specific nature or essence. As such it is one among others. Its ontic unity means it is *indivisum in se et divisum ab omni alio*, not divided in itself and divided from all other entities. It has therefore essentially a limited perfection, is a limited good, a limited actor. So God has to be thought a highest simplicity: there must be identity between his "nature" and his "being," so he has to be non-*aliud, non aliquid*.

Furthermore Thomas argues that God is in all creatures *per essentiam, praesentiam et potentiam*—through his essence, his presence, and his potency.[17] To understand this formula of Thomas, one has to bear in mind that God does not have an "essence" in the sense all creatures have an "essence," a nature. God is not an *aliquid*. The living God is beyond that sphere. So Thomas describes him as *ipsum esse subsistens*, giving this formula the sense of origin and *causa prima* of all being of creatures. So in the relationship of God's "in-*esse*" in all creatures through essence, presence, and potency, there is no reciprocity from God to creature and from creature to God at all. There is no relation added to God by God's "in-*esse*" in the creatures. In the words of John of the Cross, reassuming St. Thomas, God *is* God and the creatures. God is in all creatures through God's essence—in identity—being (*esse*). In the same sense God is infinite perfection and origin or cause of all perfection of the creatures. With this step of argument, human reflection reaches the limit of thinking and speaking: *id quo maius cogitare nequit.*[18] Yet for Thomas this result is the basis to understand in faith the triune God: as God is highest simplicity and infinite perfection, one has to attribute to God inner actions as *intelligere* and *velle.*[19] So there is for Thomas a certain understanding in the mystery of faith for the result of this divine inner action, the Word and the Spirit, with the inclusion of possible outer action as described for divine "being."[20]

With this characteristic of faith, Thomas places faith—*as fides qua* and *fides quae*—on the level of "transcendentality."[21] But in distinction from philosophy, the "horizon of transcendentality" is not unlocked by the question, what are the constitutive rational conditions of possibility of this or that object?[22] In faith the horizon is opened, because human beings feel themselves appealed and obliged in an absolutely free, nondeducible way by the "transcendent, hidden appearance" of the divine mystery, calling them to answer in faith.[23] The reason of faith, which is to be given from theology, is a judgment of wisdom, bringing together in the light of faith the different open aspects of truth.[24]

With this concept of faith, formulated by Thomas as fruit of a long preceding reflection and a sober and critical reception of Aristotle's philosophy, the question we asked at the beginning becomes still more acute: How can an epochal transition of faith be thought? The answer comes from history, and it is impossible here to give even only the most important names of theologians and philosophers; from the end of the thirteenth century, theologians begin to accept the univocal concept of being (*ens*) formulated by John Duns Scotus: "*Ens est id, cui non repugnat esse.*"[25] *Ens* is conceived here as rational transcendental concept, which is the first and most fundamental of all concepts, without which nothing can be understood. This concept is univocal because it precedes all other concepts, but it is as well the minimum of all that is knowable. All its attributes are disjunctive; they can be demonstrated only through arguments a posteriori (*argumentatio quia*). Nonetheless, this concept is fundamental and one in God's and human's science. So this concept can be thought in a twofold manner: as *ens infinitum* and as *ens finitum*. Such a univocal concept of *ens* can in no way be attributed to God according to Thomas! The first is the concept of God, the second is the concept of creature. God as *ens infinitum* serves as philosophical principle to think the unity of the world, the systematic unity of all sciences, the ultimate point of reference for the social, cultural, and the cosmic order. God as *ens infinitum* is endowed with *potestas absoluta*: God can make all that is not contradictory in itself and contradictory to God's own will.[26] The concrete order of the world can be learned by experience. The order of salvation belongs to the realm of *potestas ordinata*. The faithful come to know the order of salvation through revelation and its witnesses.

As a consequence of this innovation in later medieval theology, the following development of theology and philosophy[27]—up to the time of the Enlightenment—is characterized by a fundamental *theistic* concept of God[28] that leads to the notion of "natural theology," and from there to eighteenth-century philosophy of religion.[29] This tendency is promoted by theology and its accentuation on "nature" in contrast to "grace as super-nature."

The history of the concept of faith, starting with this medieval innovation, through the positions of the Counter-Reformation and the questions of the Enlightenment follow the main tracks as just characterized, and find a final shape in the specific problematic of neo-Scholastic theology.[30] In confrontation with modern science and its claim for unique and universal reliability, the fathers of Vatican I refer to Thomas's differentiation of faith and reason regarding their objects, their subjective potencies, and their foundation. Understood in the context of neo-Scholastic theology, it seems that the fathers imagined two parallel orders of knowledge: faith and reason. The fathers did not take into account that Thomas—differentiating faith and reason

—conceives believing and thinking in inseparable, *perichoretic* relation.[31]

This manner of conceiving faith, dominating the whole epoch from the end of the Middle Ages up to the nineteenth and twentieth century, cannot be thought anymore in a rational way within the new epoch of anthropocene. In the new context, this concept of faith would be reduced to a highly particular access to reality. Its formal perspective would be determined by a particular religious tradition. Why? Because there is no horizon into which the message of the gospel can unfold the largeness and depth of the eschatological promise. This is the point why Christian faith has lost trust, why the modern times is characterized by a crisis concerning belief in God. The witness of God has become untrustworthy for many and church structures have lost their meaning. What is the response of Vatican II to that crisis?

THE CONSTITUTIVE FUNDAMENTAL CHANGE OF VATICAN II

We must now clarify two items:

1) How does Vatican II respond to the above-asked question? Is there an epochal change of faith, a change of constitutive character?
2) What about continuity and discontinuity of faith in this change?

To answer the first question, yes, there is a change of *ratio fidei*, a change of the reason of faith.

We start our argument from an analysis of the four constitutions of Vatican II, because they are the main documents, whereas the other documents are complementary to them. It is an eye-catching fact that three of the main documents—*Sacrosanctum Concilium, Lumen Gentium, Dei Verbum*—in their first chapter describe the *mystery* that they want to treat in the following parts of the document.[32] *Gaudium et Spes*, the fourth constitution leads through the aspects, treated in chapters 1 to 3, to the mystery, presented in chapter 4.[33] So the new way to confess faith in modern times is the proclamation of the paschal mystery of salvation, the mystery of revelation, the mystery of the Church, the mystery of the kingdom of God within history. What does *mystery*—equivalent with sacrament—mean?

Mystery means God—*maior quam cogitari possit*—acting and self-communicating to human beings from the beginning of creation, calling them through God's word from the times of the protoancestors; continuing to call and to help human beings to live according to God's Spirit despite their sins in history; waking up faith, hope, and charity within human freedom, a faith that is fully revealed in Jesus Christ and through the outpouring of the Spirit. The divine mystery enables human beings to communicate and participate through faith in this communicative action of God, without mastering God and God's action. On the contrary: human beings performing faith receive the acting and living in God as absolute gift and grace beyond any merit. The documents of Vatican II presuppose a concept of faith that we have encountered in the reflections of Thomas Aquinas: faith as the fundamental virtue of human beings, generated through God's Word as founding *ratio veritatis et bonitatis* and—in a free way performed by human beings—through the dynamic of God's Spirit.

The language in which the documents speak of the different mysteries corresponds perfectly to the meaning of the mysteries. *Sacrosanctum Concilium* underlines that it is Christ himself who is present in the sacrifice of the Mass, who offers the sacrifice, who is acting in the sacraments; he speaks when the Holy Scriptures are read in the church; he is present, when the church prays and sings.[34] *Lumen Gentium* says at no. 1 that Christ is the light of the nations and this light shines and appears in the face of the Church. This mystery of the Church is "pre-figured" from the origin of the world, prepared in the history of Israel and the old covenant, revealed through Christ and the outpouring of the Holy Spirit. The mystery will be in perfect way accomplished at the end of times in glory.[35] *Dei Verbum* 2 teaches that the words and the deeds of the economy of salvation "bring to light the mystery they contain." The revelation of God is inseparably linked with Abraham, Moses, Mary, and Jesus of Nazareth. But the revelation of God, the word, is not simply the historical word or action of these men and women. "The most intimate truth, which revelation gives us about God is that the salvation of humankind *shines forth* in Christ (*illuscecit*), who himself is both, the mediator and the fullness of all revelation (*plenitudo totius revelationis*)." In view of the different statements about the mystery of the Church made in the other documents, *Gaudium et Spes* 40 wants to consider the mystery of the Church "insofar as the church exists in this world, lives and acts with the world." The Church is "in this world constituted and disposed...as visible and spiritual society. This mutual penetration of earthly and celestial citizenship can be understood only in faith and remains the mystery of human history, disturbed through sin until the full revelation of the glory of God's children."

THE CONSEQUENCES OF THE FUNDAMENTAL CONSTITUTIVE CHANGE

The Change of the Ratio Fidei *and the Style of Christian Life*

The preceding analysis of the way in which faith is presented in the documents of Vatican II cannot be characterized as an accidental clarification of what Christian belief is, or the solution of any particular question related to faith. In analogy to modern philosophy, which asks about the transcendental and aprioristic, constitutive conditions of every experience, *mysterium fidei* includes in an inseparable manner the performance of faith and all *that* is believed by the faithful. Mystery means a constitutive interrelation. How is the theological concept of mystery connected with the analysis of faith and the approach to God we have found in the history of theology? We started with Thomas Aquinas's analysis of the virtue of faith and then continued with a brief summary of his way of removal to think God. Both arguments lead into a movement of transcendence; they lead into the mystery. This does not mean that Thomas in his articles and questions about faith in his *Summa*

Theologiae simply presents modern insights. In the theology of Thomas there are the two movements, and their convergence. But Thomas does not start from the unifying point, from the mystery, to rethink the relation of faith and reason in the life of the faithful. He does not develop an articulated ecclesiology on this basis. Vatican II on the contrary just starts with the mystery.

In comparison with the concept of faith, dominant from John Duns Scotus and the late Middle Ages, the modern view of faith represents an epochal shift of the *ratio fidei*. The theistic concept of God, based on the univocal understanding of entity (*ens*) as the absolutely first transcendental determination, leads historically to an "analysis *fidei*," in which faith is something added to or joined by reason. In this perspective Vatican II— starting its theological reasoning from the mystery—presents innovations that seem to be in discontinuity with the Tradition of faith. As a matter of fact, these innovations are only in discontinuity with a certain historical shape of the *ratio fidei*.

The Council fathers of Vatican II—except a smaller number of bishops familiar with new developments in theology—where alerted to this change by a group of theologians who were acquainted with modern philosophy, especially with transcendental and phenomenological thinking. In his philosophical dissertation titled *Geist in Welt*, Karl Rahner had tried to find a way from Thomas Aquinas to Heidegger's phenomenological analysis, inspired in a certain way through Maréchal's attempt to bridge Kant and scholastic reflection.[36] The reception of Rousselot, of Blondel's *L'Action* and his idea of an "immanent apologetic," de Lubac's *De la connaissance de Dieu and Surnaturel* as well as the contributions of Chenu, Congar, Schillebeeckx, J. C. Murray, and Lonergan are to be named in this context[37]—to remember only a few who helped the bishops to speak of faith and the great theological themes in a new way.

What are the consequences of this fundamental change of the *ratio fidei*? To start teaching the mysteries of revelation, Church, liturgy, and history means to affirm in every instant, in every consideration, the constitutive relational identity of *fides qua* and *fides quae*. For example, the fathers of the Council cannot speak and act anymore as in the times of the

Counter-Reformation, where the whole interest was fixed on differences of the *fides quae*. For the members of Vatican II there are doctrinal differences between Catholics and Protestants, but they are seen with the eyes and in the perspective of Christian belief, hope, and charity. The bishops had to see and to acknowledge as well the broad list of positive factors, the richness of community in matters of faith, the acting of the Holy Spirit in the ecclesial communities, and so forth.

The conscious and performed union of the *fides qua* and the *fides quae* characterizes Vatican II as a whole and thus marks this Council through *a new style*. Style is the overall expression of a personal or collective human authenticity. It is an overall expression because style implies the different dimensions of bodily, social, cultural, intellectual, and spiritual life into one figure. It is evident that a style is interwoven with the great historical situation in which a given person or community lives. Necessarily, a new style, coming up in a community, leads to institutional adaptations in the community itself.[38] To distinguish a general way of life—marked by fashion, social pattern, and conventions—from style, we speak of style as an expression of human authenticity. As a consequence of the change of *ratio fidei*, Vatican II represents a new style of living the gospel. It is the great merit of John O'Malley that he introduced very early the concept of style into the discussion of the hermeneutics of Vatican II.[39] His interpretations of Vatican II demonstrate the richness of insights that this key concept provides for the understanding of its documents. Whereas O'Malley picks up the historical tradition of antique rhetoric—style makes part of the message, generally the most important part—Christoph Theobald understands style as a way to live in authenticity, as a way to live the eschatological Christ event in its unique singularity, its communal, ecclesiological form, and its thousand figures, so that this event can be realized personally in authenticity.[40]

The "Pastoral" Texts as "Constitutional" Texts

Another question is this: How does the fundamental constitutive change of the *ratio fidei* mark how the Council fathers speak in the documents of Vatican II? They themselves say it: in a pastoral way. This was the invitation of John XXIII, calling the bishops to celebrate a "pastoral council."[41] This was the axiom to which the bishops appealed over and over again in discussions concerning the prepared schemes or later proposals of the conciliar commissions. A lot of research took place to determine the use of the term in the historical sense.[42]

Now we know that there is a significant difference between the use of the word *pastoral* in traditional theological, especially neo-Scholastic, language and the language in which John XXIII and the Council fathers employed it. Hence our question: Has this difference to do with the change of *ratio fidei* as characterized, and with the key word *mysterium,* in which the Council fathers resume the coincidence of *fides qua* and *fides quae* as the starting point of their theological teaching? This question is of outstanding importance, because the whole "battle for meaning" has its focus in this problem.[43] On February 15, 2013, Cardinal Walter Brandmüller published an article in *L'Osservatore Romano* on "Conflicts in Postconciliar Interpretation," continuing to maintain in his argument the former understanding of *pastoral* as application of dogmatic truth in practice.[44] Indeed, the change of the *ratio fidei* provides the answer to this question. If the teaching of faith in the documents of Vatican II start from the relational identity of *fides qua* and *fides quae,* that is, from the mystery of God, revealing Godself in and through faith—the transcendent commitment of the faithful to God—than the proclamation and the teaching of faith cannot avoid and abstain from this spiritual and divine unification. The nonbeliever addressees—insofar as they are possible believers—are constitutive partners of the mystery just as the faithful. The bishops as well cannot abstain from their own position in faith: they have to proclaim the gospel. Their position and task—as representatives of the apostles—is also a constitutive moment of the mystery.

How can this form of speech act be characterized in an adequate conceptual way to mark the difference between the former way of speaking in dogmatic definitions and the new pastoral way to speak? We proposed the term *constitutional* texts.[45] The documents of Vatican II represent constitutional texts. From antiquity on, the words *constitution* and *constitutive* have not only a juridical, medical, and logical sense. They are quite familiar for everybody knowing Aristotelian and medieval history of philosophy and theology. *Materia et forma, actus et potentia* are *constitutive* inner *principia entis* of every substance. The constituent parts are necessary for the *constitution* of every entity. The underlying idea of this rich use is formulated by William of Ockham: the constituent stands *pro omni illo, quod est de essentia et quidditate alicuius, ita quod ipsum sine ille esse non posset*—for all that is *of* the essence and *of* the nature (what it is), so that itself could not be without that.[46] From Kant on, the philosophical discussion changes. Philosophers discuss the constitutive transcendental forms of thinking and rules of language under which experiences, knowledge, and empirical actions are possible. Habermas, analyzing "universal pragmatics," speaks of the constitutive rules for communicative speech acts.[47] Relating to Searle's *Speech Acts* and connected studies, he distinguishes two forms of communication through language: "discourse" and "communicative action."[48] In *discourse* the propositional content is dominant, and the communicative interaction is virtualized. In discourse we treat matters that possibly exist, and we suppose that all intelligent subjects have virtual access to this form of communication. *Communicative action* on the other hand is a form of speaking in which the intersubjective relation marks and mediates the propositional matter, which makes part of the communicative action. Society is constituted through communicative action, communicative speech acts. Society and all societal things do not exist without communicative action. In ordinary language communicative action requires discourse as well, insofar as propositional matters, communicated in communicative action, can be questioned and have to be validated through discourse, which means through recourse to the possibility of the propositional matter.

These concepts and the underlying differentiations are indispensible in clearing up in a conceptual way what pastoral speaking means in Vatican II. The traditional language of dogmatics and of dogmatic definitions—especially since the Council of Trent—was dominantly marked by a spirit of discourse.

Leading motivations of theology were the legitimation of different theological matters by recourse to Scripture and oral Tradition, and the discussion and determination of theological matters in their inner possibility. The communicative action, which faith is itself, was fairly virtualized. Max Seckler called the leading concept of revelation of Vatican I an *instruktuions-theoretisches Modell*, not a *kommunicatives Modell* as in Vatican II. "Objectivity" was reigning. How to distinguish both ways of talking? How to distinguish the differences of the texts? If one reads the preface of the constitution *Dei Filius* of Vatican I, it is evident that the bishops introduce the following declaration by a constitutive speech act.[49] The presupposition of this speech act is that the pope and the bishops, sitting together with him in the ecumenical Council, deciding and judging, possess the theological and juridical legitimation to perform this constitutive speech act. In this sense the following propositional content is marked by this speech act, which can be questioned and can be justified. It is an "ordinary, limited" speech act, because if a question about this issue arises, the whole accent will be laid on the question of the legitimacy to perform this act and the question, whether the propositional content is exactly represented. This produces the "spirit" of discourse and the leading motivations of theology, as we described them. Revelation seems to be a divine communication, reaching human beings essentially through episcopal instruction.

When the bishops of Vatican II start their theological teaching, they talk straight from the beginning of the mystery of God, the paschal mystery, the Church as the mystery of God's people, the mystery of God's revelation, and the mystery of history. These are their constitutive speech acts, these are the communicative actions they perform. The introductory words or prefaces and the first chapters of the conciliar constitutions of Vatican II about the mystery are giving the rule for all the subsequent chapters. They treat subsequent "constituent parts" of the mystery.[50] What is the specific way that these speech acts of Vatican II are different from the speech acts, for instance, in Vatican I? They do not refer to a "horizontal" intersubjective relationship between different persons. In the constitutive speech act—or communicative action—of Vatican II there reigns a so-to-say "multidimensional" communicative action: the incomprehensible initial and absolutely founding communicative action of God, the Father, realized through the Son and the Holy Spirit, and the founded communicative action of human beings, answering the gift of existence and the call to respond to God in faith, praise, and acknowledgment. It is a constitutive speech act that integrates all human activities, the whole reality, and thus constitutes all in faith. This initial speech act is as well the dominating rule to speak of the subsequent parts of the mystery with their own set of communicative actions. It is a new way to see the modern world, its epochal changing, and its appearing problems: the fact, for instance, that the different religions are living together in one society, often in one state, in one great cultural ensemble; the fact that the new generation of young people are living in a new cultural and social context, and so on. The mystery of God opens as well the possibility to look in a new way at the Church as a whole within this mystery, to which this modern world belongs as well as a part.

This constitutive rule of talking and of teaching, when compared to former times when this way of thinking and talking was not known, makes it necessary to address in another way certain topics. The reason is that the occurring propositional moments are now positioned and integrated in a specific interrelation that opens a new view and other possibilities to understand them. The following list marks some outstanding points of so-called discontinuity between Vatican II and the preceding Tradition of the Church:

Dignitatis Humanae certainly marks a change in a seventeen-hundred-year-old tradition of church-state symbiosis. Freedom of religion is seen and confessed in a much more radical form, because of a more comprehensive view of God's salvific action.

Nostra Aetate talks of the relationship with other religions in a different way than the Church did in the centuries before, because of God's auto-communication to humankind from the protoancestors on, and the continuing maintenance of God's covenant with Israel.

Gaudium et Spes opens a new approach to affirm a mutual and perichoretic relationship between the modern world and the Church, which is the sacrament of the reign of God.

Lumen Gentium, Sacrosanctum Concilium, and *Apostolicam Actuositatem* mark the profound rediscovery of the people of God, their royal dignity, their priestly and prophetic mission, and their competence to participate and perform the paschal mystery of Christ in the Eucharist, the sacraments, and the liturgy.

Lumen Gentium, Sacrosanctum Concilium, Christus Dominus, and *Presbyterorum Ordinis* affirm ministry in the Church as service for the people of God, so that the whole Church can achieve its mission, endowed with authority in and for the church.

Lumen Gentium and *Ecclesiarum Orientalium* affirm the fundamental plurality of the churches in the Church, as well as a plurality in the interpretation of the apostolic Tradition, as in liturgy and theology.

Lumen Gentium and *Unitatis redintegratio* acknowledge the duty to promote the reintegration of the separated churches; actual members of separated churches and ecclesial communities, born in these communities, cannot be accused now as sinful schismatics; notwithstanding the lack of complete unity, the Holy Spirit uses separated churches as means of salvation. All these new views are seen from the perspective of God's salvific action that founds and empowers faith, hope, and charity. At the same time, this view does not ignore the differences between the ecclesial communities, the differences in understanding of faith. It clears up active and intersubjective relationships.

In this theological way of speaking, dogmatic definitions do not occur. They are not possible in this type of *Sprachspiel,*[51] because this *Sprachspiel* clears up constitutive connections within the multidimensional intersubjective communication. If the Council fathers use this *Sprachspiel* they do not renounce their authority. On the contrary, they use their full authority as they declare it themselves—for instance in the preface of *Dei Verbum*:

> Hearing the Word of God with reverence and proclaiming it with faith...following in the footsteps of the Council of Trent and of the First Vatican Council this present Council wishes to set forth authentic doctrine of divine revelation and how it is handed on, so that by hearing the message of salvation the whole world may believe, by believing it may hope, and by hoping it may love. (*DH* 4201)

It is convenient and adequate to call the texts of Vatican II constitutional texts, because they are texts resulting from constitutive speech acts that reign and determine in a radical way the whole manner of speaking and teaching faith through the Council.

A last observation regarding the beginning of our inquiry: faith in God and God's salvation of humankind cannot be understood, except through human reason; cannot be expressed and confessed, except through human language; cannot be affirmed, except through human freedom; that is, faith is always realized through limited means, connected and used with awareness of these limitations and the confidence in the incomprehensible grace and self-communication of God overcoming all human limitations. So faith can be thought only as *ratio fidei*: *ratio* rooted in sensitivity and articulated in spoken language is the historical way to discover reality, to discover truth. This *ratio* in its historical forms does not alter faith as mystery, God-given relation—witnessed by the prophets[52] and revealed by God's Son[53]—but provides understanding of faith.

Notes

1. Vatican Council II, Message of the Council Fathers; see *Acta Synodalia*, 52 vols. (Vatican City: Typis Polyglottis Vaticanis, 1970–99), vol. I/1, 230–32.

2. See *Sacrosanctum Concilium* 4.

3. See *Lumen Gentium* 1; *Unitatis Redintegratio* 1; *Ad Gentes* 1; *Nostra Aetate* 1; *Apostolicam Actuositatem* 1, etc. It is not accidental that the hints to "modern times" etc. occur straight in the initial passages of the documents.

4. *Gaudium et Spes* 33.

5. See *Gaudium et Spes* 7.

6. See Karl Polanyi, *The Great Transformation: The Political and Economic Origins of Our Time* (Boston, MA: Beacon Press, 1944).

7. See Wolfgang Welsch, *Unsere postmoderne Moderne*, 3rd ed. (Weinheim: Oldenbourg, 1991); Jean Francois Lyotard, *La condition postmoderne: Rapport sur le savoir* (Paris: Minuit, 1979).

8. Franz Xaver Kaufmann, *Kirche in der ambivalenten Moderne* (Freiburg i.B.: Herder, 2012), 45.

9. See Niklas Luhmann, *Soziale Systeme: Grundriss einer allgemeinen Theorie* (Frankfurt a.M.: Suhrkamp, 1984). Franz Xaver Kaufmann analyzes in a brilliant way the social transformation that happened in the Church from the nineteenth to the twentieth century, demonstrating how this social functionalization was mitigated in the Church through the formation of milieus. See Kaufmann, *Kirche in der ambivalenten Moderne*, 87–104.

10. See Benedict XVI, "Encyclical Caritas in Veritate," *Acta Apostolicae Sedis* 101 (2009): 655–68, c. 2, *De humana nostrae aetatis progression*, nos. 21–33. Benedict describes the new epoch especially under perspectives of human development.

11. A remark concerning *virtue* in the *Summa Theologiae* of Thomas: Virtue refers to the *potentiae* of human beings and means the perfection into which the *potentiae* of human beings can develop. Faith is the virtue—besides hope and love—into which persons as rational beings can develop, when they—through God's revelation as *prima veritas*—accept and perform their life as God-given and in God's light. See: *STh* I-II, q. 55, a. 2; a.3; *STh* II-II, q. 2, a. 3. John of the Cross, the Spanish mystic, who belongs to the first generation of students who studied St. Thomas's *Summa Theologiae* instead of Peter Lombard's *Sententiae*, calls faith the *forma rationalis* of human beings, who are gifted with the image of God but have to realize this gift by their personal way of life.

12. Eberhard Schockenhoff, *Bonum hominis: Die anthropologischen und theologischen Grundlagen der Tugendethik des Thomas von Aquin* (Mainz: Matthias-Grunewald-Verlag, 1987), 355.

13. See Thomas Aquinas, *Super Joannis*, c. 1, l. 3. (no. 97).

14. Thomas Aquinas, *STh* II-II, q. 1, a. 2 ad 2: *Actus autem credentis non terminatur ad enuntiabile, sed ad rem.*

15. Thomas Aquinas, *Summa contra Gentiles*, I, 16.

16. See Thomas Aquinas, *STh* I, q. 30, a. 3.

17. See ibid., I, q. 8, a. 3.

18. With this argument, which is characterized here only according to its inner logic, Thomas transforms the concepts of metaphysics and cosmology of Aristotle. He paves the way to think the unmoved mover as Creator, who creates the world out of nothing. For the difference between Ibn Sina, Maimonides, and Thomas, see D. B. Burrell, *Knowing the Unknowable God: Ibn Sina, Maimonides, Aquinas* (Notre Dame, IN: University of Notre Dame Press, 1986).

19. Thomas Aquinas, *STh* I, q. 19, a. 1: *Et sicut suum intelligere est suum esse, ita et suum velle.* And as thinking is being, so it is willing.

20. See Peter Hünermann, "Tawheed—The Oneness of God in Islam," in Christoph Schwöbel, ed., *Gott-Götter-Götzen.* XIV. Europäischer Kongress für Theologie. Zürich, 11–15 September 2011 (Leipzig: Evangelische Verlagsanstalt, 2012), 173–77.

21. It is John Duns Scotus who introduces the term *scienctia transcendens* as a name for metaphysics as science. See *Quaestiones super libros Metaphysicorum Aristotelis*, prol., no. 5, ed. Viv. VII, 4f.

22. Rational metaphysical reflection starts from obvious philosophical principles that cannot be proven.

23. Thomas Aquinas was chosen as point of reference in this argument because neither in Greek or Latin patristics, nor in earlier medieval theology—see Gregory of Nyssa, Augustine, Anselm, or Hugo of St. Victor—is a similar conceptual characteristic of faith elaborated. In distinction from modern philosophy, Thomas formulates the philosophical question of the condition of possibility of world and human beings in the light of being (*esse, Sein*), calling *substance* the *analogatum princeps* of all beings (*entia, Seiendes*).

24. Thomas speaks in this context of the "instinct of faith" leading human beings to this judgment. See Max Seckler, *Instinkt und Glaubenswille nach Thomas von Aquin* (Mainz: Matthias-Grünewald-Verlag, 1961).

25. See Ludger Honnefelder, *Scientia transcendens: Die formale Bestimmtheit der Seiendheit und Realität in der Metaphysik des Mittelalters und der Neuzeit* (Hamburg: F. Meiner, 1990), 3–108.

26. This very accentuated affirmation of God's will as foundation of all order and law makes obsolete the multiple residues of antique metaphysics still present in former medieval thinking: the cyclical movements as most divine, because they turn to themselves, in this way representing the unmoved mover; the whole cosmos, regulated in all its substances by natural places (*loci naturales*) and the inborn *entelecheia*, etc.

27. Obviously there are exceptions like Meister Eckhart, Nicholas of Cusa, John of the Cross, and others.

28. The momentum of this innovation in reference to the mystery of God appears clearly in Scotus's doctrine of the Holy Trinity. It is only according to the fundamental relationship of God and the whole rational order of possible and factual entities that God generates the divine Word. So God's saying of the Word is not any more the inner-divine foundation of all cognoscibility and cognition of reality. Thomas describes this relation in an inverse way!

29. See Konrad Feiereis, *Die Umprägung der natürlichen Theologie in Religionsphilosophie* (Leipzig: St. Benno-Verlag, 1965).

30. For the neo-Scholastic view of faith, see Matthias Joseph Scheeben, *Handbuch der Katholischen Dogmatik.* Vol. 1. *Theologische Erkenntnislehre*, ed. Martin Grabmann, 3rd ed. (Freiburg 1959), 287–379.

31. John Paul II underlines this perichoretic inclusion in his encyclical *Fides et Ratio;* see the paragraphs in DH, nos. 5075–80 (DH = Denzinger–Hünermann, Heinrich Denzinger, ed, *Enchiridion symbolorum, definitionum et declarationum de rebus fidei et morum*, continued by Peter Hünermann, 42nd ed., 1st ed. 1854 (Freiburg i.B.: Herder, 2009). See Peter Hünermann, "*Fides et Ratio*—Einst und Jetzt," *Theologische Quartalschrift* 189 (2009): 161–77.

32. See *Sacrosanctum Concilium*, ch. 1, nos. 5–6; *Lumen Gentium*, ch. 1: "The Mystery of the Church," nos. 1–8; *Dei Verbum*, ch. 1: *De ipsa revelation*, no. 2; for the numerous contexts in which the term *mystery* occurs in the following chapters, as well as in the decrees and declarations of Vatican II, see Peter Hünermann, "Lateinisches Sachverzeichnis," in *Herders Theologischer Kommentar zum Zweiten Vatikanischen Konzil*, ed. Hans Jochen Hilberath and Peter Hünermann, 5 vols. (Freiburg i.B.: Herder, 2004–5), 1:896.

33. See *Gaudium et Spes*, ch. 4: "The Task of the Church in the World of This Time," no. 40.

34. See *Sacrosanctum Concilium 7*.

35. See *Lumen Gentium 1–2*.

36. Karl Rahner was only one of the members of the "Catholic School of Heidegger," which included theologians as well as philosophers such as Max Müller, Johannes B. Lotz, Bernhard Welte, Gustav Siewerth, Ferdinand Ulrich, etc.

37. See Peter Hünermann, "...*in mundo huius temporis*...Die Bedeutung des Zweiten Vatikanischen Konzils im kulturellen Transformationsprozess der Gegenwart: Das Textcorpus des Zweiten Vatikanischen Konzils ist ein konstitutioneller Text des Glaubens," in *Erinnerung an die Zukunft—Das Zweite Vatikanische Konzil*, ed. Jan H. Tück (Freiburg i.B.: Herder, 2013), 31–53, esp. 34–37.

38. See W. G. Müller, "Stil," in *Historische Wörterbuch der Philosophie*, vol. 10 (Basel: Schwabe, 1998), 150–59. The article represents a vast and critical survey from Terentius, Cicero, and Quintilianus to the contemporary publications on philosophy of style and in modern history of science.

39. See John W. O'Malley, "Vatican II: Historical Perspectives on Its Uniqueness and Interpretation," in *Vatican II: The Unfinished Agenda. A Look to the Future*, ed. Lucien Richard and Daniel Harrington (New York: Paulist Press, 1987), 22–32. He introduced the term in the second symposium (1991) to prepare the *History of Vatican II*, published then in five volumes and directed by Giuseppe Alberigo.

40. See Christoph Theobald, *La réception du concile Vatican II*. Vol. I. *Accéder à la source* (Paris: Cerf, 2009); Christoph Theobald, *Le Christianisme comme style: Une manière de faire de la théologie*, 2 vols. (Paris: Cerf, 2007).

41. See the opening speech of John XXIII, *Gaudet Mater Ecclesia*, critical and commented edition by Alberto Melloni, "Sinossi critica dell'allocuzione di apertura del Concilio Vaticano II," in *Fede Tradizione Profezia: Studi su Giovanni XXIII e sul Vaticano II* (Brescia: Paideia, 1984), 239–83.

42. See, for instance, Giuseppe Alberigo, "La svolta pastorale nel Vaticano II," in *Per una nuova pastorale ecumenica* (Naples: Dehoniane, 1990), 71–76.

43. See Massimo Faggioli, *Vatican II: The Battle for Meaning* (Mahwah, NJ: Paulist Press, 2012).

44. See the analysis and critique of Jan Heiner Tück, "Postkonziliare Interpretationskonflikte. Ein Nachtrag zur Debatte um die Verbindlichkeit des Konzils," in *Erinnerung an die Zukunft, Das Zweite Vatikanische Konzil,* 2nd ed. (Freiburg i.B.: Herder, 2013), 114–26.

45. See Peter Hünermann, "Der Text: Werden—Gestalt—Bedeutung: Eine hermeneutische Reflexion," in Hilberath and Hünermann, *Herders Theologischer Kommentar zum Zweiten Vatikanischen Konzil,* 5:5–102; Peter Hünermann, "Der übersehene Text. Zur Hermeneutik des Zweiten Vatikanischen Konzils," *Concilium* 41 (2005): 434–50; Peter Hünermann, "Der 'Text': Eine Ergänzung zur Hermeneutik des II. Vatikanischen Konzils," *Cristianesimo nella storia* 28, no. 2 (2007): 339–58.

46. Ockham, *I Sent.* 26, 3C.

47. John R. Searle introduced the term *speech act* in his famous essay *Speech Acts: An Essay in the Philosophy of Language* (Cambridge: Cambridge University Press, 1969). He distinguishes speech acts marked by constitutive rules and others, marked by regulative rules.

48. See Jürgen Habermas and Niklas Luhmann, *Theorie der Gesellschaft oder Sozialtechnologie* (Frankfurt a.M.: Suhrkamp, 1971), 213–15.

49. Communicative actions or constitutive speech acts are always introduced nominating the intersubjective relationship, which is constituted through the speech act as such. For instance: I promise to do...this or that. Within the constituted relationship the propositional content—this or that—is communicated as the following enunciation tells it. At the beginning of *Dei Filius* (Council Vatican I, 1870) the pope says, "But now, together with the bishops of the whole world who gathered in the Holy Spirit in this ecumenical council by Our authority, sit

THE LEGACY OF VATICAN II

and judge with us, and relaying on the Word of God by the Catholic Church, We have decided and authentically interpreted, written and handed down as We have received it, reverently preserved and authentically interpreted by the Catholic Church, We have decided to profess and declare from this chair of Peter..." (DH, no. 3000). See as well the introducing speech acts of the Council of Trent, DH, no. 1500; nos. 1505–7; nos. 1510–11. Another example is the speech act introducing the dogmatization of 1950 on the Virgin Mary in *Munificentissimus Deus* (DH, no. 3900).

50. See *Lumen Gentium*: ch. 2, "The People of God"; ch. 3, "The Hierarchical Structure of the Church and in Particular the Episcopate"; etc.

51. See Ludwig Wittgenstein, "Philosophische Untersuchungen," in Ludwig Wittgenstein, *Schriften* (Frankfurt: Suhrkamp, 1960), 292–94.

52. See Rom 1:2.

53. See Heb 1:2.

4

Leslie Woodcock Tentler

Contraception and the Council

A TALE OF THREE JESUIT MORALISTS

Each of the Jesuit moralists who makes an appearance in this "tale" reminds us of an important truth about the Second Vatican Council. Arthur Vermeersch, SJ (1858–1936), a Belgian who "dominated Roman moral theology" in the latter stages of his career, reminds us of the ghosts that hovered over the Council's deliberations.[1] Who doubts that the shade of Pius IX was an uncomfortable presence for the Council fathers as they sought to make their peace with a world where liberal institutions held sway? In much the same way, previous papal pronouncements against contraception, where Vermeersch had played a prominent role, came to haunt many of the fathers as this difficult issue exploded in their midst. John C. Ford, SJ (1903–89), the leading American moralist of his generation, reminds us that much of the Council's action took place outside the *aula* at St. Peter's where the formal sessions were held. Ford, who was not a Council *peritus* and seldom present in Rome during Council sessions, played a major role behind the scenes as conciliar and postconciliar maneuvering intensified around the issue of birth control. The encyclical *Humanae Vitae* (1968) attests to his influence. Richard A. McCormick, SJ (1922–

2000), a distinguished ethicist who publicly criticized *Humanae Vitae*, reminds us that the Council concluded with major issues of authority still unresolved. The crisis generated by *Humanae Vitae* represents the first and certainly most dramatic post-Council confrontation over the nature of authority in the Church.

Let us begin with Father Vermeersch, though his appearance will be brief. Appointed to the faculty of the Gregorian University in 1918, he was at the height of his prestige in 1930, when Pius XI decided to issue an encyclical on Christian marriage. Vermeersch was apparently its principal author. *Casti Connubii* was immediately occasioned by the Anglicans having voted, at a recent Lambeth Conference, to sanction the use of contraceptives in difficult marital circumstances. But it was also prompted by rumblings from Germany in support of a similar reform among Catholics and worries on the part of Roman theologians that many priests were neglecting to enforce their Church's prohibition on contraception.[2] Accordingly, the encyclical's language was both vigorous and firm. Contraception was "shameful and intrinsically vicious," according to the pope; couples who employed it, no matter their circumstances, were guilty of a "horrible crime." As for confessors, they were summoned to a newly proactive mode, which entailed both interrogation of married penitents and explicit instruction of the allegedly ignorant. No priest should "allow the faithful entrusted to [him] to err regarding this most grave law of God."[3] In an era of mass communication, *Casti Connubii* was the stuff of front-page news. Reaffirmed on a number of occasions by Pius XII, it was taught as infallible doctrine in Catholic seminaries into the early 1960s.

Given its status as an immutable teaching, contraception barely figured among the proposed Council topics submitted to Rome by the world's bishops. No American bishop mentioned it.[4] Certain European prelates, however, principally from France, Germany, Belgium, and the Netherlands, believed that the teaching had created acute pastoral problems, probably worldwide and certainly in their own jurisdictions. Their anxieties help to explain why Paul VI in February 1964 asked his secretariat of state to poll the world's bishops with regard to the status of contraception among their people. How widely was contraception practiced by Catholics and others? What was its status in law? What were the principal "doctrinal and pastoral tendencies" locally with regard to birth control? To respond to the last-mentioned question, the National Council of Catholic Bishops tapped John C. Ford, SJ—a man who, with long-time collaborator George Kelly, SJ, so dominated the field of moral theology in the United States that, in the words of Richard McCormick, "most of us regarded their agreement on a practical matter as constituting a 'solidly probable opinion.'"[5]

Ford conveyed mixed news to the bishops. Although certain European moralists had recently voiced ambiguous or even dissenting views on Church teaching, mainly occasioned by the advent of a birth control pill, this was not true in the United States. "American theologians and moralists have not defended in published articles a departure from traditional teaching on birth control." But due to a surfeit of "bootleg moral theology," a principal source of which was Dr. John Rock, "widespread confusion" prevailed among both laity and clergy. Disturbingly large numbers of Catholics appeared to believe that a change in Church teaching was imminent—a delusion fostered by the continued silence of the pope and Vatican Council II on the question. (Contraception as an issue had been removed from the purview of the Council fathers by John XXIII and assigned to an initially secret advisory commission of physicians and demographers.)[6] It was "imperative," in Ford's view, for the pope or "preferably" the Council to speak, given trends in public opinion. "There is a growing tendency on the part of the educated Catholic laity to question the whole teaching of the Church on birth control."[7]

Ford acknowledged the complex origins of the current situation, chief among them alarm at global population pressures, recent papal concessions with regard to employment of the rhythm method for purposes of family limitation, and a higher valuation among theologians "of the sexual act as an expression of conjugal love." More fundamental, however, at least in Ford's view, was "the lack of clear, cogent moral principles derived from reason to prove that contraception and contraceptive sterilization are always immoral." Ford did not doubt that contraception was intrinsically wrong, due to "the natural finality of the generative act and generative faculty" and the inviolability of what he called "the sources of life." But the recent advent of a birth control pill had muddied the waters. If, as some theologians maintained, a woman might licitly take the pill for a time in order to "normalize" an irregular menstrual cycle and thus facilitate the practice of rhythm, why might she not do so in the wake of childbirth, when women did not "normally" ovulate? The generative faculty was "not so sacrosanct we may never intervene directly at all," as Ford conceded. How far could one legitimately go in regulating the female cycle of fertility and sterility? While theologians were pondering the matter, which Ford regarded as an urgent priority, confessors were being confronted by desperate penitents whose questions they often could not answer, save by appeals to authority.[8]

In an apparent effort to prompt the pope or Council fathers to action, Ford traveled to Rome in late spring 1964. A brief visit to the American College at Louvain, where the seminarians "question[ed] the whole tradition on birth control," confirmed his sense of urgency.[9] He met with Cardinal Alfredo Ottaviani, head of the Holy Office, on June 6, when his arguments in favor of a Council statement on contraception were rebuffed. A conciliar debate over birth control would be endless, Ottaviani maintained. "Besides, so many of the Bishops knew nothing of the subject."[10] As wholehearted in his support of the traditional teaching as Ford himself, Ottaviani seems to have recognized in this straight-talking American a useful ally in what was already shaping as a Catholic war over contraception. Ford's subsequent meeting with Paul VI was almost certainly arranged by Ottaviani, a long-time friend of the pope. Ford presented the pope with a copy of the report he had recently done for the U.S. bishops, along with his recently published *Marriage Questions,* and proceeded to set him straight with regard to the birth control pill. The pill currently on the market "was *no different* from the one Pius XII condemned" in 1958, Ford explained. Thus a failure to affirm this condemnation in the clearest possible terms would not only abet the confusion that currently reigned but do irreparable damage to the ordinary magisterium. The two spoke principally in Italian, with Ford—talking "fast and furious"—occasionally resorting to Latin. The pope, whom Ford described in his diary as "affable, cordial, alert, a little tired, a little sad perhaps," appeared "to understand everything."[11]

Ford's visit probably explains his appointment, at the end of 1964, to the Papal Commission for the Study of Population, Family, and Births, popularly known as the "birth control commission." The visit was otherwise fruitless, at least from Ford's perspective. Pope Paul did subsequently issue a statement but hardly one that Ford could approve. The teaching on contraception, the Pope announced on June 23, "was under study, a study as wide and deep as possible." In the meantime, the faithful were to abide by "the relevant norms of Pius XII," since the pope did not currently have "sufficient reason" to modify them.[12] Ford was distressed—it would not be the last time—by what he saw as the pope's equivocal posture. "In the face of the pronouncement of the Holy Father, June 23, 1964, theologians are resorting to the principles of probabilism," Ford complained in March 1965. Should it be widely accepted that the traditional teaching was doubtful, confessors would be free to endorse the use of contraceptives in a variety of difficult marital circumstances or leave the decision up to the penitent. Once broadly established, such a regime would make it "almost impossible, or at least extremely difficult and fraught with practical danger" for the pope to rule definitively against contraception at some subsequent date.[13]

To head off such an eventuality, Ford renewed his efforts to prompt a vigorous papal statement. He also tried to elicit a parallel statement from the American bishops, submitting a lengthy but characteristically lucid draft to the Administrative Committee of the National Council of Catholic Bishops in August 1965. By a slim majority, however, the Committee declined to act.[14] With the matter still under study by the papal commission and the pope's own intentions unclear, indefinite postponement seemed prudent. Ford then submitted the proposed draft to Cardinal Amleto Cigognani, Paul's secretary of state, presumably hoping that he would bring it to the pope's attention.[15] One month later, in November, he wrote to Egidio Vagnozzi, apostolic delegate to the United States, requesting Vagnozzi's assistance in obtaining a private audience with the pope. By this time, Ford had a second issue he wished to discuss with the Holy Father—to wit, the drift of the papal commission on which Ford now sat. "I would like to explain the surprising attitude of some members of the Commission who are of the opinion that the Magisterium of the Church has no right to make laws or declare more laws in such a way that they are binding on the individual conscience in the individual case." He singled out Canon Pierre de Locht, whom Ford accurately described as "an influential member of the Commission." De Locht, Ford asserted, "has taught contraception to the priests and people of Belgium for some years," adding that "I have the documents to prove it."[16]

Vagnozzi was either unable or unwilling to arrange a papal audience for Ford, who traveled to Rome nonetheless. Shortly after his arrival, he was summoned to the papal chambers, presumably through the good offices of Cardinal Ottaviani, who was troubled by language in the chapter on marriage of the soon-to-be ratified "Constitution on the Church in the Modern World" (*Gaudium et Spes*). The pope apparently shared Ottaviani's anxieties, for that chapter was the primary subject of his conversation with Ford. "We spent at least three quarters of the time discussing this and the problems connected with it," as Ford recounted the audience, "and at the end he asked me to go home and write down the points which I considered absolutely indispensable to make the document acceptable, and told me to come back the next day to discuss them with him if necessary, which I did."[17] Ford's notes appear to have provided a basis for the four *modi* by means of which the pope attempted at the very last minute to substantively alter the chapter's tone and logic.[18] The chapter as drafted had spoken of marriage as a community of love and made only oblique reference to contraception. The *modi* and their accompanying letter demanded an explicit condemnation of contraception, along with a reference to *Casti Connubii* and various statements by Pius XII in its defense.

The *modi* generated a deep, if short-lived, crisis in the mixed commission charged with the chapter's final revision. Did the pope wish to preempt debate on an issue of critical pastoral importance? (The Council had already voted to approve the chapter on marriage as drafted, subject to minor amendment.) If the teaching on contraception could not be reformed, what was the purpose of the papal commission currently engaged in its study? A subsequent papal letter, prompted by an appeal from alarmed lay auditors, assured members of the mixed commission that, while the substance of the *modi* should indeed be incorporated into the text, how this was done was up to them. Freed thereby to act creatively, the mixed commission famously relegated to a footnote its single reference to *Casti Connubii* and denounced not "contraceptive arts" but "illicit practices against human generation"—a phrase so vague as to be almost meaningless.[19] "Thus the Pope's substantial intent was completely thwarted," as John Ford noted in his diary.[20] Shortly thereafter, the pope gave his blessing to the reconvening of the birth control commission with an agenda that included discussion, in Ford's words, of "natural law and birth control on a broad basis." Ford was yet again troubled by what he saw as the pope's inconsistency. "It is not logical to insist in the strongest language that the solemn doctrine of C[asti] C[onnubii] must be upheld and at the same time allow discussions to be conducted in his own commission which make sense only in the supposition that that doctrine can be rejected."[21]

Ford took extensive, if hurried, notes, during or perhaps immediately after his November 22 meeting with the pope. He and Ford evidently agreed on many issues. Although the pope was deeply concerned about population pressures in economically underdeveloped countries, he—like Ford—believed that the solution was not contraception but more equitable distribution of the world's resources. The growing legitimacy of contraception, both men feared, would eventually lead to governments imposing birth control and even abortion on unwilling populations. When Ford predicted that legalized abortion and euthanasia would inevitably follow the widespread embrace of contraception, the pope concurred. The pope was "very aware"

69

of the "new morality," Ford noted, and "was *against* it." Both men agreed that *Casti Connubii* was not substantially reformable; as Ford never tired of repeating, the authority of the ordinary magisterium was directly at stake. But the pope seemed confused, according to Ford, when it came to the pill. Moral theologians he respected—Bishop Josef Maria Reuss was specifically mentioned—were saying that it might legitimately be employed in a variety of marital circumstances. Did use of the pill not sometimes represent a temporary suppression of fertility, a state that was natural to the female for the greater part of her monthly cycle, rather than contraceptive sterilization? Not so, said Ford, invoking the inviolability of what he called life's sources. Besides, Ford argued, significant developments with regard to the rhythm method were on the medical horizon. A new drug was in the offing, one "which would *indicate* time of ovulation," thus endowing the method with pill-like effectiveness as a mode of family planning and requiring a relatively brief period of sexual abstention on the part of its users. It would be "ironical," Ford pointed out, "if [the] Church gave in just when a good solution is coming."[22]

Certain American chroniclers of the Council have credited John Ford with outsized influence over the drafting of *Humanae Vitae*, partly because of his role on the papal birth control commission and partly, in all likelihood, because of a native instinct to locate a prominent American at global center stage. (European commentators have paid him far less mind.) Ford did not have the papal access enjoyed by Cardinal Ottaviani and his curial allies, nor did his three known meetings with the pope break new theological ground. Ford did contribute substantially to the so-called minority report of the birth control commission and he did function as a consultor during the early stages of *Humanae Vitae*'s drafting.[23] But one cannot point to aspects of that encyclical that are clearly attributable to him, with the possible exception of a brief but heartfelt appeal, in the encyclical's latter pages, to "men of science," whose research, it is hoped, will render the practice of rhythm "sufficiently secure."[24] Have we an echo here of Ford's brash announcement in 1966 that "a drug" predicting the exact day of ovulation was on the horizon?

("He was very interested," Ford says of the pope's response.)[25] We know that Paul agonized over his birth control encyclical, aware that lay sentiment strongly supported reform. Was he comforted, even strengthened, in those difficult days by faith in an imminent medical breakthrough of the sort Ford had described? If so, then John Ford did indeed play a pivotal role in the encyclical's history—appropriately, for an American, as an apostle of the technological fix.

That the chapter on marriage in *Gaudium et Spes* did not, despite its papally prompted amendments, explicitly condemn the pill was trumpeted in the media as a sign of imminent reform. Ford made a final effort, again unsuccessful, to get the American bishops to clarify matters. "I think it is extremely important at the present moment to get some statement, issuing with as much authority as possible, which will help to dispel the utter confusion that exists, and which will now increase, if these popular, inaccurate press reports go unanswered."[26] Discouraged by the continued silence of the bishops' conference, he turned again to Rome, submitting the draft of a proposed papal statement—cowritten by Germain Grisez, Ford's new intellectual partner—to Archbishop Leo Binz, whom he hoped might convey it to Cardinal Cigognani or even the pope.[27] Shortly thereafter, Pope Paul offered public remarks of his own with regard to the Council's language on marriage—another Ford disappointment, given their seeming ambiguity. "It is not clear to me from the accounts in the *N.Y. Times* and the other papers just what the import of his statement is," Ford complained to Binz. "I must say it sounds rather confusing."[28]

The final meetings of the birth control commission, scheduled to run from April to June 1966, thus became for Ford the only arena where he could continue the fight. The commission had recently been enlarged, with the addition of fourteen new members, all of them archbishops. Coupled with the commission's chairmanship being assigned to Cardinal Ottaviani, the episcopal appointments stirred anxiety in reform-minded quarters. Would they stem what had already emerged in the commission as strong sentiment in favor of substantive change in the teaching on contraception? As Ford noted in the wake of an early

71

May session, the "great majority" of theologians present had voted "by a provisional show of hands" in favor of *Casti Connubii*'s reformability and against "the intrinsic malice of contraception." Cardinal Joseph Suenens, the week's presiding officer, had gone further, explicitly endorsing contraception—at least according to Ford—and inviting all "the theologians to doubt the traditional position of the Church." (I understood him to say that we had a duty to doubt it.) Those theologians who disagreed had found themselves "in a very defensive position.[29] Would the new episcopal members, scheduled to attend in June, be willing to accept what seemed to Ford close to a *fait accompli*?

The commission by this time was very large, at seventy-one members, a substantial minority of whom were lay, including three married couples. The testimony of the laymembers—most were physicians, psychologists, demographers, or sociologists— kept the discussion grounded in contemporary realities, clothing the abstract arguments of the theologians in experiential flesh. That of the married couples and especially the wives was particularly important, given that they had arrived at the session armed with abundant testimony from devout Catholics who spoke in unvarnished terms of the harm rhythm often did to marriages. Two of the wives also spoke frankly about their own experience of marital sex. Most clerical members of the commission were moved by this testimony, which seems to have played a significant role in changing certain episcopal minds. Ford, however, was not. "The young married couples have the advantage of knowing the concrete elements of the problem and the difficulties of the Church's teaching better than anyone else," he acknowledged. "But they have the disadvantage of being liable to be less objective judges in this matter because of these very difficulties." The married, in short, were "pleading their own cause." One might as well consult teenaged boys on the morality of masturbation.[30]

The June 1966 meetings of the episcopal members were occasionally stormy. But the group moved toward endorsing reform with unexpected speed, in good part for pastoral reasons. Lay testimony had had an effect, especially with regard to the rhythm method. "I am quite sure that relief must be brought to

Catholic couples," confessed Britain's Cardinal John Heenan, reckoned as a conservative, "and I cannot bring myself to accept that the thermometer and the calendar are a good way of keeping men and women from mortal sin."[31] Ford was present at the bishops' initial session—certain of the episcopal sessions were closed to all but the episcopal members—where he intervened passionately in defense of Tradition. "Like life itself, the inception of life belongs to God," Ford argued. "To attack it is to attack a fundamental human good, to intrude on God's domain. That is why the will to contracept, though essentially different morally from the will to abort, is nevertheless similar to it." Christian authorities throughout the ages had acknowledged "as it were spontaneously, that contraception violated Christian chastity and violated the inception of human life." To endorse contraception for married Catholics would not only vitiate the teaching authority of the Church. It would also open the door to permissiveness with regard to abortion. "It is noteworthy that among the Catholic theologians who defend contraception today, there are already some who defend therapeutic abortion in certain difficult cases."[32]

That Ford's eloquence had so little effect on the assembled prelates is a measure of how enormous the pastoral problem of contraception now appeared. Preoccupied with the sufferings of the "magnificent Christian couples" (the words are Heenan's) who had struggled to observe Church teaching, most of the bishops could not envision the slide toward widespread abortion predicted by Ford. With the just-adjourned Council having condemned abortion in the strongest possible terms, Ford's fears may well have seemed beside the point. Nor did Ford's frequently voiced warning that reform would fatally damage the magisterium cause the consternation one might expect. Most of the assembled prelates appeared to believe just the opposite—that a reaffirmation of the teaching after several years of practical doubt would do serious harm to the pope's authority. In the end, a substantial majority of the episcopal members—it was they alone who voted on the commission's final report—endorsed a document recommending a substantive reform of Church teaching. While marriage was of its essence oriented to procreation, the report maintained, every marital act need not be. Rearing and educating children in present-day circumstances was enormously demanding, both economically and emotionally. Parents had the right, indeed the duty, to determine how many children they might responsibly bear. Since the rhythm method had proved damaging to the marital community of love in a great many instances, it was up to Christian couples to decide which nonabortive mode of family planning was best for them.[33]

In response to what soon came to be called the commission's "majority report," Cardinal Ottaviani coordinated efforts to assemble a document in reply. Ford apparently did most of the writing, basing the draft on his summary statement to the papal commission at its meeting on May 23.[34] The "minority report," as the document came inaccurately to be known, centered on themes long central to Ford's arguments. Contraception was intrinsically evil because "the generative processes are in some way specially inviolable precisely because they are generative." The Church from its earliest days had so taught. Thus the teaching on contraception was not substantially reformable, though legitimate doctrinal development had certainly taken place—and could continue to do so—with regard to such things as the theology of sex in marriage and the employment of rhythm in the service of family limitation. The report was most eloquent, however, when it came to preserving papal authority. The text comes directly from Ford's final address to the commission:

> The Church could not have erred through so many centuries, even through one century, by imposing under serious obligation very grave burdens in the name of Jesus Christ, if Jesus Christ did not actually impose these burdens....If the Church could err in such a way, the authority of the ordinary magisterium in moral matters would be thrown into question.[35]

The drama then moved behind Vatican doors. Ford served as an advisor to Ottaviani and his mostly curial allies as they lobbied the pope, who seems to have been inclined from the first to reject his commission's recommendation, notwithstanding pleas from certain European bishops to do just the opposite. A draft of what would be the encyclical *Humanae Vitae* was apparently completed by June 1967, roughly two months after the full texts of both the "majority" and "minority" reports had been published, without authorization, in the *National Catholic Reporter.* Still the pope hesitated, apparently anxious about the encyclical's reception and worried that the draft was insufficiently pastoral. When it finally appeared, on July 29, 1968, the text had been substantially modified, some of it by the pope himself. He was largely responsible for its markedly pastoral tone and avoidance of reference to mortal sin.[36] John Ford would almost certainly have taken a harder line, having frequently argued that unrepentant users of contraception should be denied the sacraments.[37]

Nonetheless, *Humanae Vitae* marked the moment of Ford's triumph. Admirably pastoral though it was, the encyclical affirmed the ban on contraception in clear and absolute terms— terms that pointedly included the pill. But his was a pyrrhic victory, both personally and in terms of the cause to which he was so passionately devoted. Even prior to the encyclical, Ford was increasingly on the outs with his fellow moral theologians, most of whom were partisans of reform. Relations were tense with his theology faculty colleagues at Weston College, Ford told Germain Grisez in August 1967, ruing "the role I seem required to play, of frequently making myself unpopular when I don't go along with some of the decisions."[38] (The appointment of non-Catholics to teach Weston theology courses, a move that Ford opposed, was a particularly neuralgic issue.) Students that year, according to Grisez, were sometimes openly contemptuous of a man who just years earlier had been universally regarded as a giant in his field. Anger over *Humanae Vitae* apparently led to a state verging on open war. After a year's sabbatical, Ford volunteered to retire as of January 1969, and the offer was gratefully accepted.[39] Since Weston had been Ford's academic home for most of his distinguished career, the abrupt end to his classroom vocation was immensely painful.

Even more painful for Ford, very likely, was the hostile reception accorded *Humanae Vitae.* "Reactions around the world

—in the Italian and American press, for example—are just as sharp as they were at the time of the *Syllabus of Errors* of Pius IX," in the words of Bernard Häring.[40] Reactions in Catholic circles were equally sharp and frequently reflective of anguish. Theologians in the United States and subsequently in Europe took the unprecedented step of issuing public challenges to the encyclical's logic, concluding that married couples might in good conscience employ contraceptives when marital circumstances so required. Prominent lay Catholics issued statements of their own, some of them intemperate, while Catholic behavior with regard to contraception moved rapidly toward the American norm. Negative reaction to the encyclical, indeed, was so intense and widespread that one might almost speak of its having been rejected. "Non-reception became almost overnight a live theological issue," in the words of Richard McCormick, the third in our trio of Jesuit moralists. Nonreception of an authoritative papal teaching was clearly an issue that transcended the debate over birth control, having instead to do with the nature of authority in the Church. "Contraception, as a moral issue, was virtually smothered in the ecclesiological tumult," as McCormick summarized the postencyclical situation.[41]

Humanae Vitae thus occasioned a first postconciliar wrestling with the Council's principal unfinished business, which had everything to do with authority. Various Council documents had endorsed a more collegial mode of governance for a Church that in recent centuries had been characterized by an increasing concentration of authority in Rome. *Humanae Vitae* was issued without episcopal consultation and rejected the recommendations of the pope's own commission, on which a number of bishops had sat. The Council had urged the world's bishops to inaugurate structures through which priests might collaborate in diocesan governance. *Humanae Vitae* led certain bishops to punish priests who questioned its conclusions. The Council also spoke in newly appreciative terms about lay witness in the world, which necessarily entailed respect for lay autonomy and competence; it also endorsed as its reigning metaphor of Church the distinctly communal term *People of God*. But lay testimony, so instrumental in shaping the majority report of the papal commission, was effectively rejected by the pope, notwithstanding the markedly pastoral tone of his birth control encyclical. Rightly or wrongly, it seemed to a great many Catholics—laity, parish priests, and theologians alike—that the pope was attempting to exercise authority in the outdated mode of his predecessors, thereby repudiating what they took to be the Council's principal achievements.

Not surprisingly, given the stakes, the postencyclical debate was deeply polarizing. Despite his poor health, Father John Ford weighed in, asserting that *Humanae Vitae*—contrary to the claims of the pope's own spokesman—was infallible teaching.[42] He continued for the rest of his career to argue against contraception, frequently in collaboration with Germain Grisez, whose work informed the postencyclical pastoral of the U.S. bishops on "Christian Family Life." But Ford and Grisez by the late 1960s represented a distinctly minority view among moral theologians in the United States. Grisez's arguments on contraception, according to Richard McCormick's uncharacteristically acerbic assessment of the bishops' pastoral, "have been carefully scrutinized by the theological community and been found wanting, or at least very inconclusive on a number of key points."[43] McCormick himself represented the theological mainstream, both in his challenging the encyclical's principal arguments and his attention to the ecclesiological issues it raised. That he had not been consulted by the bishops in preparing their pastoral, given his prominence and the respect he enjoyed, was a measure of how divisive the postencyclical debate was proving to be.

McCormick, by his own admission, had been slow to embrace a reformist posture with regard to contraception. Trained in the manualist tradition of which John Ford was so accomplished an exponent, McCormick maintained publicly as late as 1966 that contraception was intrinsically wrong. "The teaching is there, not as a matter of counsel or opinion, but as a matter whose practical acceptance binds in conscience," as he wrote in the increasingly reformist precincts of *Commonweal*.[44] McCormick, who in 1965 became editor of "Notes on Moral Theology"—a widely-read feature of *Theological Studies* once edited by John Ford—was well-acquainted with the arguments for reform.[45] But respect for the Tradition in which he was formed—in his view, it had an admirably pastoral side—caused him to move slowly. When he announced late in 1967 that he now regarded the teaching on contraception as "in a state of practical doubt," at least in "situations of genuine conflict," it came as something of a thunderclap, given McCormick's reputation for competence and prudence.[46]

McCormick attributed his evolving views in part to Joseph Fuchs, SJ, a distinguished German moralist who served on the papal birth control commission and in that capacity reevaluated his own thinking with regard to the teaching. "Over a three-year period, Fuchs and I shared our difficulties on this question and I found myself gradually moving with him through a state of doubt to ultimate conviction that the Church's position could be and had to be reformulated." The Council itself was even more critical. "Without my explicitly adverting to it, what was really changing were basic notions of ecclesiology and eventually moral methodology. These notions had been set in motion by Vatican II, especially by its adoption of a concentric rather than pyramidal model of the Church and its heavy emphasis on the human person as central to moral reflection." The preencyclical climate— open to doubt, anticipatory of reform—made such evolution relatively painless, at least in a personal sense. Things were very different once *Humanae Vitae* appeared. "This put many of us on the spot, both on the moral issue itself, but above all on the ecclesiological implications." Having articulated his disagreement with the encyclical's moral reasoning for the December 1969 issue of *Theological Studies*, McCormick "ended up in Boston's Lahey Clinic for my efforts."[47]

Postencyclical conflict was so bitter precisely because authority was so centrally at issue. "*Humanae Vitae* became the litmus test of Catholic loyalty," McCormick correctly noted, "and dissenting scholars began to be described as 'deviant,' 'disloyal' and a host of other almost repeatable things." In the short term, the situation was deeply stressful, as McCormick's experience testifies. But it ultimately allowed theologians like him "to see many other things in a much more explicit way, things that had remained in a kind of transitional haze since the Council."

McCormick moved toward a broadened understanding of the magisterium, one in which theological dissent played a necessary role and one that proceeded in the form of a conversation involving every concerned party in the Church. "I have come to see and value lay experience and reflection and am the richer for it," McCormick wrote in 1992, adding that "the pope and bishops simply must consult those who are truly competent"—a category that might well include the laity—when it came to the application of moral principles. "Horizontal activity in this world does not belong to the Church's competence in the same way the deposit of faith does. Only with the ecclesiological moves made by Vatican II was I prepared to see this."[48]

That it took some years for McCormick to arrive at these conclusions reminds us of one final reality about the Council: for all practical purposes, it did not end in December 1965 with its elaborate closing ceremonies. The extent and meaning of the Council's reforms had still to be determined. This ongoing "battle for meaning," to borrow from Massimo Faggioli, has entailed conflict in a variety of venues, ranging from liturgy to canon law.[49] But moral theology has provided the most fiercely contested ground, as the debate over *Humanae Vitae* attests. In that debate, according to McCormick, "questions were raised about the formation of conscience, about the response due to the ordinary magisterium, about the exercise of authority in the Church, about consultative processes and collegiality, about the meaning of the guidance of the Holy Spirit to the pastors of the Church."[50] For McCormick personally, as for most moral theologians, such questions signaled a new intellectual freedom and a greater scope for creativity than would have been possible before the Council. Particularly as a medical ethicist, the postconciliar McCormick could command an audience that extended well beyond Catholics. Unlike John Ford in his heyday, however, McCormick could not assume that he spoke for, or to, a unified Catholic community. Nor was he immune from bitter attacks by fellow Catholics on his loyalty and integrity. The postconciliar Catholic world continues to be deeply divided over precisely the questions posed by the debate over *Humanae Vitae*. Our tale of three Jesuit moralists, it seems, still awaits a tidy resolution.

Notes

1. The characterization is from John T. Noonan, *Contraception: A History of Its Treatment by the Catholic Theologians and Canonists*, enlarged ed. (Cambridge, MA: Harvard University Press, 1986), 425.

2. Ibid., 425–26.

3. *Casti Connubii*, text found at http://www.vatican.va/holy_father/pius_xi/encyclicals/documents/hf_p-xi_enc_31121930_casti-connubii_en.html.

4. Joseph A. Komonchak, "What They Said Before the Council: How the U.S. Bishops Envisioned Vatican II," *Commonweal* 117, no. 21 (December 1990): 714–17.

5. Richard A. McCormick, SJ, "Moral Theology, 1940–1989: An Overview," *Theological Studies* 50, no. 1 (March 1989): 4. George Kelly died in August 1964.

6. See Robert McClory, *Turning Point: The Inside Story of the Papal Birth Control Commission* (New York: Crossroad, 1995), 40–41; Peter Hebblethwaite, *Paul VI: The First Modern Pope* (New York: Paulist Press, 1993), 298–99.

7. All quotes from John Ford, SJ, "Fourth Question: What Would Be the Doctrinal and Pastoral Tendencies in This Country?" undated but April 1964, 1–3. American Catholic History Research Center and University Archives, Catholic University, Collection 10 (NCWC papers), Box 86, folder 8. Dr. John Rock, a codeveloper of the anovulent pill, published *The Time Has Come* in 1963, in which he argued that the pill, functioning in a manner analogous to the rhythm method, was a licit means of contraception for Catholics. He was a frequent media presence at the time.

8. Ford, "Fourth Question," 4–8.

9. John C. Ford, SJ, diary of his spring–summer 1964 trip to Europe, entry for May 29, 1964. Archives of the New England Province of the Society of Jesus, John C. Ford, SJ, papers, Box 10. When I used the Ford papers, housed at Holy Cross College, they had not yet been finally catalogued. Thus all citations refer to the paper's preliminary organization, which did not include folder numbers or labels.

10. John C. Ford, SJ, "Interview with Card. Ottaviani," June 3, 1964 (handwritten notes). Archives of the New England Province of the Society of Jesus, John C. Ford, SJ, papers, Box 10.

11. John C. Ford, SJ, diary of his spring–summer 1964 trip to Europe, entry for June 6. Archives of the New England Province of the Society of Jesus, John C. Ford, SJ, papers, Box 10.

12. Quoted in John C. Ford, SJ, "First Draft: Proposed Statement on Birth Control," typescript with penciled date August 24, 1965, 6–7. American Catholic History Research Center and University Archives, NCWC papers, 10/86/8.

13. John C. Ford, SJ, "Memorandum for Archbishop [Leo] Binz," March 28, 1965. Archives of the New England Province of the Society of Jesus, John C. Ford, SJ, papers, Box 7.

14. John C. Ford, SJ to Cardinal Amleto Cigognani, October 2, 1965. Archives of the New England Province of the Society of Jesus, John C. Ford, SJ, papers, Box 8. See letters from Cardinals Joseph Ritter and Lawrence Shehan; Archbishops John Dearden, Karl Alter, John Krol; Bishops John Wright and Ernest Primeau; and Francis J. Sexton (for Cardinal Cushing) in American Catholic History Research Center and University Archives, Catholic University, Collection 10 (NCWC papers), Box 86, folder 9.

15. John C. Ford, SJ to Cardinal Amleto Cigognani, Oct. 2, 1965. Archives of the New England Province of the Society of Jesus, John C. Ford, SJ, papers, Box 8.

16. John C. Ford, SJ to Egidio Vagnozzi, November 6, 1965. Archives of the New England Province of the Society of Jesus, John C. Ford, SJ, papers, Box 8.

17. John C. Ford, SJ, "First Audience with Pope, Monday November 22 (from about 12:30 to about 1:30)," undated typescript. Archives of the New England Province of the Society of Jesus, John C. Ford, SJ, papers, Box 9.

18. Peter Hebblethwaite believes that the *modi* were drafted by Fr. Ermenegildo Lio, OFM, a Ford ally, while Ford drafted the letter that accompanied them. See Hebblethwaite, *Paul VI*, 444.

19. Ibid., 445.

20. John C. Ford, SJ, diary of November–December 1965, entry for November 26. Archives of the New England Province of the Society of Jesus, John C. Ford, SJ, papers, Box 9.

21. John C. Ford, SJ, diary of November–December 1965, later (undated) addendum to entry for November 26. Archives of the New England Province of the Society of Jesus, John C. Ford, SJ, papers, Box 9.

22. "Notes on Conversation with Pope Paul VI, November 22, 1965" (handwritten on small slips of paper). Archives of the New England Province of the Society of Jesus, John C. Ford, SJ, papers, Box 9.

23. Hebblethwaite, *Paul VI*, 469–71.

24. *Humanae Vitae*, 9. I have used a 1983 translation from the Italian by Marc Caligari, SJ, at http://www.cin.org/docs/humanvit.htm.

25. Ford, "Notes on Conversation with Pope Paul VI, November 22, 1965."

26. John C. Ford, SJ to Bishop Paul Tanner, December 17, 1965. Archives of the New England Province of the Society of Jesus, John C. Ford, SJ, papers, Box 9.

27. John C. Ford, SJ to Archbishop Leo Binz, February 11, 1966. Archives of the New England Province of the Society of Jesus, John C. Ford, SJ, papers, Box 8. Binz was a fellow member of the papal birth control commission.

28. John C. Ford, SJ to Archbishop Leo Binz, February 13, 1966. Archives of the New England Province of the Society of Jesus, John C. Ford, SJ, papers, Box 8.

29. John C. Ford, SJ, "Reflections of Father Ford on Doctors' Week (May 2–7)," undated but May 1966. Archives of the New England Province of the Society of Jesus, John C. Ford, SJ, papers, Box 8. Cardinal Suenens was one of the new episcopal members of the commission, belonging to what was initially seen as the group's liberal minority. The episcopal members did not attend commission meetings in a body until June; Krakow's Cardinal Karol Wojtyla was absent from the June sessions.

30. John C. Ford, SJ, "Reflections of Father Ford on Sessions of May 9–12," undated but May 1966. Archives of the New England Province of the Society of Jesus, John C. Ford, SJ, papers, Box 8. The analogy to teenaged boys and masturbation is Ford's.

31. Statement of Cardinal John Heenan, June 22, 1966, type-script. Archives of the New England Province of the Society of Jesus, John C. Ford, SJ, papers, Box 9.

32. Ford's intervention, which I did not find among his personal papers, is reprinted in Robert McClory, *The Encyclical That Never Was: The Story of the Pontifical Commission on Population, Family and Birth, 1964–1966*, rev. U.K. ed. (London: Sheed & Ward, 1987), 209–10.

33. "Majority Papal Commission Report," in *The Catholic Case for Contraception*, Daniel Callahan (New York: Macmillan, 1969), 149–73.

34. Hebblethwaite, *Paul VI*, 469. Hebblethwaite believes that Ottaviani himself did the bulk of the drafting, using Ford's statement as a model. But Germain Grisez, present in Rome with Ford at the time, asserts that Ford, with Grisez's assistance, was the principal author. See Grisez's website: www.twotlj.org/BC Commission.html.

35. "Minority Papal Commission Report," in Callahan, *Catholic Case*, 174–211, quotes from 184, 187. Ford's May 23, 1966 "Statement of Position" is found in the Archives of the New England Province of the Society of Jesus, John C. Ford, SJ, papers, Box 9.

36. Kaiser, *Encyclical That Never Was*, 226–27, 231, 238; Hebblethwaite, *Paul VI*, 471–72, 488, 517.

37. See, for example, Ford's "Fourth Question," 13.

38. John C. Ford, SJ to Germain Grisez, August 8, 1967. Archives of the New England Province of the Society of Jesus, John C. Ford, SJ, papers, Box 1.

39. Germain Grisez website, www.twotlj.org/BCCommission.html.

40. Bernard Häring, "The Encyclical Crisis," in Callahan, *Catholic Case*, 77. The essay initially appeared in the September 6, 1968 issue of *Commonweal*.

41. McCormick, "Moral Theology: 1940–1989," 12.

42. For a full statement of his position, see John C. Ford, SJ, and Germain Grisez, "Contraception and Infallibility," *Theological Studies* 39 (1978): 258–312.

43. Richard A. McCormick, SJ, "Flaws Mar Pastoral Comments on Contraception, Dissent According to Jesuit Theologian," *New World*, undated clipping but ca. December 1968 or early 1969. Bishop Alexander Zaleski papers, Archives of the Diocese of Lansing (MI), Folder: "NCCB Committee on Doctrine: General Correspondence, November 1968–December 1969.

44. Richard A. McCormick, SJ, "Toward a Dialogue," *Commonweal* 80, no. 11 (June 5, 1964): 316.

45. McCormick served as coeditor with John Lynch, SJ, for his first year in this role; he was subsequently sole editor until 1984.

46. See Bishop Romeo Blanchette to Most Rev. Luigi Raimondi, February 28, 1968. Bishop Alexander Zaleski papers, Archives of the Diocese of Lansing (MI), folder: NCCB Committee on Doctrine: Bishop Romeo Blanchette's Inquiry on Birth Control, March-April 1968. McCormick's statement appeared in "Notes on Moral Theology," *Theological Studies* 28 (Dec. 1967): 799–800.

47. Richard A. McCormick, SJ, *Corrective Vision: Explorations in Moral Theology* (Kansas City, MO: Sheed & Ward, 1994), 43, 44.

48. Ibid., 44, 48, 49.

49. Massimo Faggioli, *Vatican II: The Battle for Meaning* (New York: Paulist Press, 2012).

50. McCormick, *Corrective Vision*, 10.

PART II
ENGAGEMENTS
The Council and the
Public Arena

5

Richard R. Gaillardetz

Vatican II and the Humility of the Church

Christian ethics has made the recovery of virtue central to contemporary moral reflection. Recently, Gerard Mannion has suggested that contemporary ecclesiology follow suit, calling for a kind of "virtue ecclesiology."[1] Such an ecclesiology would hold together what the Church is and what the Church does.[2] His focus is on offering an ecclesiology more attuned to the shape and demands of postmodernity, one that is more elastic and open to pluralism. In his 2011 plenary address to the Catholic Theological Society of America, Paul Lakeland adopted a similar tack, presenting helpful reflections on the ecclesial virtue of humility.[3] I would like to follow suit in a consideration of the teaching of the Council. I will argue that we can find in the documents of Vatican II a solid basis for speaking of humility as an ecclesial virtue. This will require, however, some preliminary reflections on the virtue of humility itself.

BRIEF REFLECTIONS ON THE VIRTUE OF HUMILITY

The Christian ethicist Lisa Fullam has made a case for the recovery of the virtue of humility in Christian ethics. She has argued persuasively that the virtue has suffered neglect because it has been mistakenly associated with self-abasement.[4] This emphasis was particularly strong in the Augustinian tradition, where self-abasement was explicitly linked to one's sinfulness. Within that moral context, self-abasement knew no limits. This was not the approach of Thomas Aquinas, however. For Thomas, Fullam contends, self-abasement is not central to the virtue but functions merely as a corrective toward the innate human tendency toward "self-celebration." "But the practice of self-abasement is not the essence of humility, just as the virtue of sobriety cannot simply be equated with abstinence from alcohol."[5] Thomas oriented humility's self-abasement toward a healthy assessment of the truth of one's situation before God and the world. In the end, humility is concerned with honest self-knowledge. Thomas followed the Aristotelian pattern of seeing a virtue as pursuing a mean between excess and deficit. Consequently, self-abasement was not an end in itself and was not limitless but functioned as a means rather than an end where the end was accurate self-understanding.

We see this emphasis on true self-knowledge in the distinctive way in which Thomas binds the virtue of humility to the virtue of magnanimity.[6] The latter virtue is oriented toward a celebration of honor and achievement as it relates to the gifts one possesses from God. "Magnanimity makes a man deem himself worthy of great things in consideration of the gifts he holds from God."[7] Consequently, both magnanimity and humility are concerned with honest self-understanding: magnanimity honestly acknowledges one's gifts and urges one to make the greatest possible use of them, and humility honestly acknowledges one's deficiencies.[8] When paired together, humility and magnanimity can be seen as a kind of twofold virtue that urges one to a honest self-assessment of both one's gifts and deficiencies. Although in this essay I will refer only to the virtue of humility, it is always with an awareness of its integral relationship to magnanimity.

Humility is an intrinsically other-centered virtue, principally because honest self-assessment can only occur within the framework of one's relationship to God.[9] Humility, in a basic sense, is concerned with a profound reverence for the greatness of God, a reverence that inevitably brings one's own failings and inadequacies into sharper focus. At the same time, humility is also exercised in view of the goodness of all God's creatures and the gifts that they possess. As Fullam puts it, "Humility invites us not to rest in our own gifts but to look outside ourselves and to see what else God has been up to."[10]

James Keenan has noted the renewed attention to the place of humility and the other virtues in his history of modern Catholic moral theology, noting in particular its centrality in the work of twentieth century theologians like Fritz Tillmann and Bernard Häring.[11] Keenan, a leading figure in the development of contemporary virtue ethics, makes his own helpful contribution to our consideration of the virtue of humility. For Keenan the heart of humility lies in overcoming the vice of presumption. In this vein Keenan will link humility with the proper exercise of power.

> Humility is not self-deprecation, but rather the virtue for knowing the place of one's power in God's world. This is the humility of Jesus before Pilate, of Mary in the Magnificat, of Paul narrating his call, and of the incredible Mary Magdalene holding on to the risen Christ in the garden. In each instance they recognize their power in God's world and they do so as an act of indebtedness to the God who gave them this power. Humility is the virtue, therefore, that trains us in the exercise of that power. The more we practice humility, the more we understand the power that we, as leaders, are called to exercise.[12]

Keenan's explicit linking of humility and the exercise of power provides a further avenue for reflection on humility as an ecclesial virtue.

In this very brief treatment I have proposed three characteristics of the virtue of humility: (1) humility is tethered to magnanimity insofar as it is oriented toward honest self-assessment in general, and distinguished from magnanimity by its acknowledgment of one's deficiencies in particular; (2) humility is an intrinsically relational and other-centered virtue, eager to celebrate the greatness of God and the gifts of others; and (3) humility is concerned with the proper exercise of power.

VATICAN II AND THE HUMILITY OF THE CHURCH

We now turn to the teaching of the Council. There are, of course, multiple methodological approaches to the study of the Council that have been employed over the last five decades. John O'Malley has emphasized the value of genre analysis. O'Malley argues that one of the most distinctive features of Vatican II was its employment of a consistent rhetorical style he refers to as *panegyric*, "the painting of an idealized portrait in order to excite admiration and appropriation."[13] The recourse to this rhetorical genre marked a departure from earlier conciliar preferences for a more juridical style of discourse, one more inclined to render legal pronouncements and canonical penalties. The Council, by contrast, articulated an idealized account or vision of the Church intended to inspire believers and move the Church to implement the reforms necessary to realize the Council's vision in the practical order. In this essay I will argue that a principal feature of the Council's account of the Church was its consistent emphasis on the ecclesial virtue of humility.

HUMILITY AND ECCLESIAL SELF-ASSESSMENT

As we saw above, the virtue of humility requires an honest self-assessment that attends to one's deficiencies even as magnanimity attends to ones gifts. The Council is certainly not shy, nor is the larger Catholic Tradition, about affirming the gifts the Church offers the world as "universal sacrament of salvation" (*Lumen Gentium* 48). In several passages the Council emphasizes the fullness of the "means of sanctification and truth" that belong to the Catholic Church, even as many of these elements are found "outside its visible structures" (*Lumen Gentium* 8; *Unitatis Redintegratio* 3). What was most distinctive about the Council's teaching, however, was not this more modest articulation of the gifts the Church offers the world but its willingness to undergo a searching and critical ecclesial self-assessment.

The Council seemed to have recognized that ecclesial self-assessment provided a necessary foundation for authentic ecclesial reform. Within the limits of this essay, I cannot provide a comprehensive survey of every instance of the Council's call to reform and renewal.[14] Instead I offer some representative examples of the Council's determination to engage in a comprehensive self-assessment of the state of the Church as the necessary precondition for ecclesial reform.

John XXIII's Opening Address: Gaudet Mater Ecclesia

This commitment to serious ecclesial self-assessment makes its first appearance at the very outset in Pope John XXIII's opening address. The liturgy to celebrate the opening of the Council was, by today's standards, remarkable in its length. Filled with Roman ceremonial, the opening liturgy lasted over seven hours.[15] For those who remained through it all, the highlight was Pope John XXIII's remarkable address, *Gaudet Mater Ecclesia*.[16] Here, for the first time, the bishops and indeed, through the media covering the event, the entire world, heard a comprehensive articulation of the pope's hopes for the Council. After some introductory comments on the historical role of ecumenical councils, Pope John XXIII offered his reasons for calling an ecumenical Council. The Church must bring herself "up to date where required." A tame statement today, but at that time such an admission was at odds with the dominant view of the Church as a *societas perfecta*, a Church hovering serenely above the turmoil of human history. It is true that "perfect," in the neo-Scholastic sense of the claim, meant simply that the Church possessed all that was necessary for the fulfillment of its mission, but the pope chose to emphasize the Church seen as a historical reality in need of reform and renewal.

The next section of his address considered the defense of Church teaching, followed by a section on the repression of error. There we find this remarkable statement:

> At the outset of the Second Vatican Council, it is evident, as always, that the truth of the Lord will remain forever. We see, in fact, as one age succeeds another, that the opinions of men follow one another and exclude each other. And often errors vanish as quickly as they arise, like fog before the sun. The Church has always opposed these errors. Frequently she has condemned them with the greatest severity. Nowadays however, the Spouse of Christ prefers to make use of the medicine of mercy rather than that of severity. She considers that she meets the needs of the present day by demonstrating the validity of her teaching rather than by condemnations.

This passage offers the daring admission that traditional approaches to error were no longer appropriate for the Church today.

The final section turns to the unity of the Church.

> Unfortunately, the entire Christian family has not yet fully attained this visible unity in truth. The Catholic Church, therefore, considers it her duty to work actively so that there may be fulfilled the great mystery of that unity, which Jesus Christ invoked with fervent prayer from His heavenly Father on the eve of His sacrifice.

In the pope's frank acknowledgment of division in the church, there is embedded a provocative ecclesial claim. The pope could admit that the "Christian family" had not fully attained visible unity only on the assumption that non-Catholic Christians were part of that family. This new ecumenical starting point was difficult to reconcile with Pope Pius XI's exhortation to dissident non-Catholics, in the encyclical *Mortalium Animos* (1928), to return to the fold.

This short address introduced a new ecclesial tone at the very outset of the Council. It was a tone filled with hope yet sober in its self-assessment and forthright in its admission that not all was well within the Church. The pope sang, loud and clear, the first chorus in the Council's plea for greater ecclesial humility.

Sacrosanctum Concilium *and the Humble Acknowledgment of the Need for Reform*

Debates regarding the Council's liturgy constitution, *Sacrosanctum Concilium*, inevitably center on controversies related to the need and character of ongoing liturgical reform. However, as Massimo Faggioli has persuasively argued, considerations of *Sacrosanctum Concilium* must not be limited to the proper implementation of liturgical reform; this document contains, in germ, a compelling ecclesial vision, one only partially followed in the Council's subsequent documents.[17] Central to the liturgy constitution's larger ecclesial contributions is the precedent it set for ecclesial reform built on the foundation of rigorous ecclesial self-examination. The Council begins with an implicit admission of the need for reform.

> The sacred council has set out to impart an ever increasing vigor to the lives of the faithful; to adapt more closely to the needs of our age those institutions which are subject to change; to encourage whatever can promote the union of all who believe in Christ; to strengthen whatever serves to call all of humanity into the church's fold. Accordingly it sees particularly cogent reasons for undertaking the reform and promotion of the liturgy. (*Sacrosanctum Concilium* 1)

The liturgy constitution follows John XXIII in its forceful move beyond the post-Tridentine *societas perfecta* ecclesiology to one that is more thoroughly rooted in history.[18]

The Council then introduces what would be a central theme throughout the Council documents, the Church on pilgrimage:

"For what marks out the church is that it is at once human and divine, visible and endowed with invisible realities, vigorously active and yet making space in its life for contemplation, present in the world and yet in pilgrimage (*peregrinam*) beyond" (*Sacrosanctum Concilium* 2).[19] The image reinforces a sense of the Church's historical embeddedness which, in turn, opens up the possibility of authentic reform:

> The liturgy is made up of unchangeable elements divinely instituted, and of elements subject to change. These latter not only may be changed but ought to be changed with the passage of time, if they have suffered from the intrusion of anything out of harmony with the inner nature of the liturgy or have become less suitable. (*Sacrosanctum Concilium* 21)

The reality of historical change extends to the liturgical rites themselves: "The Council also desires that, where necessary the rites be revised carefully in the light of sound tradition, and that they be given new vigor to meet present-day circumstances" (*Sacrosanctum Concilium* 4). Regarding the Eucharist, in particular, the bishops insisted that liturgical revisions be undertaken such that

> the intrinsic nature and purpose of its several parts, as well as the connection between them, may be more clearly shown, and that devout and active participation by the faithful may be more easily achieved. To this end, the rites are to be simplified, due care being taken to preserve their substance. Duplications made with the passage of time are to be omitted, as are less useful additions. Other parts which were lost through the vicissitudes of history are to be restored according to the ancient tradition of the holy Fathers, as may seem appropriate or necessary. (*Sacrosanctum Concilium* 50)

In the Council's first official document it follows the pope's example in exercising an honest ecclesial self-assessment.

A Pilgrim Church Ever in Need of Reform and Renewal

We have already seen the "pilgrim" metaphor applied to the Church in *Sacrosanctum Concilium*. The constitution *Lumen Gentium* describes the Church as "clasping sinners to its bosom," even as it avoided the direct attribution of sinfulness to the Church. The painful presence of sin in the Church demands purification and the ecclesial pursuit of the path of "penance and renewal" (*Lumen Gentium* 8).[20] For the Council, this is the inevitable path of human pilgrimage.

> The church "proceeds on its pilgrim way amidst the persecutions of the world and the consolations of God," proclaiming the cross and death of the Lord until he comes. But it draws strength from the power of the risen Lord, to overcome with patience and charity its afflictions and difficulties, from within and without; and reveals his mystery faithfully in the world—albeit amid shadows—until in the end it will be made manifest in the fullness of the light. (*Lumen Gentium* 8)[21]

The theme of pilgrimage finds further exposition in chapter 7 of *Lumen Gentium*, as is evident in the very chapter title, "The Eschatological Nature of the Pilgrim Church and Its Union with the Heavenly Church." By conceiving of the Church not just as a collection of individual pilgrims but as itself pilgrim, the Council adopted a tone of deep eschatological humility. Thus the Council could write,

> The Church, to which we are all called in Christ Jesus, and in which we acquire sanctity through the grace of God, will attain its full perfection only in the glory of heaven, when there will come the time of the restoration of all things. (*Lumen Gentium* 48)

The Church lives as a people *on the way* who have the promise of God's presence and guidance but who still await the consummation of God's plan. As a pilgrim community living in history, the Church must always be willing to assess its faithfulness to the gospel. In the "Declaration on Religious Freedom," *Dignitatis Humanae*, the Council admits the Church's own role in ignoring the proper demands of religious freedom:

> In the life of the people of God in its pilgrimage, through the vicissitudes of human history, there have at times appeared patterns of behavior which were not in keeping with the spirit of the Gospel and were even opposed to it. (*Dignitatis Humanae* 12)

This rigorous examination of Church conduct, past and present, is also displayed in the "Decree on Ecumenism," *Unitatis Redintegratio*:

> In this one and only church of God from its very beginnings there arose certain rifts, which the Apostle strongly censures as damnable. But in subsequent centuries much more serious dissensions appeared and large communities became separated from full communion with the Catholic Church—for which, often enough, people on both sides were to blame. (*Unitatis Redintegratio* 3)

An honest assessment of the Church's failings is, according to the Council, a necessary precondition for any genuine ecumenical endeavor. The bishops wrote that the primary ecumenical duty of Catholics was

> to make a careful and honest appraisal of whatever needs to be renewed and done in the catholic household itself, in order that its life may bear witness more clearly and more faithfully to the teachings and institutions which have been handed down from Christ through the apostles. (*Unitatis Redintegratio*, no. 4)

The ecumenical decree then specifies what getting the "Catholic household" in order may require:

Consequently, if, in various times and circumstances, there have been deficiencies in moral conduct or in church discipline, or even in the way that church teaching has been formulated—to be carefully distinguished from the deposit of faith itself—these should be set right at the opportune moment and in the proper way. (*Unitatis Redintegratio* 6)

The Council demonstrated a consistent commitment to move from a static and immutable Church that lives on some ethereal plane in favor of a more historically grounded account of the Church. The bishops did not yield in their belief in the holiness of the Church, yet they demonstrated a willingness to undertake a much more historically responsible ecclesial assessment. They thereby pursued a path that marked out one of the central characteristics of the virtue of humility.

HUMILITY AND OTHER-CENTEREDNESS

A relational other-centeredness is a second characteristic of the virtue of humility; humility habituates us to focus not on our own accomplishments, but on the other and, preeminently, on the divine Other. Transposed into an ecclesial key, a truly humble Church would eschew any form of ecclesial triumphalism and, in the place of any hint of ecclesial self-congratulation, would give prominence to the Church's utter dependence for its life and mission on the trinitarian missions of Word and Spirit. Vatican II moved decisively in this direction, repeatedly repudiating ecclesial triumphalism. The latter move is most evident in *Dei Verbum*, the "Dogmatic Constitution on Divine Revelation."

Dei Verbum *and the Church's Receptivity to the Word*

Jared Wicks has remarked on the typical ordering of the Council documents in various editions:

Some editions place *Lumen Gentium* at the head of the Vatican II constitutions, but would not the conciliar ecclesiology be better contextualized if placed after the council text starting with "hearing the word of God reverently and proclaiming it confidently..." and ending with "the word of God...stands forever," as does *Dei Verbum*?[22]

Wicks contends that a theological reading of the Council ought to begin with the Church's humble response to a Word that is not its own. The Church must maintain a stance of receptivity to the revelation of the triune God. Consider the opening passage of the constitution:

> Hearing the word of God reverently and proclaiming it confidently, this holy synod makes its own the words of St. John: "We proclaim to you the eternal life which was with the Father and was made manifest to us—that which we have seen and heard we proclaim also to you, so that you may have fellowship with us; and our fellowship is with the Father and with his Son Jesus Christ." (*Dei Verbum* 1)

Before the Church can preach or teach with any integrity, it must first listen. It is in view of this ecclesial receptivity that the Council acknowledges that all the Christian faithful are given that supernatural instinct for the faith, the *sensus fidei*, to allow them to receive God's word, penetrate its meaning and apply it more fully in their lives (*Lumen Gentium* 12). Dependence on the revelatory word led the Council to insist that although the task of giving an authoritative interpretation of the word of God is entrusted to the magisterium, "this magisterium is not superior to the word of God, but is rather its servant" (*Dei Verbum* 10).

Dei Verbum turned away from a more propositional view of revelation as a set of truths to be mastered. This revelation stands as an invitation into relationship. The Church is called into communion with God in Christ:

> By this revelation, then, the invisible God, from the fullness of his love, addresses men and women as his

> friends and lives among them, in order to invite and receive them into his own company....The most intimate truth thus revealed about God and human salvation shines forth for us in Christ, who is himself both the mediator and the sum total of revelation. (*Dei Verbum* 2)

The Christocentrism evident in this passage plays an important role in the Council's evocation of a humbler Church more aware of its radical dependence on God's saving work. Too often overlooked are the many conciliar texts that ground the life and mission of the Church in Christ.[23] Some forget that the Latin title of the "Dogmatic Constitution on the Church," *Lumen Gentium*, "light of the nations," refers not to the Church but to Christ. That constitution opens with these lines:

> Christ is the light of the nations and consequently this holy synod, gathered together in the Holy Spirit, ardently desires to bring to all humanity that light of Christ which is resplendent on the face of the church, by proclaiming his Gospel to every creature. (*Lumen Gentium* 1)

The Church is to be focused not on itself but on Christ, the subject of the Church's proclamation.

Even as the Council insists on the centrality of Christ, it avoids a reductive ecclesial Christomonism by also recalling the mission of the Holy Spirit. *Dei Verbum* develops the fully trinitarian shape of divine revelation in its assertion that the Church's response and reception of the divine word is dependent on the action of the Spirit "who moves the heart and converts it to God, and opens the eyes of the mind and makes it easy for all to accept and believe the truth" (*Dei Verbum* 5). Ormond Rush has developed a rich theology of ecclesial reception built on the conciliar teaching that it is the function of the Holy Spirit to bring "to realization God's revelatory and salvific purposes."[24] The Holy Spirit constitutes the Church as a community of reception, wherein what is received is nothing less than the grace and revelation of Christ.

This reception must not be imagined, however, as if it were a one-time event. It is not the case that the Church simply received Christ at some definitive point in the past such that what was once received is now possessed. Rather, since what is received is not propositional information, in the first instance, but the offer of divine communion, the Church's posture of receptivity and dependence is characteristic of its entire historical existence. The Council affirms this in the second chapter of *Dei Verbum*, "The Transmission of Divine Revelation." There the bishops present Scripture and Tradition as a kind of mirror "in which the church, during its pilgrim journey here on earth, contemplates God, from whom it receives everything, until such time as it is brought to see him face to face as he really is" (*Dei Verbum* 7).

It is at this juncture that we might speak of a form of "doctrinal humility." Catherine Cornille notes that when humility is related to doctrine "it has more often been regarded as an attitude to be adopted *toward* rather than *about* the truth of Christian doctrines."[25] Individual Christians are reminded of the limits of human reason and exhorted to adopt a humble posture of docile obedience in the face of Church doctrine. Yet the Council invites us to pursue a different understanding of doctrinal humility. *Dei Verbum* 8 presents a dynamic account of Tradition's development and then offers the remarkable admission that the Church lives in history moving "toward the plenitude of divine truth." This brief clause presents revealed truth as both historically conditioned and subject to eschatological fulfillment. The Church does not so much possess revelation as it is possessed by it.

A stance of doctrinal humility is also reflected in the Council's presentation of the hierarchy of truths in *Unitatis Redintegratio* 11:

> When comparing doctrines with one another, they should remember that in Catholic doctrine there exists an order or "hierarchy" of truths, since they vary in their relation to the foundation of the Christian faith.

Here the "foundation of the Christian faith" refers to divine revelation itself.

The doctrinal humility of the Council leads it to turn away from any arrogant claim to a comprehensive grasp of divine revelation in favor of a stance of receptivity toward the revealing God.

The Dialogical Imperative of the Church

The other-centered character of humility is not limited to relationship with God but extends as well to an appreciation of the created "other." The Council's evocation of a more humble Church open to the gifts of the other is most evident in the Council's dialogical imperative. Pope Paul VI's first encyclical, *Ecclesiam Suam*, was promulgated on August 6, 1964, five weeks prior to the third session of the Council. The encyclical was dedicated almost entirely to a dialogical vision of the Church and, since it was promulgated about a month before the opening of the third session of the Council, it exerted an influence on conciliar deliberations. Its influence is certainly evident in *Gaudium et Spes*, the "Pastoral Constitution on the Church in the Modern World," which calls for an intra-ecclesial dialogue:

> Such a mission requires us first of all to create in the church itself mutual esteem, reverence and harmony, and to acknowledge all legitimate diversity; in this way all who constitute the one people of God will be able to engage in ever more fruitful dialogue, whether they are pastors or other members of the faithful. For the ties which unite the faithful together are stronger than those which separate them: let there be unity in what is necessary, freedom in what is doubtful, and charity in everything. (*Gaudium et Spes* 92)

Intra-ecclesial dialogue, that is dialogue within the Catholic Church, presumes a shared commitment to the apostolic faith, the "unity in what is necessary." Yet at the same time, it is both this unity in essentials and the "charity in everything" that frees the Church to be open to dialogue on "doubtful matters."

101

The Council was not being romantic about the demands of dialogue. It acknowledged that there would be disagreement in the Church, particularly regarding how to apply gospel values to the daily circumstances of our lives. Catholics are bound to disagree on the concrete implications of what it means to follow Jesus in their ordinary lives. When they found they were in disagreement, the bishops said,

> No one is permitted to identify the authority of the church exclusively with his or her own opinion. Let them, then try to guide each other by sincere dialogue in a spirit of mutual charity and with a genuine concern for the common good above all. (*Gaudium et Spes* 43)

The suggestion here is that a genuine openness to those with whom we disagree can yield new insight and a renewed commitment to the common good.

This spirit of dialogue was carried over into the Catholic encounters with other Christians in ecumenical relationships. This dialogue requires, on the part of Catholics, that they "become familiar with the outlook of the separated churches and communities" (*Unitatis Redintegratio* 9). In the presentation of Catholic teaching, Catholics should be cognizant of "the hierarchy of truths" that reminds us that Catholic doctrines "vary in their relation to the foundation of the Christian faith" (*Unitatis Redintegratio* 11).

This dialogical imperative was extended as well to those who belong to non-Christian religions. The Council asserted that the origins of the religious traditions of the world often lie in the effort to seek answers to the great questions that have long preoccupied the human spirit (*Nostra Aetate* 1). In its "Declaration on the Relation of the Church to Non-Christian Religions," *Nostra Aetate*, the Council affirmed that in these great religions one can find "a ray of that truth which enlightens all men and women" and it exhorted Catholics to prudent and charitable "discussion and collaboration with members of other religions" (*Nostra Aetate* 2).

Finally, we must acknowledge the dialogical spirit manifested in the Council's attitude toward the world itself. In the pastoral constitution we find a key text that captures the Council's deep ecclesial humility:

> The church is guardian of the deposit of God's word and draws religious and moral principles from it, but it does not always have a ready answer to every question. Still, it is eager to associate the light of revelation with the experience of humanity in trying to clarify the course upon which it has recently entered. (*Gaudium et Spes* 33).

This passage establishes the fundamental basis for dialogue with the world; the Church has both something to offer and something to learn from the world.

Gaudium et Spes offers an apt ecclesial example of the tethering of humility with magnanimity. In an exercise of magnanimity, the Council fathers honored the Church's gift of the good news of Jesus Christ that it offers to a wounded world in need of healing and reconciliation (*Gaudium et Spes* 37). In an exercise of ecclesial humility the Council readily acknowledged what it receives from the world:

> Just as it is in the world's interest to acknowledge the church as a social reality and a driving force in history, so too the church is not unaware how much it has profited from the history and development of humankind. It profits from the experience of past ages, from the progress of the sciences, and from the riches hidden in various cultures, through which greater light is thrown on human nature and new avenues to truth are opened up. (*Gaudium et Spes* 44)

This openness and receptivity to the world manifests that radical other-centeredness that is essential to the virtue of ecclesial humility.

HUMILITY AND THE
EXERCISE OF POWER

Finally we turn to the third characteristic of the virtue of humility. As Keenan reminded us, humility is the virtue that trains us in the exercise of power. A Church that lives out of the virtue of humility will be a Church that exercises power and authority in imitation of Christ who saw power and authority as service.

Any consideration of the Council's treatment of power in the Church must recognize its important retrieval of the long neglected pneumatological conditioning of the Church. For all ecclesial power is in some sense a participation in the presence and activity of the Spirit in the life of the Church. According to the Council it is the Holy Spirit who

> guides the church in the way of all truth and, uniting it in fellowship and ministry, bestows upon it different hierarchic and charismatic gifts, and in this way directs it and adorns it with his fruits. By the power of the Gospel he rejuvenates the church, constantly renewing it and leading it to perfect union with its spouse. (*Lumen Gentium* 4)

By baptism all the *Christifideles* are empowered by the Spirit for Christian life and ministry. Within the life of the Church, "power" can be thought of as the Spirit active in the life of believers enabling them to fulfill their baptismal call and engage in effective action in service of the Church's life and mission.

The Council did not offer any developed theological reflections on the relationship between baptismal empowerment and the particular empowerment that occurs by way of ministerial ordination. Yet it did affirm in numerous places that the exercise of ministerial power is always in service of the mission of the people of God. Power is never exercised for its own sake. The Council avoided the typical neo-Scholastic debates regarding the proper scope and limits for the exercise of jurisdictional power or of the relationship between the power of orders and the power of jurisdiction. Rather, it directed its attention toward the exercise of ministerial power configured for Christian service. Consider this key text in *Lumen Gentium* introducing the chapter on the hierarchical character of the Church:

> In order to ensure that the people of God would have pastors and would enjoy continual growth, Christ the Lord set up in his church a variety of offices whose aim is the good of the whole body. Ministers, invested with sacred power, *are at the service of their broth-ers and sisters,* so that all who belong to the people of God and therefore enjoy true Christian dignity may attain to salvation through their free, combined and well-ordered efforts in pursuit of a common goal. (*Lumen Gentium* 18)

A few paragraphs down we see another articulation of this sense of ministerial power as service: "The bishops, therefore, have undertaken along with their fellow-workers, the priests and deacons, *the service of the community*" (*Lumen Gentium* 20).[26] In the "Decree on Priestly Ministry and Life," *Presbyterorum Ordinis,* the power conferred on priests by ordination, the Council teaches, is "a power whose purpose is to build up the church. And in building up the church priests ought to treat everybody with the greatest kindness after the example of our Lord" (*Presbyterorum Ordinis* 6). The Council insists that "priests, in common with all who have been reborn in the font of Baptism, are brothers and sisters as members of the same body of Christ which all are commanded to build" (*Presbyterorum Ordinis* 9). The ministerial leadership of priests requires that they "unite their efforts with those of the lay faithful."

> Priests are to be sincere in their appreciation and promotion of lay people's dignity and of the special role the laity have to play in the church's mission....They should be willing to listen to lay people, give brotherly consideration to their wishes, and recognize their experience and competence in the different fields of

human activity....While testing the spirits to discover if they be of God, they must discover with faith, recognize with joy, and foster diligently the many and varied charismatic gifts of the laity, whether these be of a humble or more exalted kind. Among the other gifts of God which are found abundantly among the faithful...Priests should confidently entrust to the laity duties in the service of the church, giving them freedom and opportunity for activity and even inviting them, when opportunity offers, to undertake projects on their own initiative. (*Presbyterorum Ordinis* 9; see also *Apostolicam Actuositatem* 3).

Almost completely absent from the Council documents is the appearance of any notion of ministerial power presented as either a coercive/punitive power over others or as a matter of simply "ruling" over others. Rather the Council consistently opted for the language of service and collaboration and in the place of "ruling imagery" we find instead the dominance of the pastoral image of shepherding and its associative responsibilities to learn and care for one's flock (*Christus Dominus* 11, 16).

In this essay I have argued that the Council offers a compelling vision of a Church deeply shaped by ecclesial humility. Vatican II invites us to contemplate the simple face of a renewed, humble yet confident Church. This Church embraces both its divine origins and its historical embodiment. This Church acknowledges its indefectible holiness, yet is committed to honest and courageous ecclesial self-assessment. It is not preoccupied with its own gifts and contributions but remains attentive to the self-communication of God in Christ by the power of the Spirit. This Church rejects the arrogant assumption that divine truth is its exclusive possession. It sloughs off any and all pretensions to triumphalism in favor of patient and open dialogue—dialogue among Catholics, with other Christians, other religions, and the world itself. In this Church the authentic exercise of Christian power is never coercive, never abusive, never authoritarian. The Council's vision of a humble Church stands before us today as both a challenge and, sadly, a reproach.

Notes

1. Gerard Mannion, *Ecclesiology and Postmodernity: Questions for the Church in Our Time* (Collegeville, MN: Liturgical Press, 2007), 195–225.

2. Ibid., 196.

3. Paul Lakeland, "'I Want to Be in That Number': Desire, Inclusivity and the Church," *CTSA Proceedings* 66 (2011): 16–28. Lakeland further explored Mannion's ecclesial virtue of humility in "Reflections on the Grace of Self-Doubt," in *Ecclesiology and Exclusion: Boundaries of Being and Belonging in Postmodern Times*, ed. Dennis M. Doyle, Timothy J. Furry, and Pascal D. Bazzell (Maryknoll, NY: Orbis, 2012), 13–17. In that same volume, see Mannion's response to Lakeland and others, "Ecclesiology and the Humility of God: Embracing the Risk of Loving the World," 24–41.

4. Lisa Fullam, *The Virtue of Humility: A Thomistic Apologetic* (Lewiston, NY: Edwin Mellen Press, 2009), 3–4.

5. Ibid., 4.

6. Thomas relates humility to magnanimity in *Summa Theologiae* II-II, q. 161, a 1, ad. 3. He treats magnanimity directly in *Summa Theologiae* II-II, q. 129.

7. Ibid., II-II, q. 129, a. 3, ad 4.

8. For a careful analysis of how Thomas correlates these two virtues, see Fullam, *The Virtue of Humility*, 59–82.

9. *Summa Theologiae* II-II, q. 161, a 1.

10. Fullam, *The Virtue of Humility*, 132.

11. James Keenan, *A History of Catholic Moral Theology in the Twentieth Century: From Confessing Sins to Liberating Consciences* (New York: Continuum, 2010), 63–64, 92–93.

12. James Keenan, *Moral Wisdom: Lessons and Texts from the Catholic Tradition*, 2nd ed. (Lanham: Sheed & Ward, 2010), 162–63.

13. John W. O'Malley, *What Happened at Vatican II* (Cambridge, MA: Harvard University Press, 2008), 47.

14. For such a comprehensive survey, see Peter De Mey, "Church Renewal and Reform in the Documents of Vatican II: History, Theology, Terminology," *The Jurist* 71 (2011): 369–400.

15. Andrea Riccardi, "The Tumultuous Opening Days of the Council," in *History of Vatican II*, ed. Giuseppe Alberigo, trans. Joseph A. Komonchak (Maryknoll, NY: Orbis, 1997), 1:14.

16. The English translation of the pope's speech opening the Council is taken from *The Documents of Vatican II*, ed. Walter Abbott (New York: Crossroad, 1989), 1:710–19.

17. Massimo Faggioli, *True Reform: Liturgy and Ecclesiology* in Sacrosanctum Concilium (Collegeville, MN: Liturgical Press, 2012).

18. Ibid., *True Reform*, 83.

19. Translation from Norman P. Tanner, ed., *Decrees of the Ecumenical Councils* (Washington, DC: Georgetown University Press, 1990), 2:820. Curiously, Flannery translates *peregrinam* as "migrant" rather than "pilgrim."

20. As Peter De Mey has noted, commentators disagree on whether *LG* 8 justifies attributing sinfulness to the Church qua Church. De Mey, "Church Renewal," 372, n. 6.

21. The translation is from Tanner, *Decrees of Ecumenical Councils*, 2:854.

22. Jared Wicks, "Vatican II on Revelation—From Behind the Scenes," *Theological Studies* 71 (2010): 637–50, at 639. Similar calls for the theological priority of *Dei Verbum* can be found in Christoph Theobald, "'Dans les traces...' de la constitution 'Dei Verbum' du concile Vatican II: Bible, théologie et pratiques de lecture* (Paris: Cerf, 2009); Christoph Theobald, *La reception du concile Vatican II:* Vol. I *Accéder à la source* (Paris: Cerf, 2009); Ormond Rush, *Still Interpreting Vatican II: Some Hermeneutical Principles* (Mahwah, NJ: Paulist Press, 2004).

23. One sees the christological grounding of the Church in such texts as *SC* 2, 7; *GS* 22, 45; *NA* 4; *PO* 5; *OT* 16.

24. Ormond Rush, *The Eyes of Faith: The Sense of the Faithful and the Church's Reception of Revelation* (Washington, DC: Catholic University of America Press, 2009), 26.

25. Catherine Cornille, *The Im-possibility of Interreligious Dialogue* (New York: Crossroad, 2008), 27–28.

26. Translation from Tanner, *Decrees of Ecumenical Councils*.

6

John F. Baldovin, SJ

Liturgical Reform and the Public Role of the Catholic Church

On November 22, 1963, the bishops of the Roman Catholic Church, assembled for the second session of Vatican II, voted on the last draft of the "Constitution on the Sacred Liturgy (*Sacrosanctum Concilium*). A few hours later President John F. Kennedy was assassinated in Dallas, Texas. On December 4, a few weeks later, the constitution was formally approved by the Council. No doubt the Kennedy assassination loomed much larger in the world's consciousness than the approval of the liturgy constitution, but like the election of the first Roman Catholic president of the United States, the liturgy constitution was to have a significant impact on how Catholics related to the world (at least in the American context) and vice versa. It is the aim of this essay to argue that the liturgy constitution and the reform that it sanctioned had a significant impact not only on the way Catholics perceived and lived their own faith, but also on how they related to others and on how others perceived them. I suspect that one might be able to make the case for other parts of the world (especially cultures in which religious pluralism thrives), but I will concentrate on the United States.

As I begin, what theologian and canonist Ladislas Orsy has said about ecumenical councils is worth remembering:

Every ecumenical council was a historical event bringing a life cycle of the church to a closure and initiating a new one—an end and a beginning. Beyond their teaching function, the intellectual enlightenment of the church, the councils always (or mostly) left an existential impact on the church that sometimes reverberated for decades or centuries.[1]

I am going to use the funerals of three Kennedy brothers, John, Robert, and Edward, as a template for our consideration. Their differences will reveal, I believe, some interesting things about the public fortunes of Roman Catholicism in the United States.

JOHN F. KENNEDY—1963

The funeral of John F. Kennedy on November 25, 1963, took place at St. Matthew's Cathedral in Washington, DC. At the request of Mrs. Kennedy, a Pontifical Requiem Low Mass was celebrated by Cardinal Richard Cushing. As far as I can tell there was no homily, but auxiliary bishop Philip Hannan read from a number of President Kennedy's speeches, including his entire inaugural address. Schubert's "Ave Maria" and "Pie Jesu" were sung at the offertory. Cardinal Cushing celebrated a solemn high pontifical Mass in Boston two months later to the accompaniment of Mozart's *Requiem*. The funeral was planned by Sargent Shriver.

Though the entire nation and even much of the world were able to participate in the funeral via the media, the liturgical aspect of the event did not draw much attention. In any case, at this point the liturgy was not terribly "accessible" to Roman Catholics, much less others.

Within a year, however, much of this was to change. The liturgy constitution, as I have noted, was promulgated on December 4, 1963, and on September 26, 1964, within nine months (an appropriate gestation period), the office that was charged with implementing the general principles that had been affirmed by the constitution, the *Consilium*, issued the first instruction for the implementation of the reform, titled *Inter*

110

Oecumenici. In its general introduction the instruction reads as follows:

> 5. Necessary before all else, however, is the shared conviction that the Constitution on the Liturgy has as its objective not simply to change liturgical forms and texts but rather to bring to life the kind of formation of the faithful and ministry of pastors that will have their summit and source in the liturgy (see SC art. 10). That is the purpose of the changes made up to now and of those yet to come.[2]

A number of important reforms followed. National episcopal conferences (or groups of conferences sharing the same language, e.g., the International Commission on English in the Liturgy = ICEL) were charged with preparing vernacular translations. Obviously this work had already begun, since the vernacular was introduced for parts of the liturgy[3] by the First Sunday of Advent, just a few months later. Historian Mark Massa has pointed out that these reforms were also prepared by the scholarship of figures like Msgr. Frederick McManus of Boston, the first secretary of the American Bishops Committee on the Liturgy.[4] The Prayers of the Faithful were introduced. Perhaps the most striking change was to come toward the end of the instruction:

> 91. The main altar should preferably be freestanding, to permit walking around it and celebration facing the people. Its location in the place of worship should be truly central so that the attention of the whole congregation naturally focuses there.

The change in the celebrant's posture may well have been the most effective example of the reform—even more significant than the use of the vernacular since after all people could follow the liturgy with their own missals if they chose. A number of other churches, such as the Lutherans and Episcopalians, soon followed suit. Although Mass *versus populum* had never been entirely suppressed, it was extremely rare outside of Europe and gave a whole new visual presentation to Catholic liturgy.

Inter Oecumenici was followed in 1967 by an important instruction on sacred music (*Musicam Sacram*).[5] Here the most significant change was to allow generally (no. 32) what had previously been permitted as an exception: the substitution of hymns and other songs that were not contained in the liturgical texts (e.g., the introit and communion chants). This was to introduce Catholics to the possibility of singing Protestant hymns and other new compositions as part of the liturgy itself. You can see that the direction the liturgy was taking was making it look more and more like American Christian worship in general.

There were, therefore, a number of reforms that took place rather quickly after the Council: the change of the priest's posture, the introduction of the people's language for most of the liturgy, and a good deal of musical variety.

ROBERT F. KENNEDY—1968

Those early reforms characterized the situation in 1968, when our second "snapshot" took place. 1968 was the tumultuous year that saw President Lyndon B. Johnson refuse to run for a second term as president as well as the assassination of Dr. Martin Luther King Jr. on April 4. Two months later Robert F. Kennedy, brother of John and New York senator, was shot and killed while campaigning for the Democratic presidential nomination. His funeral took place at St. Patrick's Cathedral in New York City on June 8, 1968. This time the funeral was a sung requiem Mass, celebrated by Archbishop (not yet Cardinal) Terence Cooke of New York. The "Battle Hymn of the Republic" was sung by Andy Williams. Richard Tucker sang "Panis Angelicus" and Leonard Bernstein conducted the adagio from Mahler's fifth symphony. Several hymns were sung in English. Communion was received kneeling and on the tongue and purple vestments were used.

Robert Kennedy's funeral liturgy took place a year or so before the introduction of the new Roman Missal, which was promulgated by Pope Paul VI in 1969 and went into effect in 1970. The Missal itself and its pastoral and theological introduction (the General Instruction of the Roman Missal = GIRM) represented a radical departure from pre–Vatican II liturgy. It included many options, among them a choice among four eucharistic prayers instead of only Prayer I, the venerable Roman Canon, which had been the only eucharistic prayer of the Roman Rite for well over a millennium.[6] In addition the Bible readings increased tremendously, with the addition of an Old Testament reading on Sundays and a three-year cycle for the reading of Scripture on Sundays and major feasts. A weekday lectionary (on a two-year cycle) was also provided.[7]

I think it is safe to surmise that the American public found the liturgy that was celebrated for Robert Kennedy's funeral in 1968 much more accessible than the one celebrated for John Kennedy in 1963. Certainly John Kennedy's election to the presidency in 1960 signaled a sea change in general American attitudes toward Roman Catholicism, but Robert's funeral came after significant progress had been made toward Christian unity, and part of that progress was a reformed liturgy that could easily be seen to have a "family resemblance" with the worship of a number of Protestant and Anglican churches. In fact there had been a liturgical movement underway in several churches, for example, Lutheran and Episcopal, for several decades. Many churches adopted Sunday biblical readings that were virtually identical to the Roman lectionary, making it possible for pastors to meet together regularly to discuss their upcoming Sunday preaching. In addition, a number of the churches produced liturgical books that had a remarkable resemblance to the shape and content of the Roman Catholic reform, among them the Lutheran Book of Worship (1978), the Episcopal Book of Common Prayer (1979), and the United Methodist Book of Worship (1982).[8] It is particularly troubling that the current and regressive official Vatican policy on the translation of the liturgy, *Liturgiam Authenticam*, expressly eschews ecumenical contact by Catholic translating organizations like the International Commission on English in the Liturgy and, even worse, insists that its strategy aims at distinguishing

Catholic faith from other Christian ecclesial communities.[9] In the course of the past fifty years a number of common texts for worship have been agreed upon (e.g., "And also with you," the "Glory to God in the Highest," and "Holy, Holy, Holy"). The current English translation of the Roman Catholic liturgy has abandoned that project by not consulting with other ecclesial communities.[10]

The late 1960s were probably the most exciting years for ecumenism in the United States. Many people thought that some kind of reunion was just around the corner. To some extent, that enthusiasm lasted until the late 1970s, and the hopes began to fade with a reassertion of Catholic identity under a new pope, John Paul II. According to several chroniclers of the liturgical reform, the reform itself slowed down or even moved backward after 1975 when Archbishop Annibale Bugnini, the secretary of the Vatican Congregation for Divine Worship and the architect of the reform, was summarily dismissed from his position and sent to Tehran as papal nuncio.[11] In any case, ecumenism and liturgical reform went hand in hand in making Catholicism more understandable and accessible to Americans.[12]

In many ways the liturgical reform also took on a kind of Americanized character. In her study of *The Spirit of Vatican II*, American church historian Colleen McDannell traces the post–Vatican II American story through the life of her own mother moving from one town and parish to another, beginning with Erie, Pennsylvania, and ending in Ocala, Florida, where she and her husband Ken retired.[13] Her mother, Margaret, was a kind of typical post–Vatican II Catholic who accepted Church reforms, especially liturgical reforms, with enthusiasm and a great deal of commitment and participation. Her experience of the reform is mirrored in the parish church that she and her husband moved to in the early 1980s. Here is part of McDannell's narrative of the church building:

> At its dedication, Blessed Trinity was a poster child of modernist Catholicism: abstraction, simplicity, emptiness, and informality encouraged all to focus on the Mass and the assembled congregation. As with St.

Jude's Church in Colorado, the new Blessed Trinity Church was built in a fan shape with the pews arranged in a semicircle so all worshippers could see each other. Four narrow stripes of stained-glass windows with abstract symbols representing the Scripture divided a vast expanse of white wall. Bright orange carpet drew the congregation's attention to a slightly raised, spacious altar area. Rather than having any fixed artwork behind the altar, a projector was set up to show slides of religious paintings during Mass to illustrate the theme of the day's liturgy. By the time Margaret and Ken arrived in Florida, Blessed Trinity was already losing its look of Vatican II modernism.[14]

McDannell goes on to recount how subsequent pastors reconfigured the church to look more traditional. I suggest that we might think of the American Catholic Church for the most part mirroring the increasing conservatism that characterized the American culture in the 1980s, '90s, and first decade of the twenty-first century. I would certainly say that over the last several decades liturgical specialists and scholars have become somewhat more cautious and modest in their advocacy for liturgical reform—at least in general.

Although only indirectly related to the public effect of *Sacrosanctum Concilium*, it is worthwhile to consider the general reception of the Council's liturgy reforms. These reforms were inspired by the liturgy constitution itself but required implementation in the postconciliar period. Pope Paul VI, either unwilling or afraid to confront the Vatican's own Congregation for Divine Rites, established a parallel commission to implement the liturgical reform in the wake of the Council. This commission was named the *Consilium ad exsequendam constitutionem de sacra liturgia*. Paul named a noncurial Cardinal, Giacomo Lercaro of Bologna, as its president and Annibale Bugnini, CM, as its secretary. Bugnini had worked on the reform of liturgy since 1948, when Pope Pius XII established a commission to implement his encyclical, *Mediator Dei* (1947). The *Consilium* made use of liturgical experts (historical, theological, and pastoral) from all over the world. At the same time national episcopal conferences began the work of translating the texts that were being produced by Rome. In the case of English, French, and German, a number of episcopal conferences combined to appoint international teams of translators.[15]

From the outset the liturgical reform experienced resistance.[16] Very few bishops had voted against the constitution (the final vote was 2147–4) but others joined the ranks of the doubters and opponents as the various "Instructions" for implementing the reform were published.[17] Some of the most traditional among them objected very strongly to the addition of three new eucharistic prayers to the venerable Roman Canon as well as the translation of the eucharistic prayer into the vernacular at all. While many, like Joseph Ratzinger, thought that the "Tridentine Mass" needed reform, such as translating the readings into the vernacular and having them read from an ambo, some objected to the new three-year Sunday order of readings, which abandoned the traditional lectionary of the Roman Rite. That lectionary had a one-year cycle with almost no readings from the Old Testament. In terms of the Church's relation to the rest of the world, some non-Catholics objected to the loss of Latin in the liturgy, realizing that the Church was clearly showing a new face. In addition, a number of Catholics in Great Britain in particular felt that the new liturgy lessened the distance between Catholics and Anglicans and Protestants. In this they were clearly correct. The liturgical reform certainly made the differences between Catholics and other Christians seem much less extreme. This may be one of its most public effects.

In a fine review of the state of the reform, Gerard Austin finds several areas in which the reform was well received.[18] They are the following: a renewed ecclesiology based on baptism rather than office, the entire Church—head and members—as the subject of the liturgical action, and the use of the vernacular. On the other hand, he notes three areas in which the reform has not fared so well. I mention them here since I am in complete agreement with his assessment. The first area is the interrelation between the priesthoods. The ecclesiology promoted by *Sacrosanctum Concilium* required a thorough rethinking of the relation between ordained and nonordained in the Church.[19] The lack of a truly renewed theology of the ordained ministry continues to bedevil the Catholic Church. A second area where the Council's liturgical reform has not been well received is in what Austin calls the relation between the *res* and the *res et sacramentum*. I could not agree more. Let me explain. Austin uses the traditional terms from scholastic theology *res* and *res et sacramentum* to illustrate the fact that the grace (or as I call it, *the point*) of the sacrament of the Eucharist (its *res*) is the unity of the Body of Christ. That grace relies on a prior condition that comes about through the enactment of the sign. This is called the *res et sacramentum*. In the case of the Eucharist, this is the real presence of the Body and Blood of Christ in the consecrated bread and wine. The conciliar reforms placed the emphasis correctly on the outcome, the grace of the sacrament, whereas much of the recent reaction has insisted on stopping at the real presence. This *can* be the problem when eucharistic adoration is emphasized over against celebration. No good Catholic theologian would argue against the real presence, but the true genius of the reform requires that our attention be focused on the ultimate goal of the Eucharist, which is our unity in and with Christ.[20]

With regard to our focus here, however, Austin's most pertinent observation has to do with the relation between the liturgy and our attitude toward the world. Austin insists that *Sacrosanctum Concilium* be interpreted not solely on its own, but in relation to all of the Council's sixteen documents, including the final document, "The Pastoral Constitution on the Church in the Modern World." For Austin, truly engaging the liturgical reform requires embracing the Council's openness to the world. He refers to Karl Rahner's understanding of the liturgy as the symbolic, focused realization of the "liturgy of the world."[21] I would add that the way the post–Vatican II liturgy is celebrated promotes a positive view of the world. I often say (half-jokingly) that hell emptied out in the past fifty years. That is, the liturgical reform went hand in hand with a shift from a cultural Catholicism that emphasized sin and the fear of hell to one where a much more positive engagement of faith and appreciation of God's love for the world in Christ was required. In the process, purgatory also seems to have disappeared in favor of instant canonization. The shift I am describing can easily be seen in funeral liturgies, which prior to the Council had focused on the deceased and his or her fate in the hands of God (*Dies Irae*), and afterward more on Christian hope and the grief and consolation of the mourners.[22]

Negative reaction to the post–Vatican II liturgical reforms reached a kind of crescendo with the election of Pope Benedict XVI in 2005 and its apex with Benedict's *motu proprio, Summorum Pontificum* of 2007.[23] Benedict greatly liberalized the permission to use the pre–Vatican II Mass, claiming (somewhat problematically) that it had never been abrogated. This move encouraged not only the traditionalists who rejected the reformed Mass of Paul VI *tout court* but it also brought renewed enthusiasm to those who did not want a wholesale return to the preconciliar liturgy but rather a "reform of the reform."[24] Many more conservative Catholics rejected not the *Sacrosanctum Concilium* itself but rather its development in the rites as the Vatican reformed them as well as the subsequent pastoral implementation of those rites.[25]

McDannell's study also highlights another aspect of the reform that coincided with cultural and social developments: the increasingly important role of women in Church and society. Many of those who became liturgical experts and received degrees at schools like Notre Dame, Catholic University, and St. John's Collegeville were women—religious and lay alike. Although a woman (or any layperson for that matter) may not hold jurisdiction in the Catholic Church, many women have achieved influential positions with regard to the liturgy, especially a number of notable women who became professors of liturgy in major university faculties or seminaries: Mary Collins, Kathleen Hughes, Mary Margaret Kelleher, and Teresa Berger, to name some of the most prominent.

That liturgical specialists have tended to overreach their brief and impose their own understanding of the vision of Vatican II on ordinary church folk is the theme of a recent sociological study by David Maines and Michael McCallion.[26] The authors, though clearly biased on my reading of the work, argue that liturgists, particularly in the Archdiocese of Detroit where their surveys took place, tended to impose their wills on the people. I am sure that one can point to a number of cases where this has happened, as the authors do in a rather scathing chapter titled "Bob the Liturgist." I am not sure how one would compare the campaign of liturgical specialists in the North American context (we need to include Canada here) but my suspicion is that the liturgical renewal became significantly Americanized, given a new sense of freedom and possibility after Vatican II.

Indeed one astute observer, Francis Mannion, claimed that the liturgical reform had been (even if unconsciously) thoroughly adapted to North American culture. In an important 1988 essay Mannion argued that three aspects of American culture profoundly affected liturgical celebration. These were the subjectification of reality, the intimization of culture, and the politicization of society.[27] The first is a result of the Enlightenment's "turn to the subject" and the consequent individualism so rampant in modern culture. The second has to do with the notion that "warmth is God," in other words, that only close intimacy is really genuine and that therefore only small-group worship is authentic. The last of these factors he relates to the tendency to turn everything into a political battlefield in contemporary society. There is great merit in Mannion's argument. Liturgy and culture do constitute a two-way street. In the past fifty years, Catholic liturgy has gained a new visibility and stature in American culture. At the same time, the culture has affected the liturgy. It seems to me that much of the opposition to the contemporary Catholic liturgical reform has to do with a rejection of contemporary culture and particularly with the challenges it poses to traditional morality.

The funeral of Senator Robert Kennedy took place around the peak of enthusiasm about the reform of the liturgy— although the reforms had by no means settled in 1968. The Roman Missal of Paul VI was not published until 1969. A full English translation of the Missal did not appear until 1973. And a number of the reformed sacramental rituals, like the Rite of

119

Penance and the Rite of Christian Initiation of Adults, had not yet appeared.

Let us therefore fast-forward some thirty years to the funeral of Senator Edward Kennedy, the last surviving Kennedy brother in 2009.

EDWARD M. KENNEDY—2009

The funeral of Edward Kennedy, longtime Massachusetts senator, took place on August 29, 2009, at the Basilica of Our Lady of Perpetual Help (the Mission Church), Boston. Rev. Donald Monan, SJ, the former president of Boston College, was the celebrant and Rev. Mark Hession, the Kennedy pastor from Cape Cod, was the preacher. Cardinal Sean O'Malley of Boston presided in choir.

Even though not a sudden and nationwide tragedy like the assassinations of his brothers, Ted Kennedy's funeral was widely broadcast, another event that drew national attention. For this reason it can serve as our third touch point in discerning the impact of the Vatican II liturgical reform on public life.

In addition to the "star quality" of the music that marked John's and Robert's funerals (Susan Graham sang "Ave Maria," and cellist YoYo Ma accompanied tenor Placido Domingo who sang "Panis Angelicus"), some aspects of the liturgy itself reflected the current state of Roman Catholicism vis-à-vis American public life. For example, there was heightened attention around which Catholic politicians might receive holy communion. Receiving communion had (has) become a battleground for many conservative Catholics who judge that Catholic politicians who oppose the Church's teaching on issues like abortion and same-sex marriage should be refused communion. Indeed, the United States Conference of Catholic Bishops has weighed in on the issue (albeit in a very nuanced manner that allows individual bishops to make their own determination on the issue).[28] Although the media were not allowed to film the communion procession—at least on the side of the church where the dignitaries were located—it was quite clear that Cardinal O'Malley left the sanctuary to offer the greeting of peace to President and Mrs. Obama as well as to Vice President and Dr. Biden. Vice President Biden is a Catholic whose position on abortion as well as same-sex marriage is at odds with the Church. How prominent Catholics participate in liturgy has clearly become a matter of public interest.

On the other hand, the funeral liturgy was a good example of contemporary Roman Catholic worship, a liturgy whose "accessibility" could appeal to the sensibilities of most Americans. As a student of the liturgy, I have to add that a broadcast liturgy like this one was somewhat of a missed opportunity in that some standard "Catholic best practices" were not employed. I mean that, regretfully, the Eucharistic acclamations (Holy, Holy, Holy, etc.) were not sung; nor was the responsorial psalm sung.[29] On the other hand, the majority of the Kennedy family (as well as those on the right side of the church where the communion procession was televised) appeared to receive communion in the hand.[30] The color of the vestments (white) was another indication of how Catholic attitudes had changed with regard to funerals—and death in general.

All in all (with the exception of the issue of the reception of holy communion), there was not a great deal that was remarkable about the last of our three Kennedy funerals. Perhaps this was a sign that the liturgical reform, at least as an American cultural phenomenon, has taken root and become a normal part of the national culture.

CONCLUSION

I am aware that in choosing to focus on three Kennedy funerals I have only told part of the story of the public effect of the Vatican II reform of the liturgy. In the first place, I have largely passed over the 1970s, '80s, and '90s, when a great deal of liturgical ferment and reaction to it happened. (I might, for example, have spent some time on the funeral of Jacqueline Kennedy on May 24, 1994, during which the hymn "We Gather Together," sung to the rather upbeat Dutch tune, *Kremser*, served as the processional hymn.) Second, in focusing on the Kennedy funerals I have limited myself to three liturgical events that, although broadcast nationally, took place in the American Northeast. Thus I have neglected the American Midwest, South, and West. A great deal more liturgical experimentation took place in the Midwest and West, and so I think it's safe to suggest many more ecumenical possibilities emerged there. Third, I have neglected the relation between the reform and other cultures in the United States, in particular Latino cultures, in which the introduction of Spanish greatly aided general cultural assimilation and development.[31] A similar study of the effect on the reform on African American Catholic communities could shed some light on how black Catholics in the United States have been able to relate more closely with their Protestant brothers and sisters. The reader can imagine that to do justice to our subject a much larger study would be required, and I would be very happy indeed if a scholar were to pick up on the Latino side of the equation.

Be that as it may, I think we can draw four general conclusions from the foregoing:

1. The liturgical renewal and revolutionary reform inspired by Vatican II's "Constitution on the Liturgy" was far from a purely internal church matter. How the church worships inevitably affects it face toward the world and the attitudes that Catholics have toward the world. At the same time, the culture has had a significant impact on Catholic worship.

2. In the American context on which we have focused, translating the liturgy into the vernacular greatly aided the "normalization" of Catholicism in American life. This process had begun much earlier, of course. It had been aided by the fellowship created in World War II and the increase of Catholics in the middle class in the 1950s. It was quite clearly symbolized by the election of President John F. Kennedy in 1960. (Our study has capitalized on the great irony of President Kennedy's assassination and funeral coinciding so

closely with the official approval of *Sacrosanctum Concilium.*)

3. Each of the public figures whose funerals I have used to frame this study were ardently committed to the public good and in particular to peace and social justice—especially with regard to racial discrimination. Their lives of service can also remind us that the liturgical reform made the justice dimension and consequences of the liturgy all the more evident. As Robert Hovda once wrote, "What do you mean we need more peace liturgies? Peace liturgies are the only kind we have."[32] The relation between the liturgy and ordinary life—with the implication of the struggle for peace and justice—is probably the most unrealized and unappreciated promise of the post–Vatican II liturgical reform. Here the liturgy truly has the potential to mirror what God wants the world to look like—a plain translation of the kingdom of God. The reformed Catholic liturgy has the potential of helping people to realize the value of communion, peace, and equality, but we have a long way to go before we help people to make the connection between the communal dimension of the liturgy and life.[33] The stubborn perception that one must make a choice between being a partisan of the liturgy and being a partisan of social justice is unfortunate indeed.

4. In pluralistic societies like the United States, the liturgical reform had the added effect of greatly aiding ecumenical efforts. That effort has clearly cooled off with the circling of the wagons that has taken place over the past thirty-five years since the election of Pope John Paul II, and especially over the past eight years with the election of Pope Benedict XVI. For this reason, a number of people have concluded that Vatican II is dead.[34]

The recent election of Pope Francis, however, shows promise of reversing the conservative tide of the past thirty or so years that brought the forward movement of the liturgical reform to a halt. In his recently published interview for a number of Jesuit publications, Pope Francis has made it quite clear that he supports the forward movement of the reform:

> The work of the liturgical reform has been a service to the people as a re-reading of the Gospel from a concrete historical situation. Yes, there are hermeneutics of continuity and discontinuity, but one thing is clear: the dynamic of reading the Gospel, actualizing its message for today—which was typical of Vatican II—is absolutely irreversible.[35]

As I hope we have seen, *Sacrosanctum Concilium* should not be read without regard to the rest of the Council. It certainly would be a pity if we restricted ourselves to a literalist or fundamentalist reading of the conciliar documents like it. These documents need to be read in an intratextual manner, as well as in the context of the subsequent reform that put them into practice.

As the attention given to the fiftieth anniversary of the Council, including the fiftieth anniversary currently of the liturgy constitution, reveals, Vatican II is far from dead. The liturgical reform's interaction with contemporary culture is indeed a work in progress.

Notes

1. Ladislas Orsy, *Receiving the Council: Theological and Canonical Insights and Debates* (Collegeville, MN: Liturgical Press, 2009), 77.

2. See http://www.adoremus.org/Interoecumenici.html#sthash.d8SOkXph.dpuf.

3. Nos. 57–59. Permission to translate the eucharistic prayer was to come later.

4. Mark S. Massa, *The Catholic Revolution: How the Sixties Changed the Catholic Church Forever* (New York: Oxford University Press, 2010), 25ff.

5. http://www.vatican.va/archive/hist_councils/ii_vati can_council/documents/vat-ii_instr_19670305_musicam -sacram_en.html.

6. The Missal of Paul VI provoked a strong reaction in some traditionalist Catholic circles, but that is another story. For example, see Laszlo Dobszay, *The Bugnini Liturgy and the Reform of the Reform* (Front Royal, VA: Catholic Church Music Associates, 2003); and Klaus Gamber, *The Reform of the Roman Liturgy: Its Problems and Background*, with an introduction by Cardinal Joseph Ratzinger (Harrison, NY: Una Voce Press and The Foundation for Catholic Reform, 1993). See also John Baldovin, *Reforming the Liturgy: A Response to the Critics* (Collegeville, MN: Liturgical Press, 2008).

7. Hitherto, weekday readings had only been provided for Lent in the Roman Rite.

8. I should add that the process of reform among the Protestant and Anglican churches had begun well before Vatican II, as was made clear by Professor Paul F. Bradshaw in a paper delivered at the International Symposium on Liturgy and the Arts in May 2013, sponsored by the Monastery of Bose, Italy. That paper will be published in the proceedings of the conference.

9. Congregation for Divine Worship and the Discipline of Sacraments, Fifth Instruction, "For the Right Implementation of the Constitution on the Sacred Liturgy of the Second Vatican Council," *Liturgiam Authenticam*: On the Use of the Vernacular Languages in the Publication of the Books of the Roman Liturgy, March 28, 2001, http://www.vatican.va/roman_curia/congrega tions/ccdds/documents/rc_con_ccdds_doc_20010507_litur giam-authenticam_en.html (Hereafter, LA.) LA no. 98 even forbids collaboration between so-called mixed commissions. The insistence on a peculiar sacred vocabulary and how it relates to other Christians is my interpretation of the intent of LA no. 27; see also nos. 49–50. LA no. 104 directly contravenes *Sacrosanctum Concilium* no. 36, in which the authority to translate is given directly to episcopal conferences, subject to Vatican approval (*recognitio*).

10. See "The Reims Statement: Praying with One Voice; On Common Texts and Lectionary in the Life of the Churches," of the ecumenical English Language Liturgical Consultation (www.englishtexts.org), August 16, 2011.

11. See Annibale Bugnini, *The Reform of the Liturgy 1948–1975* (Collegeville, MN: Liturgical Press, 1980); Piero Marini, *Challenging Reform: Realizing the Vision of the Liturgical Renewal, 1963–1975*, ed. Mark Francis, John Page, and Keith Pecklers (Collegeville, MN: Liturgical Press, 2007).

12. On the current state of ecumenism, see Orsy, *Receiving the Council,* 46–54.

13. Colleen McDannell, *The Spirit of Vatican II: A History of Catholic Reform in America* (New York: Basic Books, 2011).

14. Ibid., 209–10.

15. Eleven episcopal conferences (Australia, Canada, England and Wales, India, Ireland, New Zealand, Pakistan, the Philippines, Scotland, South Africa, and the United States) formed the International Commission for English in the Liturgy (ICEL) in 1964. The intriguing history of ICEL has yet to be written, but see John Wilkins, "Lost in Translation: The Bishops, the Vatican and the English Liturgy," *Commonweal* 132 (2005): 12, 16, 18–20; Maurice Taylor, *Being A Bishop in Scotland* (Blackrock: Columba Press, 2006), 131–38; Paddy Kearney, *Guardian of the Light: Denis Hurley; Renewing the Church, Opposing Apartheid* (New York: Continuum, 2009), 106–24, 161–69.

16. See Bugnini, *Reform*, 277–301.

17. See Marini, *Challenging Reform*, and Baldovin, *Reforming the Liturgy*.

18. Gerard Austin, "The Reception of the Liturgical Reform of the Second Vatican Council," *Liturgical Ministry* 17 (2008): 49–57.

19. This has been noted by Massimo Faggioli, *True Reform: Liturgy and Ecclesiology in Sacrosanctum Concilium* (Collegeville, MN: Liturgical Press, 2012).

20. I make the same point in my "Is the Liturgy Hitting Its Target?" *The Jurist* 72 (2012): 453–65.

21. Austin, "The Reception of the Liturgical Reform," 55; see Karl Rahner, "Considerations on the Active Role of the Person in the Sacramental Event," *Theological Investigations XIV* (New York: Crossroad, 1973), 161–84.

22. See John Baldovin, "Three Funerals (and a Film)," in *Postmodern Worship and the Arts*, ed. Doug Adams and Michael E. Moynahan (San Jose, CA: Resource Publications, 2002), 129–35; Ansgar Franz, "'Everything Is Worthwhile at the

End?' Christian Funeral Liturgy amidst Ecclesial Tradition and Secular Rites," *Studia Liturgica* 32 (2002): 48–68.

23. For an earlier survey of rejection of the Council, see Daniele Menozzi, "Opposition to the Council (1966–84)," in *The Reception of Vatican II*, ed. Giuseppe Alberigo, Jean-Pierre Jossua, and Joseph A. Komonchak, trans. Matthew J. O'Connell (Washington, DC: Catholic University of America Press, 1987), 325–48.

24. On *Summorum Pontificum*, see John Baldovin, "Reflections on Summmorum Pontificum," *Worship* 83 (2009): 98–112; Chad Glendinning, "Was the 1962 *Missale Romanum* Abrogated? A Canonical Analysis in Light of *Summorum Pontificum*," *Worship* 85 (2011): 15–37. On the "reform of the reform," see Thomas Kocik, ed., *The Reform of the Reform? A Liturgical Debate: Reform or Return* (San Francisco, CA: Ignatius Press, 2003).

25. These groups are very active on the internet. See, for example, The New Liturgical Movement (http://www.newliturgicalmovement.org/) or Rorate Caeli (http://rorate-caeli.blogspot.com/).

26. David Maines and Michael McCallion, *Transforming Catholicism: Liturgical Change in the Vatican II Church* (Lanham, MD: Rowman and Littlefield, 2007).

27. M. Francis Mannion, "Liturgy and the Present Crisis of Culture," *Worship* 62 (1988): 98–123. For a similar cultural critique, see Mark Searle, "Private Religion, Individualistic Society and Common Worship," in *Liturgy and Spirituality in Context: Perspectives on Prayer and Culture*, ed. Eleanor Bernstein (Collegeville, MN: Liturgical Press, 1990), 27–46.

28. For a recent statement, http://www.usccb.org/_cs_upload/7594_1.pdf. This statement was issued after Pope Benedict made remarks about abortion and politicians in a visit to Argentina in March 2012.

29. Reciting the responsorial psalm happens at many Catholic funerals, probably because of the concern that as many of those close to the deceased as possible might have an active role in the celebration. But that is a subject for another essay.

30. Unlike the Kennedy family weddings, no one appeared to be drunk.

31. Virgilio Elizondo and Timothy Matovina, *Mestizo Worship: A Pastoral Approach to Liturgical Ministry* (Collegeville, MN: Liturgical Press, 1998); James Empereur and Eduardio Fernandez, *La Vida Sacra: Contemporary Hispanic Sacramental Theology* (Lanham, MD: Rowman & Littlefield, 2006); Timothy Matovina, *Latino Catholicism: Transformation in America's Largest Church* (Princeton, NJ: Princeton University Press, 2012). One could even claim, in light of the recent upsurge in desire for the traditional Latin liturgy, that the future of Roman Catholic liturgy in America is more Latino than Latin!

32. See John Baldovin, ed., *Robert Hovda: The Amen Corner* (Collegville, MN: Liturgical Press, 1994), 170–76.

33. Luis Maldonado deals with this issue very ably in "Liturgy as Communal Enterprise," in Alberigo et al., *The Reception of Vatican II*, 309–21.

34. I recently took part in a webcast panel titled "Vatican II: Dead or Alive?" http://www.youtube.com/watch?v=55eC7YY-JSY.

35. Antonio Spadaro, "A Big Heart Open to God: The Exclusive Interview with Pope Francis," *America*, September 30, 2013.

7

Lisa Sowle Cahill

Vatican II, Moral Theology, and Social Ethics

From the standpoint of moral theology and ethics, the Second Vatican Council represents a new type of dialogical "openness to the modern world," a collaborative approach to reading "the signs of the times." The Council embraced "all men [and women] of good will" in a common effort to discern what are, and how to address, "the joys and the hopes, the griefs and the anxieties" of individuals and societies in a newly global era.[1] However, the consequences of this engagement might not have been exactly what the Council fathers expected, for they have been multiple and multidirectional. Whenever a government intervenes in a complex system, it risks exemplifying the law of unintended consequences.[2] This especially has proven to be the case with the new, more active, more authoritative role of the laity in moral theology, ethics, and public Catholicism; yet it is also true of the renewed biblical orientation in Catholic ethics. And it might be said of the Council's general posture of political engagement that many of the results envisioned or at least hoped for have not been realized.

The effects of Vatican II may be explored by identifying three conciliar developments, and posing a question about the long-range significance of each. The first development is the openness of the Church to the modern world. The question is whether, fifty years later, optimism or pessimism about the effects of that engagement is warranted. To what extent have its apparent initial aims been met? The second development is that natural law and the gospel have become the double premises of the Church's public role. This complicates the content of the message, however, raising further questions of knowledge and authority. Who interprets these two sources, and who decides what their meaning should look like in practice? The third development is the empowerment of the laity. But a follow-up question is, what are the laity actually doing? Here again, we may find some surprises.

OPENNESS TO THE MODERN WORLD

Perhaps more than anything else, and certainly in the areas of ethics and politics, Vatican II represents openness to the modern world in reading and responding to the signs of the times. The motif of aggiornamento, announced by John XXIII in a speech introducing the Council,[3] is perhaps more significant in ethics than in any other area, with the possible exception of interreligious dialogue.

In "The Pastoral Constitution on the Church in the Modern World" (*Gaudium et Spes*), the "Problems of Special Urgency" that title the chapters of part 2 all have to do with ethics and politics. They include marriage and family, the development of culture (covering themes of dignity of the person, the common good, and humanism), socioeconomic life, political community, and peace and the community of nations. Even though *Gaudium et Spes* is a Catholic teaching document, it is addressed to "the whole human family,"[4] which is envisioned to be an amenable partner in addressing the world's critical problems. The "world"—not only the Church—is created in love, fallen to sin, but also "emancipated now by Christ." Therefore Christians, Catholics, and the Church as an institution are called to "foster the brotherhood of man."[5] A commitment to solidarity and justice are part of the mission of the Church, a mission that is not only *to* the modern world, but also *with* the modern world.

Gaudium et Spes opens by alluding to modern people's

"joys and hopes, griefs and anxieties," and names multiple forms of injustice. Yet the overarching emphasis is not on existential suffering and evils to be feared, but on natural human goodness, solidarity, and gospel liberation. Certainly in the massive press coverage that its sessions received, as well as in its reception by the general public and by the Catholic faithful (whether admirers or detractors), the Council's approach to the modern world has been perceived to exude energy, optimism, and engagement. To most people, Vatican II embodies a Catholicism that is more collegial, more global, more empowering of the laity, and more ready to learn from those beyond the Church's borders than had ever been the case before.

But was the Council's apparent optimism about engaging the world for the global betterment of human societies warranted? *Gaudium et Spes*, despite recognizing the global extent of human suffering, is in some ways very '60s—hopeful and upbeat about putting our collective shoulder to the wheel and producing widespread social change as the result of our public engagement on social questions. Moral and social virtues can be promoted in individuals and in society. "Thus, with the needed help of divine grace, men who are truly new and artisans of a new humanity can be forthcoming."[6]

In 1996 David Hollenbach gave a presidential address to the Society of Christian Ethics called "Social Ethics under the Sign of the Cross." His message was the importance of confronting the fact that our efforts not only require sacrifice, but also may result in apparent defeat and even death.[7] Hence, in light of the world's suffering and anguish, the "inexorable and unavoidable issue" that must be faced is the classic problem of evil. Is there an ultimate power that sustains existence, and if so, is it "hostile or friendly"?[8] Does that power enable successful human responses to the suffering around us?

Unfortunately, despite the transformationist agenda of Vatican II and of Catholic social teaching in general, the evidence of history does not clearly substantiate hope for comprehensive, progressive global change for justice. It is true that there are certain human goods that are recognized across cultures, such as adequate nutrition, shelter, protection from physical violence, meaningful work, opportunities for families to stay together and nurture their children, and political participation. Globally, there has been progress toward respect for human equality and social justice in some areas such as human rights, women's rights, and the environment.[9] Yet while most people and societies assert their own moral right to participate in basic goods, virtually all persons and societies are willing to deny them selectively to others whom they deem less worthy. Progress toward the universal common good acclaimed by every pope since John XXIII is piecemeal, uneven, and unstable. To take the example of violent conflict, wars between nations have decreased since the 1950s, but civil conflict has made up the gap, with the result that most war-related deaths today are civilian. Moreover, even after formal peace accords are signed, conflicts have a very high chance—by one estimate about 40 percent—of breaking out again into violence.[10] And although extreme poverty has declined worldwide,[11] the gap between the richest and the poorest has widened.[12]

Here in the United States, to look more narrowly, most Catholics are not, in fact, all that committed to addressing human ills like economic inequality and threats to life. According to Catholic University's Center for Applied Research in the Apostolate (CARA), 80 percent claim that helping the poor is important to Catholic identity, but 60 percent believe that one can be a good Catholic without personally doing anything to help the poor.[13] In *Racial Justice and the Catholic Church*, Bryan Massingale shows how racism is and always has been endemic in the U.S. Catholic Church, despite lip service to the contrary.[14] Despite the Catholic magisterium's clear and repeated teachings on protection of life, the Public Religion Research Institute has found that 53 percent of Catholics think abortion should be legal in all or most cases; 51 percent think the death penalty is acceptable.[15] The challenge today to the Church's public political engagement is to be realistic about the intractability of personal, social, and structural exploitation, violence, and apathy; yet socially engaged, committed to solidarity, and hopeful about the future.

According to Hollenbach, "We need hope in the possibility of solidarity and hope that human aspirations are not ultimately futile...hope in the possibility of the ultimate fulfillment of all that is most deeply human."[16] He sees the source of this hope as ultimately religious, and links it both to the doctrine of creation and to the cross. The cross embodies divine compassion for all forms of human suffering, and in it "we discover a source of hope that outstrips all our ability to plan, to control, and to succeed."[17] Hollenbach states clearly that he does not think only Christians or only religious people can have hope or be committed to social justice. Yet Christian symbols seem best to capture those possibilities. In and through the cross we see that suffering and death, grief and anguish, that come as the price of solidarity with the oppressed are actually signs of grace and signs that the mission of Christ identified by the Council is being realized and will be a force for good.[18] "Social ethics under the sign of the cross...both responds to and reveals a God who is Friend even in the midst of the afflictions of history," making credible "the Christian hope in resurrection and the final victory of joy."[19]

What remains to be further drawn out or explicated are the answers to two questions. How do these symbols, theologically mediated through texts and discourses, actually come to inspire practical trust, hope, solidarity, and committed action in the real world? And how is this the case when the work is shared among people of differing worldviews? The instigation or inspiration of wider participation in the Church is a necessary part of answering these questions, and of meeting the challenges of hope, solidarity, and commitment in a disappointing and desperate world. These are points to which we will return when developing the changed role of the laity after Vatican II.

NATURAL LAW AND GOSPEL

The Council, especially *Gaudium et Spes,* expands on the natural law tradition of moral theology and politics, globalizing it; and at the same time, it heightens the gospel identity of the Church and its members. The message and the mission are human *and* Christian; grounded in natural law *and* Scripture;

addressed to the "brotherhood of man" *and* shaped within the "body of Christ."

A longstanding characteristic of Catholic moral theology and ethics—going back at least to Thomas Aquinas—is that basic moral goods, responsibilities, knowledge, and principles are considered to be "reasonable" and to correspond to human "nature." Although sin corrupts both reason and nature, which are redeemed only in Christ, a universal natural morality can still establish a constructive meeting ground for ethics and politics. At its most basic, natural law is simply the idea that human beings are similar enough in needs and priorities to agree at a fundamental level about what constitutes basic human goods, and what are the minimum requirements for cooperative social life.

In 2009 the International Theological Commission (ITC), an international group of thirty theologians appointed by the pope, produced a document called "In Search of a Universal Ethic."[20] The ITC argues that a renewal of natural law ethics in a more historically conscious vein is necessary to support "planetary responsibility" and "global solidarity."[21] The ITC acknowledges the need for constant revision of specifications of human goods, norms, and rights in light of cross-cultural exchange. If natural law is to serve as a moral and political compass in pluralistic societies and internationally, then it must not be presented in the "rigid form" that it has sometimes assumed in the past.[22] The formulation of norms of the natural law calls for modesty, prudence, and dialogue with those who need not share the Catholic or Christian worldview.[23] Christian identity should inspire commitment to work with others to secure the global common good.[24]

At the same time, the Council's "Decree on Priestly Formation" (*Optatum Totius*) calls for moral theology to be "nourished" by Scripture.[25] The Council's call for renewal of the liturgy[26] enhances the gospel dimensions of moral theology as well. Increasingly liturgy is seen as an occasion of moral formation, and a place where the community is prepared to bring gospel values to the public venues where Catholics participate with others in building the common good. A theological leader in this regard since the Council is Louis-Marie Chauvet, who has argued that the sacramental theology of the Church needs to be completely reconceived to account for the effect of sacramental participation in the Christian life, and the Christian life as a response to God's initiative in the sacraments.[27]

The recovery of the gospel basis and ecclesial dimension of moral theology and social ethics has provided a way to anchor and express Catholic community identity, and sense of personal belonging. A Christian way of life includes and can be concretely expressed not only by liturgy and prayer, but also in a moral and social "lifestyle" of discipleship—whether that be religious orders, pro-life movements, the Catholic Worker, Catholic social services like Catholic Charities and Catholic Relief Services, parish outreach groups, basic Christian communities, prison ministries, or the Jesuit Volunteer Corps.

But to what degree and how does this gospel identity, a communal or ecclesial identity, enter into the public sphere, for example in addressing the central issues of Catholic social teaching, such as poverty, human rights, war and peace, and the equal rights of women? The combination of natural law and gospel in the mode of aggiornamento produces a major tension around which identity or source will control in which situation, or with what audience.[28] We have thus seen some highly conflicted debates about who "owns" Catholic identity and its social-moral expressions, how to interpret natural law and Scripture, and which provides the normative bottom line on which issue.

One way in which the gospel has changed social ethics is by the introduction of the "preferential option for the poor," based on Jesus' ministry of the reign of God (Mark 1:14) and his care for the poor and outcast. The preferential option for the poor means more than justice as equality or equal access, and more than liberal freedom as noninterference. It means a special priority and affirmative action for those who are most left out of the common good. Coming from liberation theology, this phrasing is more explicit in Paul VI, John Paul II, and Benedict XVI—and certainly appears likely to be in Francis I. For example, John Paul II defines "the *option* or *love of preference* for the poor" as having special primacy in the exercise of Christian charity, and as extending beyond individual actions to include "our *social responsibilities*," including economic justice, and decisions and policies at the national and international levels.[29] Though not so directly stated, the option for the poor finds precedents in *Gaudium et Spes* as well, for that document reminds us that it is a matter of justice "to come to the relief of the poor."[30] Not all have been equally receptive to the preferential option for the poor, however. The idea that this is an evangelical priority with a social justice dimension, backed by the ministry of Jesus himself, has seemed to some either to reduce the gospel to a program of social reform, or to threaten the notions of fairness held by many in modern capitalist societies— such as just desert, merit, or even opportunistic success.

Turning to the side of so-called personal ethics, new readings of the natural law have shifted what used to be some defining "Christian" viewpoints, for instance ideas of sex and gender purportedly based on the Genesis accounts of creation and fall. The premise of a natural and just equality between the sexes has emerged since the Council, though not without difficulty. New insights into natural law as requiring the dignity of all persons, human rights, justice, and the common good have influenced traditional Catholic teachings about the subordination of women to men and the priority of procreation as the meaning of sex. Now men and women are at least in theory seen as equal, and sex is also and equally for the purpose of expressing and enhancing love. Since the Council, we have seen growing appreciation of the goodness of marriage and family as spheres of holiness and Christian flourishing, as well as John Paul II apologizing for sexism in the Church, and thanking the women's liberation movement.[31]

Interestingly, the ITC report on a universal ethics based on natural law applies the inductive approach to specific applications or instantiations of moral goods and principles to issues in social ethics, like environmental justice, and is open to new readings of global responsibility. Yet it invokes standard magisterial teachings about sex, procreation, and contraception as evidence that basic norms of the natural law are recognized.[32] The ITC leaves aside the numerous allegations that these teachings do not adequately capture the real nature of sex, procreation and gender equality, true justice, or a genuine appropriation of the gospel. Instead, regarding many specifics of sexual morality, it falls back on ecclesial authority and analyses reached in the past and still marked out by the magisterium as defining what it means to be a Catholic.[33]

This leaves unanswered many questions about whether the Roman Catholic Church has really come to terms with the full social equality of women, in family, society, and Church. The complementarity model of gender and "special genius of women," along with motherhood as women's most important vocation—which is not asserted of fatherhood for men—are still provoking many critical responses.[34] Moreover, global cultural differences on sex and gender ideals and norms are huge.

Given such tensions, there are at least two different ways of looking at Catholic identity since Vatican II. Several authors—notably Massimo Faggioli, Joseph Komonchak, and Ormond Rush—have described an "Augustinian" direction and a "neo-Thomist" direction, an analysis that can be applied to interpretations of the Council and to the Church in the public arena, as well.[35]

Keeping their distance from the aggiornamento of Vatican II, the Augustinians see the Church as a haven of grace in a sinful world: Catholics should be bringing the experience of a real but transcendent God to an increasingly secular public and emphasizing the distinctive moral and religious practices that set them apart. For Augustinians, the Church is faith-community oriented more than public-engagement oriented. Social service is a work of the Church, especially of laypeople, but broad social transformation is not the real program.

At the time of the Council and after, key theologians driving this train of thought included Hans Urs von Balthasar, Cardinal (and future pope) Joseph Ratzinger, and Cardinal Henri de Lubac, SJ. The issue was raised with new force during the pontificate of Benedict XVI through some of his encyclicals, especially his 2005 *Deus Caritas Est* (God Is Love) and his 2009 *Caritas in Veritate* (Charity in Truth), which prompted debate about whether he saw justice as truly the mission of the Church and whether his teaching lens was the global Church or the rapidly secularizing countries of Western Europe.

The progressive neo-Thomists, on the other hand, have been represented by Karl Rahner, SJ, the Dominicans Marie-Dominique Chenu and Cardinal Yves Congar, and John Courtney Murray, SJ. They have stressed the created goodness of the world, history, politics, and the sciences, and affirmed that grace is already and everywhere present in our world. Also important to neo-Thomists is historical consciousness, in light of which they believe that our knowledge of truth is "constantly emerging," not a finished product that has already been revealed, known, and taught. "Truth has its objectivity, but it is only gradually being grasped by us in our judgment over time, through experience, and with maturity."[36] This also applies to Catholic moral teaching, which does not arrive independently of "the human processes necessary for authentic learning and teaching...divine assistance must be conceived of as working through these human processes," which are not suddenly or uniquely replaced by a divine power when the magisterium speaks.[37]

Among the neo-Thomists, there is a sense of positive engagement and learning—perhaps most visibly from the natural and social sciences—in areas such as sex and gender, economics, evolution, and the environment. In this perspective, Catholic social teaching is reclaimed and promoted, and the preferential option for the poor is seen as an agenda for political action and structural change.

Today, fifty years after Vatican II, we may be witnessing the emergence of a third vision of the Church, one with more appeal to the post–Vatican II generations. This model might be termed neo-Franciscan. It has been around since the pontificate of John Paul II, and is not necessarily to be equated with the outlook of the new Pope Francis. Like St. Francis, it prioritizes small faith communities and personal devotion and service. A theologian from the Vatican II era who signals some of these themes—Scripture, the Holy Spirit, and a life of Christian virtue centered on Christ—is the Belgian Dominican Servais Pinckaers.[38] Another theological figure who has shaped the thinking of some in this model is the Protestant theologian Stanley Hauerwas, who calls

Christians to a countercultural witness to the cross of Christ.[39] Yet these Catholics are also inspired by figures such as Dorothy Day and Oscar Romero.

A neo-Franciscan public agenda for the Church would take shape in care for the poor, nonviolence, environmental concern, and dialogue with other religions to accomplish goals. St. Francis, after all, made it his special mission to care for lepers, embraced a life of voluntary poverty, composed a poem in praise of "Brother Sun and Sister Moon,"[40] and crossed crusaders' lines to meet peacefully with the sultan of Egypt.[41] A contemporary neo-Franciscan approach would stress an evangelical identity in the world. It would be strong on Christian "holiness," prayer, and ritual, but, consistent with Catholic Tradition, it would not represent a sect-type Church, which is to say, one that withdraws from politics and renounces all "worldy" values. Yet neo-Franciscans, in my view, need to—but do not always—incorporate the strong commitment to structural justice found in Catholic social teaching. Pope Francis may reinforce this note. When he hosted a meal for the poor in Assisi a few months after his election, he called for the Church today to become a "Church of the poor" (a phrase not long ago identified by the Congregation of the Doctrine of the Faith as unacceptable in Jon Sobrino's liberation theology),[42] and called attention to social injustices such as unemployment, world hunger, and the plight of migrants and refugees.[43]

THE ROLE OF THE LAITY

We often think of Vatican II as empowering the laity. For example, according to the journalist Robert Blair Kaiser, who reported on the history, substance, and politics of the papal birth control commission, "Vatican II attempted to write a Charter for a People's Church," representing a "passing of power from old elite institutions to the people," so that they are no longer "the unthinking pawns of others," but are "acting persons in their own right."[44] To Kaiser, Vatican II represents "the radical equality of all believers."[45] In reality, the Council's message on the laity was more than a bit mixed, and quite ambivalent about just how far the institutional Church (papacy and episcopacy) is willing to go in recognizing the voice and authority of the nonordained.

According to *Lumen Gentium*, "In matters of faith and morals, the bishops speak in the name of Christ, and the faithful are to accept their teaching and adhere to it with a religious assent of soul."[46] Since all the baptized are "consecrated by the Holy Spirit," it cannot be denied that the "layman" may have the knowledge or competence to "express his opinion on things which concern the good of the church."[47] Hence the "sacred pastors" should promote the "responsibility of the layman." However, the layperson's voice is in no way independent, and should always be channeled "through the agencies set up by the Church for this purpose."[48] Although the laity are envisioned as participating in the Church's work of salvation, this work does not occupy the ecclesial core or center. Instead the laity evangelize by going "out," as it were, into worldly vocations, where they are "preoccupied with worldly cares."[49]

The "Decree on the Apostolate of Lay People" is somewhat more promising, insisting that the apostolate of the laity should be "intensified and broadened." The laity have their own spheres of expertise, offering opportunities for Christian witness, and also for carrying out the dialogue with Church and culture. "With a constantly increasing population, continual progress in science and technology, and closer interpersonal relationships, the areas for the lay apostolate have been immensely widened particularly in fields that have been for the most part open to the laity alone."[50] Nevertheless, this document too tends to envision the laity as being "trained" by the official curators of doctrine to "manifest" its truth to an outside world.[51]

In 1987 John Paul II hosted a synod on the laity in Rome, on the occasion of which he authored an "apostolic exhortation," *Christifidelis Laici*. Almost a quarter century after the Council, the laity are therein regarded as contributing to, not just learning from, the institutional Church; their growing activity on behalf of the Church is praised. Indeed, greater "collaboration" among priests, religious, and laity is to be desired. In particular, the "Holy Spirit continues to renew the youth of the Church" and "has inspired new aspirations towards holiness and the participation of so many lay faithful." Most of the examples given by John Paul II are intra-ecclesial, such as participation in the liturgy and ministries, but he also mentions "the fuller and meaningful participation of women in the development of society."[52]

In terms of explicitly Christian and Catholic public engagement of the laity on behalf of the Church, the United States perhaps presents more opportunities than many other societies, including Western Europe. Unlike Western Europe, but like many areas of the global South, the United States is still a relatively religious country. Our public officials frequently invoke the name of God, religious figures can be media pundits, and the lobbying of religious bodies is actually of note and concern to voters, public officials, and candidates for election. Rick Warren of the Saddleback Church hosted a presidential debate, Bill O'Reilly is a national television personality, and Peter Steinfels has authored a religion column for the *New York Times*. We in the United States enjoy a remarkably healthy and widespread network of Catholic colleges and universities, as well as Newman Centers and other forms of presence in "secular" (religiously pluralistic) institutions. Catholic institutions reach out into the community and the larger social and political spheres in many ways—student internships, community partnerships, legal aid clinics, and as employers, to name a few. Catholic institutions of higher learning are most definitely sites of being Church and of "public Catholicism," engaging Catholic intellectual Traditions with contemporary fields like economics, history, philosophy, and science; founding centers and institutes for the study of society, ethics, and politics; and sponsoring speakers on everything from gender equality, to the ethics of genetic research, to climate change, to the plight of immigrants and refugees worldwide. The point to emphasize, however, is that lay activism can and does go in quite different directions, both progressive neo-Thomist and neo-Augustinian, and now perhaps also neo-Franciscan. Yes, we have Sr. Simone Campbell's cross-country "Nuns on the Bus" campaign in favor of Catholic social teaching–informed politics, the Boston College School of Ministry's 2013 Symposium on "The Legacy of the Second

Vatican Council," and dozens or hundreds of progressive-minded theologians, both clerical and lay. In the 2012 national election, about 90 percent of the faculty and staff of Catholic universities who donated to the presidential campaigns gave to President Barack Obama, despite the U.S. Bishops' strenuous campaign against his administration's new health care legislation, the 2010 Affordable Care Act (ACA).[53]

The United States has also seen a huge influx of new Catholics of Hispanic heritage, who are demographically younger and tend to side more than white Catholics with progressive policies and causes.[54] In 1990, 80 percent of Catholics were non-Hispanic whites, while in 2013, 63 percent of Catholics are whites, 29 percent are Hispanics, and almost half—48 percent—of Catholics under 30 are Hispanic.[55] This younger, more ethnically diverse face of Catholicism will certainly affect the nature and style of lay participation and the issues identified by Catholics as important to their religious and political commitment.

Meanwhile, on the other side, we also have very powerful conservative lay voices such as George Weigel (Ethics and Public Policy Center), Richard Doerflinger (Associate Director of Pro-Life Activities at the United States Conference of Catholic Bishops), and Robert E. George (Princeton University), whom the *New York Times* pictured with President George W. Bush and called "this country's most influential conservative Christian thinker."[56] These are some of the intellectual and political powerhouses behind the public engagement of the current United States Conference of the Catholic Bishops (USCCB).

Lay-led organizations are influential as well. The Cardinal Newman Society, regarded by some as providing "a great service to the Catholic Church in America," is notable for its high-pressure and often successful efforts to police the Catholic "orthodoxy" of classroom content, campus lecturers, and even websites.[57] A coalition of well-funded conservative Catholics and evangelicals is driving a "religious liberty" attack on same-sex marriage, antidiscrimination laws, and access to contraception through Obama's health care reform law.[58] Multiple Catholic universities, law schools, and law professors have hosted or participated in sessions on—and often advocacy of—the religious liberty campaign.[59] The lay group The Catholic Association paid for ads against the ACA and for the USCCB's anti-Affordable Care Act "Religious Liberty Campaign" on Fox News and in the *Wall Street Journal.*[60]

While the more traditionalist voices may insist on the importance of respecting and protecting the authority of the institutional magisterium, what they are doing in practice is defining and redefining what the content of that teaching will be. The emphasis of the U.S. episcopacy on, for example, gay marriage, abortion, and contraception, diverges markedly from the equal or greater emphasis of recent and current popes on poverty, peace, and the economic obligations of wealthy nations to less privileged ones. Yet it matches the priorities of conservative funders such as the Knights of Columbus and the Beckett Fund for Religious Liberty.[61]

In his analysis of Catholic conservative power in American politics, Peter McDonough argues that in the 1990s, Catholic conservatives took advantage of the success of social conservatives in politics, the appointment of conservative bishops by John Paul II, a longstanding American tolerance for income disparities, and a strong cultural tradition of individualism to sideline progressive Catholic calls for social justice. Catholic neoconservatives are advancing the influence of the Church in politics under the paradoxical banner of keeping the government from intruding on the Church. Meanwhile the progressive message on such things as women's ordination, priestly celibacy, or global poverty and world peace fails to grip most U.S. Catholics at the existential level of their daily struggles, while in sexual matters people can follow their own consciences. Hence progressives are less involved and adamant than their conservative opposition, and less visible and forceful on the Catholic political scene.[62]

Even more significant than these diverging voices is the fact that lay involvement—in the actual life of the Church, beyond the scholars, movement leaders, and culture war elites— is in decline. We may debate whether the laity are empowered, but how many of them even care enough to invest personally in the reforms of Vatican II? According to statistics from CARA, the

143

number of American Catholics is decreasing, women are leaving the Church at a higher rate than men, and only 15 percent of the millennial generation—born between 1979 and 1993—attends Mass regularly. The attendance rate of this last generation of Catholics, coming of age in the twenty-first-century, is the lowest of all generations surveyed. Even most Hispanics, whose attendance rate is higher than non-Hispanics, do not see weekly Mass attendance as necessary to being a good Catholic. The majority of Catholics say they want a more democratic Church, yet only a minority say they are interested in getting more involved in their parishes.[63]

The legacy of Vatican II is mixed with regard to public engagement on morality and politics, but enhanced lay responsibility and lay activism are crucial to realizing the Council's vision of aggiornamento, and to doing so with a lively yet charitable pluralism of vision. Tim Muldoon sees Vatican II as forwarding a new age of the Church, having roots in earlier phenomena such as the development of the "third order" of lay Franciscans in the thirteenth century, the formation of women's religious orders in the seventeenth through nineteenth centuries, and the flourishing of lay associations and communities from the middle ages through the Vatican II period. The most important form of Christian spirituality in the present day is "a lay-led movement of engagement with the secular world."[64] Now, as Carolyn Weir Herman confirms, "in both the secular and ecclesial realms, the laity are called to manifest the authority that comes to them through baptism and confirmation and in this way properly share in Christ's prophetic ministry."[65]

While the rate of attrition of younger Catholics from sacramental participation and from adherence to Catholic moral and political teachings is significant, Pope Francis's refreshing message of personal dedication to the poor and to social justice may have the potential to reinvigorate their interest and commitment. Across the mainline U.S. Christian denominations, younger members are walking away from their ecclesial birthplaces because, unlike their elders and the teachings typically accented by their churches, they take gender equality for granted, approve same-sex unions, accept racial and ethnic diversity, recognize the presence of God in other faiths, and are concerned about global poverty and the environment.[66] If these values are to find expression in renewed interest in organized religion, peer communities of worship, solidarity, and fellowship will be essential. Catholic outreach and lay activism must go beyond the traditional parish framework if they are to attract and keep a new Catholic constituency. Social and political action in the name of justice and the gospel will surely be essential aspects of "being Church" for tomorrow's Catholics. Joining forces with others in the same cause is a key way to shape identity, community, and hope for the future.

As *Gaudium et Spes* reminds us, "Christians have shouldered a gigantic task" in seeking to enlarge the practice of justice in the modern world. But it is precisely in embracing this challenge as our own that we discover "the gift of the Holy Spirit" and are blessed with "a lively hope." It is here too that gospel-inspired transformations, real and hoped for, expand beyond the Church and join Catholics with other Christians, with non-Christian religious believers, and with nonbelievers, in a common cause. According to Vatican II and subsequent Catholic teaching,[67] the presence and power of the Divine are experienced wherever there is genuine love of and commitment to the neighbor. The Spirit of the one God sustains all who work for justice in good faith. Only by mediating the Church's moral, social, and political message to the world's cultures in a positive, active way will we, the Church, be able to make a difference in the struggle against human suffering, a struggle we share with other faiths and worldviews. This struggle is not only a requirement of justice; it is the calling of all who claim faithfulness to Jesus' ministry of the reign of God; and it both springs from and inspires hope for a better world.

Notes

1. These phrases refer to the Council's "Dogmatic Constitution on the Church in the Modern World" (1965). The precise wording *openness to the modern world,* frequently used to characterize the Council, does not appear as such. However, the title phrase *modern world* also occurs in the title of chapter

4, "The Role of the Church in the Modern World," and is repeated several times in the document. The subsequent phrases occur in nos. 4, 22, and 1, respectively.

2. Robert K. Merton, "The Unanticipated Consequences of Purposive Social Action," *American Sociological Review* 1 (1936): 894–904.

3. See the text of the announcement of the Council of January 25, 1959, by John XXIII published in *Acta Apostolicae Sedis*, February 2, 1959.

4. *Gaudium et Spes* 2.

5. Ibid., 3.

6. Ibid., 30.

7. David Hollenbach, "Social Ethics under the Sign of the Cross," *Annual of the Society of Christian Ethics* (1996): 3–18. This address became chapter 4 of David Hollenbach, SJ, *The Global Face of Public Faith: Politics, Human Rights, and Christian Ethics* (Washington, DC: Georgetown University Press, 2003).

8. Hollenbach, *Global Face*, 60.

9. See Margaret Keck and Kathryn Sikkink, *Activists beyond Borders: Advocacy Networks in International Politics* (Ithaca, NY: Cornell University Press, 1998); and Kathryn Sikkink, *The Justice Cascade: How Human Rights Prosecutions Are Changing World Politics* (New York: W. W. Norton & Company, 2011).

10. See Virginia Page Fortna, "Inside and Out: Peacekeeping and the Duration of Peace after Civil and Interstate Wars," *International Studies Review* 5 (2003): 97–114.

11. Nikhila Gill, "Extreme Poverty Drops Worldwide," India Ink blog, *New York Times*, March 4, 2012, http://india.blogs.ny times.com/2012/03/04/extreme-poverty-drops-world wide/?_r=0. Gill cites the 2012 World Bank Development Report.

12. Save the Children, *Born Equal: How Reducing Inequality Could Give Our Children a Better Future*, 2012, www.savethechil dren.org.uk/sites/default/files/images/Born_Equal.pdf.

13. A research team, commissioned by the *National Catholic Reporter* (NCR), which included William D'Antonio of The Catholic University of America (CUA), Mary Gautier of the Center for Applied Research in the Apostolate (CARA) at Georgetown University, and Michele Dillon of the University of New Hampshire, completed its fifth survey of American Catholics in 2011. The principal findings of the survey were

published in *NCR*'s October 28–November 10 edition under the title "Persistence and Change," http://ncronline.org/American Catholics. This research was also published as William V. D'Antonio, Michele Dillon, and Mary Gautier, *American Catholics in Transition* (Lanham, MD: Rowman & Littlefield, 2013).

14. Bryan N. Massingale, *Racial Justice and the Catholic Church* (Maryknoll, NY: Orbis, 2010).

15. Public Religion Research Institute, "American Catholics in 2013," http://publicreligion.org/research/2013/02/fact-sheet-american-catholics-in-2013/.

16. Hollenbach, *Global Face*, 66.

17. Ibid., 68.

18. David Hollenbach, "Joy and Hope, Grief and Anguish," *America* 193 (2005): 12–4.

19. Hollenbach, *Global Face*, 69.

20. International Theological Commission, "In Search of a Universal Ethic: A New Look at the Natural Law" (2009), http://www.vatican.va/roman_curia/congregations/cfaith/cti_docu ments/rc_con_cfaith_doc_20090520_legge-naturale_ en.html.

21. Ibid., no. 1.

22. Ibid., no. 33.

23. Ibid., no. 52.

24. Ibid., no. 116.

25. "Decree on Priestly Formation" (*Optatum Totius*, 1965) 16.

26. "Constitution on the Sacred Liturgy" (*Sacrosanctum Concilium*, 1963).

27. See Louis-Marie Chauvet, *Symbol and Sacrament: A Sacramental Reinterpretation of Christian Existence*, trans. Patrick Madigan and Madeleine Beaumont (Collegeville, MN: Liturgical Press, 1995).

28. David Hollenbach, SJ, "Commentary on *Gaudium et Spes* (Pastoral Constitution on the Church in the Modern World)," in *Modern Catholic Social Teaching Commentaries and Interpretations*, ed. Kenneth R. Himes et al. (Washington, DC: Georgetown University Press, 2005), 277.

29. John Paul II, "On Social Concern" (*Sollicitudo Rei Socialis*, 1987), no. 42.

30. *Gaudium et Spes* 69; cf. 63.

31. John Paul II, "Letter to Women" (1995), http://www.vati can.va/holy_father/john_paul_ii/letters/documents/hf_jp-ii_let_29061995_women_en.html.

32. International Theological Commission, "In Search of a Universal Ethic," nos. 34, 49.

33. See Andrea Vicini, "*The Search for a Universal Ethic:* The International Theological Commission's 2009 Document on Natural Law," in *Human Nature and Natural Law,* ed. Lisa Sowle Cahill, Hille Haker, and Eloi Messi Metogo (London: SCM Press, 2010), 115.

34. On these issues, see John Paul II, "On the Family" (*Familiaris Consortio,* 1981), and "On the Dignity and Vocation of Women" (*Mulieris Dignitatem,* 1988).

35. See Massimo Faggioli, *Vatican II: The Battle for Meaning* (Mahwah, NJ: Paulist Press, 2012), ch. 4; Joseph A. Komonchak, "The Church in Crisis: Pope Benedict's Theological Vision," *Commonweal* 132 (June 3, 2005): 11–14; and Ormond Rush, *Still Interpreting Vatican II: Some Hermeneutical Principles* (Mahwah, NJ: Paulist Press, 2004), 15.

36. James F. Keenan, SJ, *A History of Catholic Moral Theology in the Twentieth Century: From Confessing Sins to Liberating Consciences* (New York: Continuum, 2010), 113. The emergence of "historical consciousness" in Catholic moral theology since Vatican II is often traced to the influence of Bernard Lonergan. See also Charles E. Curran, *Catholic Moral Theology in the United States: A Brief History* (Washington, DC: Georgetown University Press, 2008), 103–4.

37. Richard R. Gaillardetz, "The Groupe des Dombes Document 'One Teacher' (2005): Toward a Postconciliar Catholic Reception," *Theological Studies* 74 (2013): 45.

38. Servais Pinckaers, OP, *The Sources of Christian Ethics,* trans. Sr. Mary Thomas Noble, OP (Washington, DC: Catholic University of America Press, 1995). See also Craig Steven Titus, "Servais Pinckaers and the Renewal of Catholic Moral Theology," in *Journal of Moral Theology* 1 (2012): 43–68.

39. See for example, Stanley Hauerwas, *A Community of Character: Toward a Constructive Christian Social Ethic* (Notre Dame, IN: University of Notre Dame Press, 1991).

40. St. Francis of Assisi, "Canticle of Brother Sun and Sister Moon," http://www.catholic.org/prayers/prayer.php?p=183.

41. See Jon M. Sweeney, *Francis of Assisi in His Own Words: The Essential Writings* (Orleans, MA: Paraclete Press, 2013).

42. Congregation for the Doctrine of the Faith, *Notification on the Works of Father Jon Sobrino, SJ* (2006), http://www.vati

can.va/roman_curia/congregations/cfaith/documents/rc_con_
cfaith_doc_20061126_notification-sobrino_en.html, no. 2.

43. BBC World News Europe, "Pope Francis Urges Church to
Focus on Helping Poor," October 4, 2013, http://www.bbc.co.uk/
news/world-europe-24391800.

44. Robert Blair Kaiser, "Vatican II Attempted to Write a
Charter for a People's Church," in *Revisiting Vatican II: 50 Years
of Renewal*, ed. Shaji George Kuchuthara (Bangalore:
Dharmaram College, 2013), 44.

45. Kaiser, "Vatican II," 49.

46. "Dogmatic Constitution on the Church" (*Lumen
Gentium*) 25.

47. Ibid., 10.

48. Ibid., 37.

49. Ibid., 33–34, 37.

50. "Decree on the Apostolate of the Laity" (*Apostolicam
Actuositatem*, 1965) 1; cf. no. 31 on the lay responsibility to
"engage in conversation with others, believers or nonbelievers."

51. *Apostolicam Actuositatem* 30–31.

52. John Paul II, *Christifideles Laici* ("On the Lay Faithful in
the Church and the World," 1988) 2, http://www.vatican
.va/holy_father/john_paul_ii/apost_exhortations/documents
/hf_jp-ii_exh_30121988_christifideles-laici_en.html.

53. Editor, "Despite 'War on Catholics,' Faculty and Staff at
Catholic Universities Gave Overwhelmingly to Obama," *Catholic
News USA*, December 6, 2012, http://www.cathnewsusa.com/
2012/12/despite-%E2%80%98war-on-catholics%E2%80%99-fac
ulty-and-staff-at-catholic-universities-gave-overwhelmingly-to-
obama/.

54. See Gary M. Segura, "Latino Public Opinion &
Realigning the American Electorate," *Daedalus* (Fall 2012):
98–113.

55. Juhem Navarro-Rivera, "Pope Francis and Hispanic
American Catholics," Public Religion Research Institute website,
March 18, 2013, http://publicreligion.org/2013/03/pope-francis-
and-hispanic-american-catholics/.

56. David D. Kirkpatrick, "The Conservative-Christian Big
Thinker," *New York Times*, December 16, 2009, http://www.ny
times.com/2009/12/20/magazine/20george-t.html?page
wanted=all.

57. Dan Morris-Young, "Cardinal Newman Society Takes on Watchdog Role for Catholic Identity," *National Catholic Reporter*, November 21, 2012, http://ncronline.org/news/faith-parish/cardinal-newman-society-takes-watchdog-role-catholic-identity.

58. Jay Michaelson, "Redefining Religious Liberty," May 28, 2013, http://www.politicalresearch.org/redefining-religious-liberty/.

59. See for example a 2012 Georgetown conference on "Catholic Perspectives on Religious Liberty," http://berkleycenter .georgetown.edu/events/catholic-perspectives-on-religious-liberty.

60. Peter Nicholas and Daniel Lippman, "Catholic Group Targeting Obama," *Wall Street Journal*, June 20, 2012, http:// hausercenter.org/npnews/?p=4928.

61. See Dennis Coday, "Knights of Columbus Leader: 'Catholics Can No Longer Accept Politics as Usual,'" *National Catholic Reporter*, June 26, 2012, http://ncronline.org/news/politics/knights-columbus-leader-catholics-can-no-longer-accept-politics-usual, in which the supreme knight of the Knights of Columbus equates Catholic social teaching with support of the traditional family and opposition to abortion, mandated insurance coverage of contraception, and gay unions; and the website of the Beckett Fund, where a priority in the defense of "religious liberty" is again opposition to existing U.S. law defining birth control as preventive care that health insurers are mandated to cover (http://www.becketfund.org/hhs/).

62. Peter McDonough, *The Catholic Labyrinth: Power, Apathy, and a Passion for Reform in the American Church* (New York: Oxford University Press, 2013).

63. See sources in n13 above.

64. Tim Muldoon, "Introduction: Catholic Identity and the Laity," in *Catholic Identity and the Laity*, ed. Tim Muldoon, College Theology Annual Volume 54 (2008): 11.

65. Carolyn Weir Herman, "The *Sensus Fidei* and Lay Authority in the Roman Catholic Church," in Muldoon, *Catholic Identity and the Laity*, 162.

66. Robert D. Putnam and David E. Campbell, *American Grace: How Religion and Divides and Unites Us* (New York: Simon & Schuster, 2010).

67. See "Declaration on the Relation of the Church to Non-Christian Religions" (*Nostra Aetate*, 1965); and "On the Unicity and Salvific Universality of Jesus Christ and the Church" (*Dominus Iesus*, 2000), http://www.vatican.va/roman_curia /congregations/cfaith/documents/rc_con_cfaith_doc_2000080 6_dominus-iesus_en.html. The former envisions a lasting covenant between God and the Jews; the latter presents Christianity as the superior religion, but also sees Christ as present to adherents of other traditions.

8

Bradford E. Hinze

Vatican II and U.S. Catholic Communities

PROMOTING GRASSROOTS DEMOCRACY

For most of the defining achievements of the Second Vatican Council, we find the seeds of ressourcement and aggiornamento taking root and breaking ground in the midst of "the long nineteenth century" and especially during the decades before the Council—in biblical studies, the patristic revival, Thomistic and medieval studies, and in the liturgical movement. The same can be said about efforts to engage with the struggles of the poor and laborers by promoting grassroots democracy through civic involvement on pressing social, political, and economic issues. An array of social movements was nurtured and legitimated by the emergence of Catholic social teaching. Together this development of practice and doctrine contributed to conciliar debates that resulted in an official Catholic promotion of democracy. This achievement by the Council in turn legitimated the further advancement of grassroots democracy in local churches already underway, and gave these movements a new impetus and stronger intellectual justification.

This chapter explores U.S. Catholic parish and diocesan communities' involvement in community organizing as a means to promote grassroots democracy, against the backdrop of what transpired at the Council and in comparison to other forms of Catholic Action. I will focus on the participation of Catholics in faith-based community organizing groups that began in earnest over twenty years before the Council, groups that from the beginning included people from diverse Christian communities, other faiths, and alternative worldviews.

The phenomenon of local forms of synodality or conciliarity in parishes and dioceses is closely related to the Catholic promotion of grassroots democracy. I wish to point out that connection here, even though it cannot be sufficiently explored. There is evidence of analogies, and more substantively, a mutually beneficial synergism between the advance of grassroots democracy by local Catholic communities and the involvement of lay Catholics with the clergy in processes of communal discernment and decision making that advance the pastoral mission of parishes and dioceses through councils and synods. Local churches can learn from community organizations advancing grassroots democracy, and such community organizations can likewise benefit from practices of local synodality.

NARRATING CATHOLICISM AND DEMOCRACY: HIGHROADS AND LOW

There are a number of different ways of approaching the legacy of Vatican II in terms of the promotion of democracy. It is customary to take the high road, pointing out grand vistas, key figures, and important documents. Bryan Hehir takes this pathway, in the footsteps left a generation before by John Courtney Murray, by examining official Catholic teachings.[1] Usually this story moves from Pope Gregory XVI's critique of the liberal rights of freedom of conscience in his 1832 encyclical *Mirari Vos*, to the statement from Pius XII's "Christmas Messages" of 1944 that reads, "A democratic form of government appears to many people as a natural postulate imposed by reason itself," followed by Pope John XXIII's natural law defense of the promotion of justice in terms of human rights in his 1963 encyclical *Pacem in*

Terris, and culminates with *Gaudium et Spes* and *Dignitatis Humanae* in 1965. Vatican II provides a landmark formulation. Although the term *democracy* was not used in *Gaudium et Spes*, as Michel Schooyans delineates, the document rejected "despotic, totalitarian, dictatorial governments" (*GS* 74ff.), and affirmed the "freedom to choose type of government and leaders (no. 74),...human rights (no. 26),...the equal dignity of all people (no. 29)," and made "an appeal for the participation of all" (nos. 31, 75), so to "provid[e] all citizens without any distinction with ever improving and effective opportunities to play an active part in the establishment of the juridical foundations of the political community, [and] in the administration of public affairs" (*GS* 75).[2]

Another commonly traveled high road focuses on those Catholic philosophers, theologians, and intellectuals who played influential roles in advancing human rights, economic justice, in particular just labor practices, and the doctrines of freedom, human rights, and democracy. John A. Ryan, Jacques Maritain, and John Courtney Murray figure prominently on this path. Sometimes included are other contributions by European Catholic exiles from Germany, France, Italy, and Spain in the late 1930s into the United States who began to defend constitutional democracy, democratic politics, and civil liberties as they condemned the policies of Mussolini in Italy, Hitler and the Nazis in Germany, Marshal Pétain and the Vichy regime in France, and Francisco Franco in Spain.[3]

Emile Perreau-Saussine has recently developed an alternative to these common narratives in *Catholicism and Democracy: An Essay in the History of Political Thought*. Perreau-Saussine offers a more complex reading of the shift from Vatican I to Vatican II on the issue of democracy. One of his key arguments is that the ultramontanist tendency associated with Vatican I and the polycentric liberal impulses of Vatican II represent "two poles between which the Catholic Church oscillates in the age of democracy,...but these two poles are complementary and can be successfully integrated within a single perspective."[4] Most importantly, these two positions are in agreement "that there was something irreducibly secular about the modern state" and target this fact either for condemnation or collaboration.[5]

I am particularly interested in the way Perreau-Saussine interprets the role of various forms of Gallicanism in France. He seeks to show that the Gallican vision, which emphasizes the importance of the church and laypeople in political life, ultimately influenced the teachings of the universal Church at Vatican II. By exploring the synergism between Gallicanism, a conciliarist approach to church structure and governance,[6] and grassroots democracy in France, he lends support to my own conviction about the dynamic relation between local synodality and grassroots democracy. Though the author, a political scientist, shows no interest in exploring the ecclesiological issues pertaining to the impact of Gallicanism on the structures of lay participation in the life and mission of the local church, these connections cannot be ruled out. Moreover, is it only a curious contingency that bridges certain impulses among the adherents of Gallicanism in the nineteenth century and some key figures advancing lay participation in the Church associated with *nouvelle théologie* in the twentieth century?[7] I think not. John Coleman observed thirty years ago that "almost all of the innovative theologians in *nouvelle théologie* had, somewhere in their backgrounds, close contacts with Catholic Action movements," with Yves Congar and Marie Dominique Chenu offering important examples of engagement in what Coleman calls strategic theology.[8] One of the inferences that can be drawn from Perreau-Saussine's and Coleman's arguments is that in France the synergism of local synodality and grassroots democracy begins to manifest itself.

Many take these high roads following the contributions of official teachings and intellectuals, but I wish to take the low road into poor and working-class neighborhoods of the United States where Catholics wrestled with concerns about employment, wages, housing, education, and health care, and cultivated practices of civic virtue through grassroots community organizing. The pilgrims who embarked on these low roads, beginning in the mid-twentieth century, have been preceded by Catholics who have participated in social movements as activists, as proponents of labor unions, and in political parties in Europe, the United States, and Latin America, including proponents of Social Catholicism in the nineteenth century[9] and many groups associated with Catholic Action in the twentieth.

TWO IMPORTANT DEVELOPMENTS AT VATICAN II

Before examining faith-based community organizing, it is helpful to consider two important crossroads at Vatican II: the group of bishops who became advocates for "the Church of the poor," and the widespread attention given to Catholic Action. Both efforts are relevant for the study of Catholic community organizing.

Church of the Poor Group

Catholic community organizing was inspired initially by an interest in the Church speaking out and acting up about the concerns of poor and working-class people, often in dense urban neighborhoods with high percentages of poverty, hunger, and crime, and also in rural settings among migrant farm workers and the black civil rights movement. Catholic community organizing can rightly be identified as an effort to become a Church of the poor, to be in solidarity with the poor, and to be collaborators with the poor in advancing grassroots democracy.

A month before the Council convened, Pope John XXIII inspired a group of bishops especially concerned about the poor, when, in an address to the world, on September 11, 1962, he declared that "confronted with the underdeveloped countries, the Church presents itself as it is and wishes to be, as the Church of all, and particularly as the Church of the poor." The expression "Church of the poor" was subsequently echoed often during the Council, especially during the first two periods of the Council in 1962 and in 1963.[10] It became a particular rallying cry for a group of fifty bishops, many from Francophone regions in Europe and Africa, as well as bishops from Latin America, who met on numerous occasions to discuss how to promote the concerns of the poor.

When this group initially met in 1962, the first item raised by Bishop Georges Mercier of the Missionaries of Africa concerned the development of poor countries, an issue deeply intertwined with questions about economic and political democracy. During the third period of the Council, in the fall of 1964, this group put forth a document with two motions, eventually approved by over five hundred bishops, that was "secretly" given to Pope Paul. One motion urged that more attention be given to the importance of "Simplicity and Evangelical Poverty" as a way of promoting the Church of the poor commended by John XXIII. A second motion concerned the "Primacy in our Ministry for the Evangelization of the Poor."[11]

Explicit attention to promoting democracy among the poor appears to be missing in this report prepared under the direction of Cardinal Giacomo Lercaro, Archbishop of Bologna, who was asked by Pope Paul VI a year earlier in October 1963 to explore how the work of the Church of the Poor group might be used in the decrees. The first doctrinal part of this report developed a critique of affluent society and spoke about the mystery of evangelical poverty as addressing challenges of the times in light of scripture and christology. The second part was practical and urged that bishops should embrace simplicity of life and evangelical poverty, priests should be selected to work among the poor, and laity, clergy, and religious should fast and abstain and give money to the poor. However, in Norman Tanner's judgment, "There is no real evidence of the reception of the report!"[12]

Catholic Action

To clarify the distinctive contribution of faith-based community organizing, it is helpful to note both the historical and theoretical intersection between faith-based community organizing and Catholic Action—including intersections among the membership—and the differences between their respective methods and aims. At the time of the Council it was widely acknowledged by Council fathers and theologians alike that the people of God theology provided deeper theological moorings for lay involvement in the mission of the Church in the world, for which they used the term *Catholic Action* that had been heralded by Pope Pius XI in 1931 as "the participation of the laity in the apostolate of the hierarchy."[13]

The difficulty before and during the Council, as described by Étienne Fouilloux, was that there was

> sometimes quite [a] lively debate between what was called "general" Catholic Action, Italian in origin, which took no account of special conditions of life in its parish-based mass-movements (men, women, young people, girls), and what was called "specialized" Catholic Action, which was broken down into groups (workers, farmers, students, sailors...) and was national in structure. The first of these two sometimes suspected the second of introducing (horrible to say) the class struggle into the bosom of the Church.[14]

General Catholic Action fostered a paternalistic approach to the laity's participation in the hierarchy's apostolate, passively obedient to bishops' directives and active as foot soldiers in culture wars. Specialized forms of Catholic Action, and I will use the groups influenced by Belgian Father Joseph Cardijn as my key examples, developed a more inductive method and encouraged more active lay leadership in collaboration with the clergy. A larger set of questions was surfaced by Gustavo Gutiérrez and others in Latin American about the limitations of Catholic Action and lay apostolic movements already before and during the Council, and as I will comment further below, these questions were more widely discussed in Europe and in the United States beginning in the 1970s.[15]

Noting the features of specialized forms of Catholic Action as it took shape under the leadership of Cardijn will enable us to clarify the shared and distinctive features of faith-based community organizing as this took shape in the United States. In the second decade of the twentieth century Cardijn began to organize workers near Brussels, drawing on the labor encyclicals of

Popes Leo XIII and subsequently Pius XI. After World War I he launched the Young Christian Workers (*Jeunesse ouvrière chrétienne*—often referenced as JOC), in which small groups were trained to use Cardijn's method of see-judge-act (*Voir, Juger, Agir*) in small circles composed of workers, farmers, students, and academics. These groups were initiated into a discipline of a "review of life," a group practice and process in which participants discussed what they were observing about the social conditions or facts encountered in daily life; offered judgments or assessments of these realities based on gospel values and Catholic social teaching; surfaced plans of action or strategies to address these situations; and then picked one to carry out. Cardijn's approach became known as the Jocist method and was immensely influential in Europe and around the world. JOC became the poster child of Catholic Action, and was what Pius XI had in mind when in 1931 he commended Catholic Action as "the participation of the laity in the apostolate of the hierarchy."

In the 1960s, Gustavo Gutiérrez rendered this judgment about Catholic Action in the context of his reflections about options for the Latin American Church: "The kind of apostolic movement represented by the Catholic Action groups among the French workers—that is, communities of Christians with different political options who meet for a *revision de vie* in the light of the faith—is, as such, not viable." Why? "The model of the Workers' Catholic Action is valid in a more or less stable society where political commitments can be lived out publicly."[16] Gutiérrez concedes that specialized Catholic Action has its place, but its strategies of public protest and political engagement in repressive Latin American countries risked reprisals, torture, and death. With this contrasting context in mind, let us return to the situation in Europe and in the United States.

Young Christian Student (YCS) groups, initially national groups in Belgium and France beginning in the late 1920s, but eventually international, followed the specialized method of Cardijn and met regularly in small groups for a "review of life," discussion of social conditions in light of gospel values, and considerations of ways of acting. The International Movement of Catholic Students (IMCS/Pax Romana), going back to 1921, has likewise offered a particularly influential international example of Catholic Action, but one distinct from YCS, and at the time more indebted to the Italian Christendom paradigm.[17]

Two examples of specialized Catholic Action in the Cardijn mode emerged in the United States: the Young Christian Workers, begun in the late 1930s and active until 1970, and the Christian Family Movement, established in the 1940s in Notre Dame, Indiana, and Chicago, Illinois.[18] Monsignor Reynold Hillenbrand and Fr. John (Jack) Egan of the Archdiocese of Chicago promoted the development of these two groups and became prominent advocates of the Jocist method.

Some bishops at the Council resisted specialized Catholic Action associated with Cardijn. At the World Council of Lay Apostolate in October 1957, Cardinal Suenens of Belgium voiced the opinion that the name *Catholic Action* was too narrowly associated with particular social action groups that promoted activist and sometimes confrontational practices, such as the Young Christian Workers, rather than being associated with a groups more focused on spirituality. This complaint was repeated at Vatican II.[19]

The Second Vatican Council commended Catholic Action explicitly, yet in a concession to critics defined it broadly (*AA* 20), specifying four criteria for such groups: apostolic aim, cooperation with hierarchy, laity acting in organic unity, with hierarchical mandate. The Council thus affirmed a plurality of forms of organizations under the category of Catholic Action.

After the Council, especially during the pontificates of John Paul II and Benedict XVI, growing attention was given to new ecclesial movements like the Opus Dei, Neocatechumenal Way, the Charismatic Renewal, Cursillo, Focolare, Sant'Egidio, and Comunione e Liberazione, among others.[20] This begs the question: Are these new ecclesial movements expressions of Catholic Action as judged according to the criteria developed by the Council? Moreover, how might they differ from examples of special Catholic Action?

Massimo Faggioli provides a useful framework to consider these questions. He has explored the tension between an ecclesiology of the local church, which was recovered at Vatican II, with its promotion of a participatory (synodal) model of governance in the diocese and parish, and a centralized ecclesiology that is focused on the authority of the pope, the Vatican, and the papal magisterium, which has been accentuated during the pontificates of John Paul II and Benedict XVI. The emphasis on the local church corresponds to many examples of special Catholic Action in the Cardijn model, whereas a devotion to the pope is often found in new ecclesial movements. Consequently, although the new movements are frequently considered as fruit of the Council, Faggioli raises a concern about the loss of connection with parishes and dioceses that frequently mark these new movements. New ecclesial movements' success, he cautions,

> comes at the expense of the ecclesiology of the local Church, thus helping to undermine the quest [at Vatican II] for a new balance between center and periphery in modern-world Catholicism....[This is evident in their] scant awareness of the relationship between collegiality and the bishops's role.., and by [their use of] a nonsynodal model of governance within their communities.[21]

Following this claim, even if there are some new ecclesial movements that are exceptions to this pattern, I would maintain that, in contrast to many expressions of new ecclesial movements, faith-based community organizing is true to the deepest impulses of the Council in its attention to the local church. Moreover, Faggioli's argument lends credence to my contention that there is a vital synergism between the promotion of grassroots democracy and local synodality.

FAITH-BASED COMMUNITY ORGANIZING

In the United States, faith-based community organizing in the tradition of Saul Alinsky shares the concerns of the Church of the Poor group at Vatican II, but with explicit interests in promoting grassroots democracy as an instrument for addressing social, economic, and political issues pertaining to poverty and injustice. These groups also share certain social concerns with the Cardijn model of Catholic Action pertaining to the plight of the poor and laborers.

Community organizing in the Alinsky tradition does not involve forming small study groups devoted to the review of life.[22] Yet, like Catholic Action in the Cardijn tradition, community organizers do promote practices of see-judge-act in local communities within parish and diocesan contexts. Moreover, faith-based community-organizing groups promote the cultivation of skills and group practices for collective deliberation in ways that relate both to democratic decision-making in civic society and in the Church, and to synodal styles of parish and diocesan governance and pastoral planning in parishes and dioceses.[23]

An Unlikely Patron Saint for Catholics

The vast majority of faith-based community organizing groups in the United States draw their inspiration from Saul Alinksy, the agnostic and occasionally irreverent son of Jewish parents of Russian descent who came to form lifelong collaboration and friendships with Catholic intellectuals, bishops, priests, and parishioners. He was raised in the slums of Chicago and eventually pursued graduate studies at the University of Chicago; his research on organized crime and juvenile delinquency was influenced by the ethnographic methods of Robert Park and the social philosophy of George Herbert Mead. Subsequently he became a union organizer trained by the labor leader John L. Lewis.[24] He also became friends with Myles Horton, one of the cofounders of the Highlander School of education for social change.[25]

In the late 1930s Alinsky began to collaborate closely with Catholics and Protestants and Jews in Chicago to organize a coalition of parishes and congregations, unions and clubs that would address a range of problems facing the inhabitants of the worst slums in the United States; the result was what came to be called the Back of the Yards Neighborhood Council in 1939, which brought about effective changes in the workplace and in the neighborhoods. Based on that experience, Alinsky wrote a book in 1946, *Reveille for Radicals*, which offered a vision of people's organizations to promote the self-interests and common good of local citizens. In 1940 he established the Industrial Areas Foundation (IAF), a training program for community organizations.[26] Alinsky's closest disciples were originally primarily men, Catholics, Methodists, Baptists, African Americans, Jews, and people like himself with no particular religious outlook. Together they trained thousands of community organizers in the United States and eventually around the world, resulting in a new generation of leaders that includes women, Pentecostals, Muslims, and people of other faiths. Alinsky-style community organizations shared some of the same concerns of Cardijn versions of Catholic Action, but by contrast from the beginning were ecumenical, interreligious, and included members who were not religious, and employed considerably different methods.

Catholic Activists in Ecumenical, Interfaith, Pluralistic Coalitions

Alinsky's personal relationships with Catholic clergy and laypeople reveal the depth and significance of the personal connections these men and women discovered between their respective concerns for building just democratic civic communities. He became friends and allies with Chicago auxiliary bishop Bernard J. Sheil, who was an outspoken proponent of social justice and just labor practices and the founder in 1930 of the Catholic Youth Organization, which at that time was associated with promoting youth involvement in social action. Alinsky met philosopher Jacques Maritain, one of the most influential Catholic proponents of democracy in a pluralist society, several years after Maritain published *Integral Humanism* (1938). Their friendship began early in the 1940s; Maritain learned about and came to greatly appreciate Alinsky's work with, and role as founder of, the Back of the Yards Neighborhood Council.[27] In fact, it was Maritain who urged Alinsky to write *Reveille for Radicals* (1946), which recounted the lessons learned during the

163

formation of this council. For over twenty-five years they exchanged letters.

Also during the 1940s Maritain suggested that Alinsky contact John (Jack) Egan, a Chicago diocesan priest in his early thirties at the time, a chaplain for the Young Christian Workers and the Young Christian Student movements, and soon to be a key figure in the Christian Family Movement. All of these organizations utilized Cardijn's Catholic Action method, which Egan had learned and been inspired by during his seminary coursework with Monsignor Reynold J. Hillenbrand. Egan represents one of a number of key connections between Catholic Action in the Cardijn model and Alinsky's community organizing. Of this connection, historian Beryl Satter has suggested "while Catholic Action shared Alinsky's emphasis on gathering facts in order to understand a community, it also stressed the importance of formulating a moral response to a situation—a difference that would have significant consequences."[28] In light of the fact that Alinsky was an agnostic with no interest in religious symbols, as he put it, this judgment makes sense; but it merits further consideration, in part because of the fact that so many Catholics found his approach so compatible with their own social and religious outlook.

Besides clergy and intellectuals like Sheil, Maritain, and Egan, there were many Catholics who became community organizers: former Benedictine seminarian Ed Chambers became the point person for the Industrial Areas Foundation; Michael Gecan and John Baumann, SJ, founder of People Improving Communities through Organization (formerly Pacific Institute for Community Organization) (PICO) in 1972; Ernie Cortes, founder of Communities Organized for Public Service in San Antonio, Texas, in 1974, who then moved out to the United Neighborhood Organization in East Los Angeles in 1976; Greg Galuzzo became executive director of Gamaliel Foundation in 1986, and the list continues. In addition to Sheil, there were an increasing number of bishops who became avid supporters of community organizers in the tradition of Alinsky and encouraged their clergy to work closely with them and in some cases to be trained by them. In the decade after the Back of the Yards Neighborhood Council was launched, Alinsky started new organizations in the Woodlawn area of Chicago, in St. Paul, Minnesota, Kansas City, Omaha, Los Angeles, and Lackawanna, New York, and more widely in New York City.[29] While the first generation of organizers was predominantly male, it is a sad fact that no one has devoted attention to researching and writing about the women, including many woman religious, who were actively involved as organizers, staff members, trainers, and eventually as executive directors of coalitions.

The National Office of Catholic Charities, through the leadership of Monsignor John O'Grady, and the Catholic Campaign for Human Development became major financial supporters of the work of Alinsky in addressing problems of urban poverty. He was recognized as a proponent of a model of democracy that recognized the centrality of self-interest, power dynamics, and agitation, but that was also thoroughly consistent with Catholic social teaching on the dignity of the human person, human rights, the common good, and the principle of subsidiarity.

Today, five large national faith-based community organizing training networks are active in the United States: the Industrial Area Foundations (begun in 1940), People Improving Communities through Organization, National People's Action (1972), Gamaliel, and Direct Action and Research Training Center or DART (1982).[30] By 1999 there were 133 community organizations in 33 states across the country. These federations have about four thousand institutions as official members. In 1999 about 3,500 (or 87.5 percent) of those institutions were religious congregations, and about 1,155 (32.92 percent) across the United States were Catholic, the largest single church-affiliated group.[31] Surveys distributed in 2011 to 189 active organizations, with a return rate of 94 percent, gathered data from 178 institution-based community organizations located in 39 states with 4,145 member institutions and about 3,233 (78 percent) of the member institutions being congregations.[32]

Comparisons of data from 1999 and 2011 show an overall ten-year growth rate of 42 percent in community organizing institutions. (Interestingly, just as Catholic Action groups in the

United States like Young Christian Workers and Christian Family Movement were disbanding during the 1970s, faith-based community organizations continued to grow significantly.) In 2011 approximately 1,326 (32 percent) were mainline Protestant, 1,119 (27 percent) Catholic, and 995 (24 percent) black Protestant. New efforts by community organizations have been made to reach out to the Evangelical and Pentecostal congregations as well as to Unitarians, Jews, and Muslims, as well as with other nonreligious groups. According to the 2011 study, the drop among Catholic parish involvement from 33 percent to 27 percent during this decade reflects the fact that "the United States Conference of Catholic Bishops has de-emphasized community organizing in the training and promotion of the clergy," even though it has "continued to provide approximately $8 million per year to fund community organizing efforts through the Catholic Campaign for Human Development (CCHD)—their primary domestic anti-poverty program."[33] Over the past few years the American Life League, a pro-life organization with a budget of over $6 million, has initiated a smear campaign against the CCHD's contributions to antipoverty projects employing faith-based community organizing.[34] The United States Catholic Conference of Bishops has, however, rejected publicly this effort to undermine the credibility of faith-based community organizing.

WHAT DOES GRASSROOTS DEMOCRACY ENTAIL?

Maritain and Alinsky

We arrive at the most important question. One way to address this is to compare and contrast Jacques Maritain's understanding of democracy with what we can infer from Alinsky's work. Bernard Doering clarifies the differences well. Alinski commends "the right of free association of citizens to undertake action and organize institutions to determine their own destiny," and defends "the necessity of community organizing as mediating structures between the individual and the state, structures that help the government do what it is supposed to do."

Maritain, on the other hand, concentrates on "the distinction between the individual and the person, the primacy of the individual conscience in a religiously and politically pluralist democracy,...the primacy of the common good, and...the source of authority residing in the people, who accord that authority to the government that acts in their name."[35] On this basis the two recognized a great affinity in outlooks and "a kindred spirit."

Maritain would go so far as to see in Alinsky's work an inchoate "love for the human being and for God," even though he knew Alinsky would never admit the latter. He was critical of Alinsky's analysis of power for its failure to incorporate an analysis of moral power and the power of love. Alinsky's analysis remained secular or temporal and had no room for a moral or spiritual framework. Here Maritain's distinction of spiritual and temporal planes comes to the forefront. Nevertheless, Maritain treasured Saul Alinsky's work with the Back of the Yards Neighborhood Council as an advocate and provocateur of democracy among the poor and the marginalized.

Alinsky's approach would not, of course, be susceptible to the same criticisms leveled against Maritain's "new Christendom" and "two planes view" (distinguishing the temporal and the spiritual planes) of history. There is only one history for Alinsky, with no risk of spiritual or communal diversions. And yet Maritain believed, as he communicated in a personal letter to the author after his first reading of Alinsky's *Reveille for Radicals*, that "this book is epoch-making. It reveals a new way for *real* democracy, the only way in which man's thirst for social communion can develop and be satisfied, through freedom and not through totalitarianism in our disintegrated times....You are a Thomist, dear Saul, a practical Thomist!"[36] Maritain's review of the book in the *New York Post* reiterates his enthusiastic endorsement of Alinsky's method:

> Democracy does not work with amorphous, unorganized people; that is why democracy necessarily requires political parties. It also requires that from the very bottom people organize themselves naturally, spontaneously, in the everyday life of their basic communities,

so as to participate really and actively in the political life of the nation, and so that the achievements of this life may really be *their* work and *their* achievements. Such deep-seated civic consciousness is the best way to rejuvenate the very life of political parties, and to make stable the primary foundations of government by the people and for the people.... [Alinsky] explains in a remarkable manner how the intensity with which a small community, thus organized from within a living whole, becomes definitely aware of its power of initiative and its common good, naturally develops into concrete awareness of the common good of the nation and the common good of the international community.[37]

What have Catholic advocates of democracy found appealing in Alinsky's method of grassroots organizing? On one level it is its motivation. As Alinsky responded to Egan's question at their first meeting about how he got into this work, "Oh, Jack, I hate to see people get pushed around."[38] At the level of principle, they found in him someone with a profound sense of the dignity of each individual, and a commitment to the rights of individuals to speak up for themselves in civil society and in the political arena on matters of a living wage, housing, and eventually racial justice, health care, and education. For many of his Catholic followers Alinksy's approach to self-interest was transposed into a commitment to promoting the common good against the economic and power elites in a community by adhering to the principle of subsidiarity.

Neither Alinsky nor his followers became advocates of class conflict or identity politics; instead, a fundamental tenet for them is that no one should be excluded from work, housing, and most importantly from active participation in the political process and from engagement in civil society.[39] Grassroots democracy is about challenging destructive powers at work in communities by developing relational power that can call into question and hold accountable wielders of destructive power, and building more positive power relations by expanding social capital.

Basic Ingredients in Cultivating Grassroots Democracy

More than democratic principles of human dignity, equal rights, solidarity, or the common good, faith-based community organizing in the Alinsky tradition emphasizes the cultivation of a set of skills and practices associated with democratic decision making. Certain basic ingredients involved in these skills and practices merit comparison with Cardijn's see-judge-act method. Four basic components are found in leadership training manuals for community organizing used by the IAF, PICO, Gamaliel, and other networks, and have been analyzed by scholars working in the fields of history, the social sciences, and education. These are the following:

- First, building solidarity, or what social scientists call social capital, through one-on-one conversations about basic concerns in one's personal and social life in order to identify what Alinsky called one's self-interest.
- Second, selecting an issue that merits attention based on the initial round of one-on-one conversations, sharpened through research and analysis by community leaders and the community organizing staff, and confirmed through deliberation among wider circles of the community in a second round of one-on-ones or small group meetings.
- Third, identifying a person in authority and with some power in the targeted institution to engage about this issue.
- Fourth, engaging and holding accountable persons in roles of leadership through a public encounter between the group and the person in power, in order to set in motion social change.

These building blocks of a democratic process can serve many purposes. At the most basic level, one-on-one conversations provide a context for individuals to speak personally about their aspirations and concerns with another human being, to tap into desires and disturbances—in other words, to speak about fundamental aspirations and laments of their daily lives. Such informal communication provides participants the impetus to form relationships, build bonds of solidarity, and become actively involved with each other in areas of mutual concern.

What grievances by poor and working class people drive grassroots democratic movements? If we go back to the first meeting of the Back of the Yards Neighborhood Council launched by Alinsky, we find the following report from a local newspaper: "Unemployment, education, delinquency, housing and health were introduced as issues to be taken up in greater detail by the council at future meetings."[40] These same issues preoccupy poor and working-class people today. We can elaborate on them as follows.

Education and schools—Many parents and guardians are vigilant about their children's education. They are quick to complain about the need for school reform, better teachers, a wider curriculum, more after-school programs, and a smaller class size. In some cities, people complain about the advancement of a culture of criminalization in school disciplining procedures, which cultivates what has been called "the school to prison pipeline."

Economy—Levels of unemployment remain high across the country and especially in poorer urban and rural areas. Many people must work one, two, or more minimum—or low—wage jobs to cover some of the bare necessities of life, and they still must seek out public assistance to avoid homelessness, hunger, and health problems. In the past, people addressed these issues by supporting labor unions that would negotiate higher wages and benefits with corporate management. More recently, there have been efforts to enact legislation that requires a living wage, which is often still far below what is needed to meet basic necessities and benefits. There have been protests against big-box retailers' and fast food franchises' labor practices and salary scales. In some cases pressure has been brought to bear on elected officials who approve major tax credits for developers to build new retail stores or industries; there have been calls to reject such deals and to promote public-private partnerships for new developments, worker cooperative businesses, and community benefits agreements between developers and local citizen groups.

Housing—Problems with the housing industry have been a longstanding concern among people of color and their allies in lower income neighborhoods. Faith-based community organizations have been at the forefront of work to expose practices of redlining, in which banks and lending institutions refuse home loans to people of color, and more recently the phenomenon of reverse redlining where these same groups have been targeted as vulnerable populations who can be exploited with exorbitant interest rates. People living in tenement housing have regularly been victims of absentee owners and supervisors who fail to respond to complaints about the lack of hot water, heating, the presence of rodents and cockroaches, and the lack of basic maintenance on dilapidated apartments. There are also broader concerns about the need for affordable housing, especially in light of the gentrification of poorer areas and the displacement of poor populations by hiking up rents to astronomical levels.

Race—Race is a factor in each of these problem areas—education, economy, and housing—adversely affecting African Americans, immigrants from Africa, Latin America, the Caribbean, West Indies, and from the Middle East. Moreover, race is closely intertwined with problems in health care, immigration policies, and environmental issues.[41]

In this process of surfacing areas of concern, both people's talents and wounds are recognized and honored. Community organizers devote special attention to identifying latent leadership skills in the communities, often in someone who is particularly agitated about an issue, or someone who is willing to step forward and speak up, but also can step back and listen, really listen, and learn. In the process the question surfaces, Who might be able to develop the skills to lead a meeting, speak up at a rally, or negotiate in situations of conflict? Through these democratic processes, participants learn ways to hold people accountable, not only those in positions of power and authority in government and society, but also internally among leaders and staff of the organization through extensive processes of evaluation.[42]

The 2011 survey of community organizations in the United States revealed a shift underway in the expansion of democratic tactics. In the past, the usual tactics included direct actions like occupying the office of a "shady" employer or apartment owner or bank; petition drives; public actions; and accountability sessions. There have, more recently, been increasing efforts to learn about behind-the-scenes political dynamics on an issue; to build relationships with political or economic actors; and to learn about economic and policy issues involved in order to be able to address them effectively.[43] A radical democratic distrust of elites has been joined by a more representative approach to democracy. Conflict, the hallmark of Alinsky's model of community organizing, still has a strategic role to play, but negotiations and partnerships with a range of stakeholders in the community, including business and government elites, do as well.

One of my major conclusions is that this overall set of practices and skills utilized by faith-based community organizing to cultivate civic virtue in grassroots democracy merits comparison with the model of see-judge-act advanced by Joseph Cardijn.[44] The four steps delineated above—one-on-ones, cutting an issue, identifying a target, and holding people accountable in the pursuit of social change—could be transposed into a Cardijn three-step idiom: (1) see by means of heightened awareness of concerns through solidarity; (2 and 3) judge what issues are most pressing and how to address these issues by means of social analysis and reflection; (4) act in concert by holding accountable and challenging people in authority to respond to the social reality in light of the common good. Developing a process of ongoing collective awareness, discernment, decision making, and evaluation can be detected in both the heirs of Alinsky and the followers of Cardijn's model. The inroads made by both have been beneficial, but there are deeper complicating factors involved in promoting grassroots democracy that must also be acknowledged, and that merit further attention.

Democratic Practices and Power Relations: Two Frameworks

In this final section, let me raise several of the issues that merit further investigation by introducing two multivariant interpretive frameworks for assessing power dynamics in the advancement of grassroots democracy by faith-based groups. The first framework has been widely used to analyze examples of Catholic Action, but it also can be employed to assess faith-based community organizing. Kevin Ahern draws on the work of Gustavo Gutiérrez and Dean Brackley to distinguish four models of Church involvement in society, each of which has influenced IMCS/Pax Romana over the course of its history.[45] The *Christendom Model* combines an Augustinian theology with an antiliberal and antimodern traditionalist (associated with French *Integrism*), Church-centered outlook that justifies the need for the Church's intervention in society (IMCS/Pax Romana operated with this model between the 1880s and the 1930s). Jacques Maritain is associated with, second, a *New Christendom Model* based on his critique of the Christendom model and his defense of the relative autonomy of the temporal order (this influenced IMCS/Pax Romana 1930s–1950s) and, third, a *Distinction of [Spiritual and Temporal] Planes Model* (1950s–1960s), which views the two planes as united, but emphasizes the priority of the Church's spiritual mission. Fourth, a *Liberation Model* accentuates the role of the Church in promoting social justice (1960s to present).

The Christendom Model is not associated with the emergence of faith-based community organizing in the Alinsky tradition; the bishops that supported this work did not have *integrist* convictions. Although Alinsky and Maritain were certainly friends and shared certain convictions about democracy, one would never assume that the New Christendom and Two-Planes Models, associated with Maritain's position, were basic tenets or influential for Alinsky's core community organization leadership. To what extent the New Christendom and Two-Planes Model provided a working frame of reference for clergy, women religious, or lay Catholics involved in community organizing during the Alinksy era would be difficult to ascertain. Yet it seems more than likely that Maritain's views offered a useful framework for some activists, and especially for their episcopal and clergy allies and collaborators. Certain forms of Catholic Action came under the influence of what Ahern calls an *Integral Liberation Model* beginning in the 1960s. Without a doubt, liberationist views received attention and were debated among those involved in community organizing in the United States, as reflected in the work of Ed Chambers and Ernie Cortes. Still, liberationists' critical engagement with Marxist categories and modes of analysis ran contrary to Alinsky's and Maritain's aversion to Marxist class conflict analysis. In their eyes, social conflict is necessary and can serve a useful (moral) purpose, but class conflict is not the solution.

A second multivariant framework engages more recent historical and theoretical approaches to offer further valuable modes of analysis focused specifically on how the relationship between democratic practices and power is understood by Alinsky and his heirs. This entails deeper historical analysis of the sources and diverse theoretical approaches. Here, a first avenue is provided by Alinsky's own writings and, as Luke Bretherton has explored, how his early work influenced his understanding of social relations, and I would argue by extension, power.[46] A second approach is associated with IAF community organizers Ed Chambers and Leo Penta, both of whom draw on the work of Hannah Arendt and process thinker Bernard Loomer to discuss the use of power. A third theoretical trajectory is developed in Richard Wood's analysis of social capital and the cultural power of religious symbols, myths, and rituals. A fourth pragmatic and ethnographic approach has been developed by Jeffrey Stout in his analysis of how power is operative in community organizing as an instance of grassroots democracy. A fifth trajectory is associated with Michel Foucault's writings on discourse and power, and his later writings on democracy. Stout has argued that community organizing in the Alinsky tradition provides a more viable and intelligible approach to the use of power in democratic society than that offered by Foucault's analysis. Stout concedes that

Foucault's analysis can offer further insights into how power operates in groups and societies, but that community organizers have far more to offer.[47] Though distinct, these five perspectives need not be viewed as contradictory.

The first four models—Alinsky, Chambers and Penta, Wood, and Stout—I would argue need to be held tension with the work of Michel Foucault and other poststructuralist writers who bring to the surface difficult questions about democracy and power. It must be acknowledged that much Catholic theology and spirituality harbor a conflict-averse mentality and devote little consideration of structures and practices of ecclesial and civic accountability. By contrast, faith-based community organizing reflects a keener awareness of the positive role of conflict, especially as it pertains to situations of confrontation and accountability in social action and communal life. On this count, each of these four approaches illuminates the legacy of Alinsky and are compatible with certain views of liberation theology. There have been, however, more radical critiques of democratic practices and theories and liberationist viewpoints leveled by contemporary critical theorists, including Foucault, Derrida, postcolonial theorists, and Walter Mignolo, and decolonialists. Here I agree with Jeffrey Stout that community organizing remains a valuable resource for promoting grassroots democracy over against any position that would dismiss it. However, because of the pernicious problems of transgenerational poverty created by structural racism and sexism, I believe these diverse critical theorists, as Stout himself concedes, have valuable contributions to make that do not jettison the resistance, resilience, and results of community organizers. Here, a preferential option for poor and working-class people, who themselves remain committed to advancing grassroots democracy, offers more than sufficient justification for continuing to explore the vital resources provided by community organizing.

To conclude, I have considered U.S. Catholic parish and diocesan promotion of grassroots democracy through faith-based community organizing in the context of Vatican II's Church of the Poor group of bishops and the conciliar treatment of Catholic Action. These local U.S. Church-based groups offer, on the one hand, rich resources for promoting lay and clergy collaboration in the Church's work with the poor, both locally and globally. On the other hand, these groups approximate and can be seen as a further development of the Cardijn model of Catholic Action. How precisely these U.S. efforts compare with Latin American liberationist theology, ministry, base communities, and parishes is a topic that merits further consideration.

Faith-based community organizing has been developing the practices and skills necessary for advancing grassroots democracy, and thus merits wider attention among lay and clerical ecclesial ministers. Significantly, many of these same practices and skills are needed to advance local forms of synodality in parishes and dioceses, in council development, in pastoral planning, and in other forms of participatory governance.

Notes

1. Michel Schooyans, "Democracy in the Teachings of the Popes: Preliminary Report," *Proceedings of the Workshop on Democracy, 12–13 December 1996*, Pontifical Academy of the Social Sciences, 11–40, http://www.pass.va/content/dam/scienze sociali/pdf/miscellanea1.pdf; Paolo G. Carozza and Daniel Philpott, "The Catholic Church, Human Rights, and Democracy: Convergence and Conflict with the Modern State," *Logos: A Journal of Catholic Thought and Culture* 15, no. 3 (2012): 15–43; Paul E. Sigmund, "Catholicism and Liberal Democracy," *Catholicism and Liberalism: Contributions to American Public Philosophy*, ed. R. Bruce Douglass and David Hollenbach, SJ (New York: Cambridge University Press, 1994), 217–41; J. Bryan Hehir, "The Modern Catholic Church and Human Rights: The Impact of the Second Vatican Council," *Christianity and Human Rights: An Introduction*, ed. John Witte Jr. and Franklin S. Alexander (Cambridge: Cambridge University Press, 2010), 113–34; J. Bryan Hehir, "Post-Conciliar Catholicism and Democracy," lecture at the symposium "Democracy in the Shadow of Constantine," Fordham University, June 12, 2013.

2. Schooyans, "Democracy in the Teachings of the Popes," 26.

3. John T. McGreevy, in *Catholicism and American Freedom: A History* (New York: W. W. Norton, 2003), lists the following exiles: "Germans F. A. Heremns, Goetz Briefs, Dietrich von

Hildebrand, Heinrich Rommen, Heinrich Brüning, Waldemar Gurian, Fraz Mueller, and Theodore Brauer, Spains' Alfredo Mendizábal, Italy's Father Luigi Sturzo, and France's Maritain, Yves Simon, and Paul Vignaux" (197).

4. Emile Perreau-Saussine, *Catholicism and Democracy: An Essay in the History of Political Thought*, trans. Richard Rex (Princeton, NJ: Princeton University Press, 2012), 2.

5. Ibid., 2; also see 14, 67.

6. See Brian Tierney, "Church Law and Alternative Structures: A Medieval Perspective," *Governance, Accountability, and the Future of the Catholic Church*, ed. Francis Oakley and Bruce Russett (New York: Continuum, 2004), 49–61.

7. For representatives of Gallicanism, see Perreau-Sassine, *Catholicism and Democracy*, 69–80.

8. John A. Coleman, *An American Strategic Theology* (New York: Paulist Press, 1982), 140–41.

9. Proponents of Social Catholicism include Adrien Albert Marie de Mun and Francois-René de La Tour du Pin, Marquis de la Charce, who formed in 1871 *L'Oeuvre des Cercles Catholique d'Ouvriers*; Marc Sangnier, who established the newspaper *La Démocratie* and started in 1894 the liberal Catholic group The Furrow; The Fribourg Union brought together lay Catholic intellectuals in October between 1885 and 1891 to discuss difficult social issues pertaining to industrialization and the labor question, which contributed to the encyclical *Rerum Novarum*. In the mid-twentieth century a Spanish priest, José María Arizmendiarrieta, promoted economic democracy through the establishment of worker cooperatives in the Mondragon Corporation in the Basque region, drawing on Catholic social teaching.

10. See *History of Vatican II*, ed. Giuseppe Alberigo, trans. Joseph A. Komonchak, 5 vols. (Maryknoll, NY: Orbis, 1995–2006); on the Church of the Poor during the first two periods of the Council, see 2:200–3, 3:164–65.

11. Norman Tanner, "The Church in the World (*Ecclesia ad Extra*)," in Alberigo and Komonchak, *History of Vatican II*, 4:382–86, at 383–84. A preliminary document included "an introduction by M. McGrath on the problems of poverty in the contemporary world, a theology part by Y. Congar, and a practical part by J. Wright" (384, no. 174); the final report can be found in Giacomo Lercaro, *Per la forza dello spirito: Discorsi conciliari del*

card. *Giacomo Lercaro* (Bologna: Edizioni Dehoniane, 1984), 157–70.

12. Tanner, "The Church in the World," 385.

13. Letter of Pius XI to Cardinal Bertram, November 13, 1928, in *Clergy and Laity: Official Catholic Teachings*, ed. Odile M. Liebard (Wilmington, NC: McGrath, 1978), 30–34, at 31.

14. Étienne Fouilloux, "The Antepreparatory Phase: The Slow Emergence from Inertia (January, 1959–October, 1962), in Alberigo and Komonchak, *History of Vatican II*, 1:55–66, at 78.

15. Gustavo Gutiérrez, *A Theology of Liberation: History, Politics, and Salvation* (Maryknoll, NY: Orbis 1988), 39–40, 59–60.

16. Ibid., 60.

17. Kevin J. Ahern, "Structures of Grace: Catholic Nongovernmental Organizations and the Mission of the Church," (PhD diss., Boston College, 2013), 135–93; see Buenaventura Pelegri, *IMCS-IYCS: Their Option, Their Pedagogy* (Kowloom, Hong Kong: Asian Secretariat, International Movement of Catholic Students, 1979).

18. Mary Irene Zotti, *A Time of Awakening: The Young Christian Worker Story in the United States, 1938–1970* (Chicago: Loyola University Press, 1991); Jeffrey M. Burns, *Disturbing the Peace: A History of the Christian Family Movement, 1949–1974* (Notre Dame, IN: University of Notre Dame Press, 1999).

19. Jan Grootaers, "The Drama Continues between the Acts: The 'Second Preparation' and Its Opponents," in Alberigo and Komonchak, *History of Vatican II*, 2:359–514, at 443–45.

20. For a general overview, see Brendan Leahy, *Ecclesial Movements and Communities: Origins, Significance, and Issues* (Hyde Park, NY: New City Press, 2011); for a historical and theological assessment, see Massimo Faggioli, *Breve storia dei movimenti cattolici* (Roma: Carocci editore, 2008) and the English translation, *Sorting Out Catholicism: A Brief History of the New Catholic Movements* (Collegeville, MN: Liturgical Press, 2014); Massimo Faggioli, "Between Documents and Spirit: The Case of the 'New Catholic Movements,'" in *After Vatican II: Trajectories and Hermeneutics*, ed. James L. Heft (Grand Rapids: Eerdmans, 2012), 1–22; Massimo Faggioli, "The Neocatechumenate and Communion in the Church," *The Japan Mission Journal* 65 (2011): 31–38.

21. Faggioli, "Between Documents and Spirit," 16.

22. On Catholic Action, see Yves Congar, *Lay People in the Church* (Westminster, MD: The Newman Press [first French edition, 1951], 1967), 249–399; Jeremy Bonner, Christopher D. Denny, and Mary Beth Fraser Connolly, eds., *Empowering the People: Catholic Action before and after Vatican II* (Bronx, NY: Fordham University Press, 2013).

23. My particular thesis advances in an ecclesiological key the work of two sociological studies by Richard Wood and Mary Ann Flaherty, *Renewing Congregations: The Contribution of Faith-Based Community Organizing* (Syosset, NY: Interfaith Funders, 2003), http://www.piconetwork.org/tools-resources/doc ument/0012.pdf; and *Faith and Public Life: Faith-Based Community Organizing and the Development of Congregations* (Syosset, NY: Interfaith Funders, 2004), http://repository.unm. edu/bitstream/handle/1928/10664/Faithpercent26PublicLife.pdf ?sequence=1.

24. On John L. Lewis, see Sanford D. Worwitt, *Let Them Call Me Rebel: Saul Alinsky, His Life and Legacy* (New York: Random House, 1989; Vintage Edition, 1992), 41–45.

25. On Alinsky and Horton, see my essay, "The Prophetic Mission of the Local Church: Community Organizing as a School for the Social Imaginary," in *Ecclesiology and Exclusion: Boundaries of Being and Belonging in Postmodern Times*, ed. Dennis D. Doyle, Timothy J. Furry, and Pascal D. Bazzell (Maryknoll, NY: Orbis, 2012), 226.

26. Saul D. Alinsky, *Reveille for Radicals* (Chicago: University of Chicago Press, 1946; New York: Vintage, 1989); *Rules for Radicals* (New York: Random House, 1971; Vintage Edition, 1989); Nicholas von Hoffman, *Radical: A Portrait of Saul Alinsky* (New York: Nation Books, 2010).

27. Bernard Doering considers who might have introduced Maritain to Alinsky in Bernard Doering, ed., *The Philosopher and the Provocateur: The Correspondence of Jacques Maritain and Saul Alinsky* (Notre Dame, IN: University of Notre Dame Press, 1994), 4, no. 2.

28. Beryl Satter, *Family Properties: Race, Real Estate, and the Exploitation of Black Urban America* (New York: Holt, 2009), 120. For more details on Alinsky and Egan, see Margery Frisbie, *An Alley in Chicago: The Ministry of a City Priest* (Kansas City, MO: Sheed & Ward, 1991), 22–27.

29. On how race was a crucial factor in Alinsky's work, see John T. McGreevy, *Parish Boundaries: The Catholic Encounter with Race in the Twentieth-Century Urban North* (Chicago: University of Chicago Press, 1996), 111–32.

30. On the Industrial Area Foundation, see Edward T. Chambers, *Roots for Radicals: Organizing for Power, Action, and Justice* (New York: Continuum, 2003); on Ernesto Cortes, IAF, and COPS, see Mary Beth Rogers, *Cold Anger: A Story of Faith and Power Politics* (Denton, TX: University of North Texas Press, 1999), and Mark R. Warren, *Dry Bones Rattling: Community Building to Revitalize American Democracy* (Princeton: Princeton University Press, 2001); on the Gamaliel Foundation, see Dennis A. Jackobsen, *Doing Justice: Congregations and Community Organizing* (Minneapolis, MN: Fortress, 2001); on Pacific Institute for Community Organization (PICO), see Richard L. Wood, *Faith in Action: Religion, Race, and Democratic Organizing in America* (Chicago: University of Chicago Press, 2002); Luke Bretherton emphasizes Alinsky's friendship with Catholic philosopher Jacques Maritain and the compatibility of his views with Augustine's theology of the secular, *Christianity and Contemporary Politics: The Conditions and Possibilities of Faithful Witness* (Malden, MA: Wiley-Blackwell, 2010), 71–125.

31. Mark R. Warren and Richard L. Wood, *Faith-Based Community Organizing: The State of the Field* (January 2001), http://comm-org.wisc.edu/papers2001/faith/faith.htm; see part 3.

32. Brad Fulton and Richard L. Wood, "Interfaith Community Organizing: Emerging Theological and Organizational Challenges," *International Journal of Public Theology* 6 (2012): 398–420, at 402, 407.

33. Ibid., 408 and 409, no. 18.

34. Faith in Public Life, a center for faith groups promoting issues of justice, compassion, and the common good that was formed in 2006, issued in June 11, 2013, "Be Not Afraid? Guilt by Association, Catholic McCarthyism and Growing Threats to the U.S. Bishops' Anti-Poverty Mission," http://www.faithinpublic life.org/wp-content/uploads/2013/06/FPL-CCHD-report.pdf.

35. Doering, *The Philosopher and the Provocateur*, xix.

36. Ibid., 11.

37. Ibid., 19.

38. Worwitt, *Let Them Call Me Rebel*, 270.

39. Maritain was pleased that Alinsky had no inclination to Hegelian dialectic and Marxist class conflict theory, and Ernesto Cortes expressed reservations about liberation theologians' use of Marxist theory and even the role of base communities that were not sufficiently parish based. See *Cold Anger*, 127–42.

40. As quoted in Worwitt, *Let Them Call Me Rebel*, 68.

41. For a fuller list, see Wood, *Faith in Action*, 80.

42. Ibid., 34–49, 164–71.

43. "Building Bridges, Building Power," 20. Richard Wood noticed in 2002 a new trend among faith-based community organizing was emerging that was indebted to the heritage of representative democracy. "This cultural shift both reflects and allows the organizations' practice of partnership and negotiation vis-à-vis institutional leaders in the political and economic arenas....Radical democratic distrust of elites would make partnership and negotiation with political elites morally and politically suspect." But certain networks (like PICO) have taken a step beyond Alinsky's legacy by "partial[ly] embrac[ing]...a more representative understanding of democracy [that] makes such partnership imaginable and desirable" (Wood, *Faith in Action*, 178).

44. Similar comparisons could be made with the method of the pastoral circle as developed by Joe Holland and Peter Henriot, *Social Analysis: Linking Faith and Justice* (Maryknoll, NY: Orbis, 1984); Frans Wijsen, Peter Henriot, and Rodrigo Mejía, eds., *The Pastoral Circle Revisited: A Critical Quest for Truth and Transformation* (Maryknoll, NY: Orbis, 2005).

45. Ahern, *Structures of Grace*, 138–66; Gutiérrez, *A Theology of Liberation*, 39–40, 59–60; Dean Brackley, *Divine Revolution: Salvation and Liberation in Catholic Thought* (Maryknoll, NY: Orbis, 1996), 68–70.

46. See Luke Bretherton, *Resurrecting Democracy: Faith, Citizenship and the Politics of a Common Life* (Cambridge: Cambridge University Press, 2014).

47. For my initial foray into this topic, see Bradford Hinze, "Talking Back, Acting Up: Wrestling with Spirits in Social Bodies," *Interdisciplinary and Religio-Cultural Discourses on a Spirit-Filled World: Loosing the Spirits*, ed. Veli-Matti Kärkkäinen, Kirsteen Kim, and Amos Yong (New York: Palgrave MacMillan, 2013), 155–70.

PART III
FIGURES
The Jesuits and Vatican II

9

Jared Wicks, SJ

Augustin Cardinal Bea, SJ
BIBLICAL AND ECUMENICAL
CONSCIENCE OF VATICAN II

In 1990, twenty-five years after Vatican II ended, Bavarian television presented a program about the Council in which a
reporter posed questions to two individuals who had experienced Vatican II as theological experts, Professor Hans Küng and
Cardinal Joseph Ratzinger. The final question was whether the
Church of 1990 was not in need of a similar reinvigorating
breakthrough, even of a Third Vatican Council.

Küng welcomed the idea and hoped to live to see Vatican
III, especially for taking up issues suppressed at Vatican II, like
birth control and clerical celibacy. New issues need attention,
like the role of women in the Church's ministry. Above all, a new
Council should present faith as truly liberating from the
depressed conditions of 1990. But Ratzinger cautioned that
ecclesial renewal has to first grow over time and then be harvested. Vatican II harvested the renewal movements of the
decades before 1960. Renewing liturgical, biblical, and ecumenical developments had been ignited by pioneering individuals
and then developed in small groups pressing for change in the
Church's formulation of doctrine, in its worship, and in relations

with other Christians. Ratzinger did not see, in 1990, this kind of necessary preparation.[1]

My chapter on the German Jesuit Augustin Bea will relate first a newly discovered work by him in the 1920s and then sketch how in the 1950s he learned from two pre–Vatican II renewal movements. Then, under the impact of Pope John XXIII and Bea's becoming a cardinal in late 1959, he fused what he had learned into a coherent outlook and conviction, making him a major player in the Council—even as its "biblical and ecumenical conscience." Bea was not a pioneer of renewal, but instead an alert observer who forgot nothing of what he heard with interest. When he became a cardinal, he had a store of insights and convictions, gained from some pioneers and groups of change promoters, which prepared him well for the mission given him by Pope John XXIII, which Bea carried out energetically at the Council.

BEA'S EARLY SERVICE IN THE SOCIETY OF JESUS AND THEN FOR THE HOLY SEE IN 1926

Augustin Bea lectured on Scripture for thirty-four years at the Pontifical Biblical Institute, but his scholarly preparation for such teaching was minimal. His Jesuit superiors valued his talents for organization and personal governance. As soon as he started teaching Old Testament at the Valkenburg Jesuit theologate in 1918, he became the province's prefect of studies as well, overseeing the programs of the German Jesuit scholastics. At age forty, in 1921, he became the founding provincial of the new Southern German Jesuit Province, with residence in Munich, where he became well known to the nuncio to Bavaria, Eugenio Pacelli. In one exchange with Father General Ledochowski, Bea the provincial said he would not be sending young German Jesuits to Rome for special studies, because German graduate programs were far superior to the Roman programs in theology and Scripture. The general responded by calling Bea after only three years as provincial to Rome in 1924, precisely to set up adequate graduate programs for Jesuits, while he also taught at the Biblical Institute and the Gregorian. The historian of the Biblicum, Maurice Gilbert, notes that in the 1930s, the Old Testament courses were taught by Frs. Vaccari and Bea, "both being not so well trained in the subject."[2]

A notable revelation of Bea's early outlook and values is a recently published report of 1926, written by Bea on commission by the Roman Curia's Congregation for Seminaries. It sketched the condition of the Church in Germany, especially of German centers of Catholic theological education.[3] Bea was sharply critical of the university faculties of theology, in which most seminarians followed a three- or four-year program before they spent a year or two in a bishop's seminary for pastoral formation. Most of the faculties were state sponsored, with the bishops having no role in appointing professors—something to change through concordats with the Holy See. The theology professors privileged scholarship and spent too many class hours on topics of their research, to the detriment of completing the course content. Their fascination with historical controversy trumped their handing on of the Church's doctrine, so that for future priests St. Thomas Aquinas remained *terra incognita* and the priests were ill prepared to communicate to the people the beauty and consolation of Catholic truth. Biblical studies in the Catholic faculties were worse, since they were dominated by critical philological exegesis to the neglect of theological content. The university exegetes despised the norms of the Papal Biblical Commission, while Protestant influence on interpretation was widespread, leaving future priests ignorant of God's word of life and truth.

Since all this had consequences in the parishes, Bea laid out remedial action: (1) Insist on seminarians having a six-year basic course before ordination, as canon law had set down, which should include two years of scholastic philosophy. (2) Promising seminary students should go to Rome to study at the Gregorian, Angelicum, or Biblical Institute—where programs were improving, but at the doctoral level still had to become more respectable. The Jesuit-run Innsbruck faculty of theology could also serve here. (3) In the diocesan seminaries, the teachers must come from the ranks of priests formed in scholastic doctrine in institutions recognized by the Holy See. (4) Since many German bishops knew little theology, the Holy See had to gain more influence over episcopal appointments. In dioceses with rights of election, the Cathedral Chapters did not sense the urgency of sound seminary education.

This 1926 document by Bea shows that he was not caught up in the zeal for denunciation that marked the antimodernism of the day. He argued critically out of concerns for good preaching and catechesis. But he showed no hint of the passion for Christian unity that drove him in the era of John XXIII.

BEA AS A ROMAN INSIDER— WITH LITTLE-KNOWN ECUMENICAL CONTACTS IN THE 1950s

In 1930 Bea became rector of the Biblical Institute, leading to appointments as consultor to bodies of the Roman Curia. On the Pontifical Biblical Commission, Bea contributed substantially to Pius XII's 1943 transforming encyclical *Divino Afflante Spiritu*, sharing the work with the Commission's secretary, Jacques-Marie Vosté, a Dominican protégé of Lagrange.[4] Bea served the Congregation for Seminaries (1936) and the Congregation of Rites (1950) and in 1945 he became the confessor of Pope Pius XII and of the German sisters of the papal household. Bea ended his nineteen-year tenure as rector of the Biblicum in July 1949. After this, he continued to carry a light teaching load; however, this had to compete for his time and attention with new projects of reports for the Supreme Congregation of the Holy Office.

A turning point in Bea's curriculum vitae had come in March 1949 (at age sixty-seven), with his appointment as consultor to the Holy Office.[5] There he became the valued source of information on and assessments of German theology, in which ecumenical topics loomed large. This Holy Office work was the main way in which Bea came to know certain pre–Vatican II renewal movements, specifically those promoting Jewish-Christian understanding and those quietly advancing different facets of the ecumenical process.

Early in his Holy Office service, Bea met the redaction team of the *Freiburger Rundbrief,* a quarterly begun in 1948 to circulate texts and documents in promotion of Jewish-Christian friendship and the dismantling of Christian misunderstandings and prejudicial stereotypes of Jews.[6] In 1950 Bea and Robert Leiber, SJ, Pope Pius XII's private secretary, visited the editors of the *Rundbrief* and became convinced of their orthodoxy and valuable work.[7] From then on, copies of the *Rundbrief* went to bishops and to its Roman friends in high places, like Fr. Bea, who could pass on information and emerging exegetical and theological insights on Jewish-Christian relations to Pius XII in post-sacramental conversations with the pope. Looking ahead ten years to September 1960, Bea was prepared when Pope John asked him to expand the work of the Unity Secretariat to deal with anti-Semitism and Christianity's special relation to the living religion of Judaism. Our image of preconciliar renewal pioneers and movements should include, as it did for Bea, the *Rundbrief* and similar efforts in France, Switzerland, and the Netherlands—which were harvested in *Nostra Aetate* 4.[8]

During the 1950s, a major source of Bea's information about Catholic ecumenical efforts was the archbishop of Paderborn, Lorenz Jaeger, who in the meetings of the German bishops reported regularly on Protestantism and ecumenical developments.[9] Jaeger sent Bea copies of some of these reports. In 1956 Bea thanked Jaeger for his report of that year and said it added significantly to what he (Bea) had already learned from his study of materials from the Faith and Order Conference of Lund (1952) and from the World Council of Churches assembly in Evanston, Illinois in the United States (1954).[10] Jaeger's visits to Rome regularly included conversations with Bea, in which Jaeger could, for instance, relate his experiences since 1946 as cosponsor of the Ecumenical Working Group (*Arbeitskreis*) of Evangelical and Catholic theologians.[11] Another topic with Bea was Jaeger's founding in Paderborn in 1957 of a Catholic ecumenical study center, the Johann-Adam-Moehler-Institute, which Bea appreciated for its focus on accurate study of the present-day realities of Lutheran theology and the Lutheran churches.

In the Ecumenical *Arbeitskreis*, a priest-professor of Paderborn, Msgr. Josef Höfer, comanaged the selection of papers for meetings from 1947 to 1954. That work ended when Höfer came to Rome as ecclesiastical consultor of the German Embassy. Thus, from the mid-1950s onward, Höfer and Bea had extensive conversations on ecumenical developments. Höfer's own theology of the Church stressed the ongoing influence of Christ the head and of the Holy Spirit to assemble and guide the ecclesial body of Christ. Höfer also held a broader conception of incorporation into the body and the Church than Pius XII had formulated in the encyclical *Mystici Corporis Christi* (1943).[12]

A third current of ecumenical information for Bea began to flow in 1952 when Johannes Willebrands came from the Netherlands to Rome for advice on a planned association of Catholic theologians involved in ecumenical efforts. After the association was approved and instituted in 1953, Willebrands reported in Rome on the annual meetings of this "Catholic Conference on Ecumenical Questions." Ostensibly the main addressee of the reports was Archbishop Alfredo Ottaviani of the Holy Office, but Willebrands also informed Bea on developments—to have a direct conduit to Pius XII until 1958. The Conference had discreet contacts with the World Council of Churches and focused some meetings major themes of World Council assemblies, such as "Christ the Hope of the World," for Evanston (1954).[13]

Pius XII's death in October 1958 and the election of John XXIII at first simplified Bea's life, since he had no more Saturday trips to the Apostolic Palace or Castel Gandolfo for the pope's confession. Bea had bouts of illness from mid-'58 to mid-'59, but his correspondence shows that John XXIII's announcement of a coming council had drawn him into studying the pope's allocutions for clarification of the ecumenical dimension.[14] In September 1959, two months before the announcement of his cardinalate, he wrote a revealing letter to Jaeger. The preparation of the Council must include drafting an ecclesiology document, which, among other points, will bring clarity on

Church/state relations. (No blank slate there for future work leading to *Dignitatis Humanae*.) The conciliar ecclesiology must state amply the role of bishops, both in responsibility for the universal Church and in leadership of the dioceses. "Centralization is certainly not a blessing for the Church." The Council should mandate that the dicasteries of the curia have prefects with specialized knowledge of their Congregation's field (still a relevant desire), along with an international band of both cardinal members and consultors. More generally, in ecclesiology the topic of the risen Christ's "royal dominion" or lordship needed development, from which one would have a better context for understanding the magisterium.[15] This would not be a "council of union" like the Council of Florence in the fifteenth century, but it could create presuppositions for gradual developments toward union.

This was from shortly before November 16, 1959, when news came that Bea would be made cardinal in a December consistory. The elevation intended to recognize his many consultations in the curia, his long leadership of the Biblicum, and his service as confessor to Pius XII. But his gathering and mulling over ecumenical topics for ten years made him into a "surprise package" for John XXIII. In his first audience as cardinal, Bea told Pope John that he felt called to dedicate his new status and authority to promoting Christian unity—much to the delight of John XXIII. In the next five months, developments followed quickly toward the institution of the Secretariat for Promoting the Unity of Christians on June 5, 1960, with Bea as President.[16]

BEA'S ROLE IN VATICAN II'S FIRST MAJOR DRAMA

I arrange my "macroaccount" of Vatican II around two major conciliar dramas. The first drama was the wide-ranging setting aside, in late 1962 and well into 1963, of most, not all, of the texts of the Preparatory Commissions composed from 1960 to mid-1962. This first drama dominates many popular accounts—and it remains fascinating. The second drama, of which Joseph Komonchak often reminds us, is that of "fissures" of serious differences between groups within the Council majority about what to feature in the major revised texts moving toward approval in 1964–65. I hope more emphasis will fall on this second drama in 2014–15, to show the marks it left on the documents and its postconciliar continuations. But what follows will clarify Bea's role as a major player in the first great drama of the Council.

I have written elsewhere about Bea's secretariat being a "proponent of *ressourcement*" during the Vatican II preparation. It produced noteworthy draft texts of ecclesiology and on the word of God in the life of the Church.[17]

The Secretariat's sixteen members and twenty consultors met in November 1960, when ten subcommissions were created to deal with major ecumenical topics. At that time, the texts of the Secretariat were foreseen as helping the preparatory commissions by ecumenical sensitizing and guidance.[18] But, in a major development, a small cluster of Secretariat texts became earmarked for submission to the Council itself, and this expanded in 1963.[19]

Even before the secretariat's second meeting in February 1961, Bea "went public" with his then-innovative interpretation of membership in Christ's body and in the Church. He challenged as incomplete the conception, based on Pius XII's *Mystici Corporis* (1943), that was then reigning in Cardinal Ottaviani's Preparatory Theological Commission. In the latter, Roman Catholics were members in reality (*in re*) of the body of Christ and the Church, by reason of the three bonds of baptismal regeneration, profession of the true faith, and not being separated for grave offenses. To be sure, outside the Church sincere seekers bent on fulfilling God's will as they know it were "ordered to" or "related to" the body and Church by their desire and so could be saved. In humankind, therefore, some were members of Christ *in re* and many nonmembers were ordered or related to Christ and the Church *in voto*.

On December 2, 1960, the Anglican Primate, Archbishop Geoffrey Fisher of Canterbury, paid a courtesy call to Pope John and afterward went to see Bea at the Brazilian College. Bea was glad to test the waters with Fisher about observers at Vatican II being sent by the other churches and confessions. But Bea also published in *La Civiltà Cattolica,* shortly after Fisher's visit, a theological justification of Pope John's reception of the Anglican Primate. Bea argued that for Catholics the practice of charity has a special character regarding other Christians, whom Pope John regularly calls "our brothers" and even "our sons."

> They are our brothers, even though separated from the Catholic faith. In fact Pope Pius XII's encyclical on the sacred liturgy, *Mediator Dei* [1947], states explic- itly that those validly baptized "are in the mystical Body and become by common title members of Christ the Priest."...Canon Law, in its turn, echoes this doc- trine when it declares that a person validly baptized becomes a member of the Church of Christ, with all the rights and duties of a Christian, save only those cases where an obstacle prevents one from the use of these rights [canon 87]. Sufficient attention has not always been paid to the fact that the Holy Father does not hesitate to call all separated Christians brothers— and even sons; and the doctrine of the Mystical Body enables us to understand why he does so.[20]

To promote more "sufficient attention" to this truth about baptized non-Catholics, Bea put his argument before a wider public in the Italian *Messenger of the Sacred Heart* for December 1960. This was to explain the January 1961 special intention of the Apostolate of Prayer, "that the truth and char- ity of Christ may remove the obstacles that still stand in the way of the reunion of all Christians in the one Church of Christ." Bea underscored that this intention was very close to the heart of Pope John, who was helped now by the special Secretariat to promote the union of Christians. Speaking of the separated Orthodox and Protestants, Bea applies to them canon 87 on the baptized having the status of "persons in the Church of Christ." He added references to three passages of St. Paul on incorpora- tion into Christ, and said that Pope Pius XII had "explicitly and categorically" affirmed their belonging to the priestly people in *Mediator Dei.* Prayer was needed so that every baptized person may enjoy to the full all the rights and privileges given in baptism in the unity of one Church.[21]

On January 21, 1961, Bea stated more fully his case for baptized non-Catholics belonging "fundamentally" to the Church, in a public lecture at the Angelicum in Rome. He explained that when *Mystici Corporis* said that schism or heresy severs the bond with the Church, Pius XII was referring to those who formally, consciously, and freely embrace separation—not those born into the other churches and communities and continuing there in good faith. The denial of belonging spoken of in *Mystici Corporis* refers to membership *"only in the full sense"* that Catholics have. But there are other levels of belonging, primarily by baptism, leading to lives influenced by God's grace and among the Orthodox blessed by the episcopate and sacraments. Among Protestants, believers are guided by God's word in Scripture to faith in Christ and worship of him.[22]

In these weeks the Secretary of the Preparatory Theological Commission, Fr. Sebastian Tromp, made diary entries on these and others of Cardinal Bea's lectures and articles. Tromp prepared a memo for Cardinal Ottaviani on Bea's departure from the narrow concept of Church belonging that was settled doctrine in the Theological Commission's Vatican II preparation.[23] But Bea actively and publically dissented, proposing a view of baptized non-Catholics that was eventually expressed as Catholic doctrine in *Lumen Gentium* 15 and *Unitatis Redintegratio* 3, and all of its chapter 3.[24]

Drama was heightened by Bea's very active role as a member of Vatican II's Central Preparatory Commission—on which I have published two dense columns.[25] I show there how Bea laid the basis, in November 1961, for the "fall" of the schema *De fontibus revelationis* a year later, when he delivered a lengthy critique of the draft *De fontibus* regarding its biblical citations and its distance from Pius XII's encyclical *Divino Afflante Spiritu* (1943).[26] Then in May 1962, in the same venue, he criticized at length the Theological Commission's *De ecclesia*, basing himself in great part on ecclesiological formulations worked out by subcommissions of the Unity Secretariat. The suggestions had gone to the Theological Commission a year before, but were not considered, much less adopted, in drafting this major text of the Vatican II preparation in ecclesiology. Bea was a major actor in beginning the dramatic leaving behind of important Vatican II preparatory documents.

BEA'S ROLE DURING THE EARLY VATICAN II DEBATES

As Vatican II opened, Bea reflected on the prepared draft texts, which he had seen in their entirety while participating in the Central Preparatory Commission. This left him deeply concerned over the notable dissonance between most of these documents and the goals that John XXIII had been formulating, which were now summarized and made more pointed in John's inaugural address *Gaudet Mater Ecclesia* of October 11, 1962. So when the directive body, the Council's Secretariat for Extraordinary Affairs, held its first meeting on October 16, 1962, it had before it a memorandum from Bea documenting the overriding pastoral purpose that John was proposing and suggesting (1) that this be communicated to the commissions as *the* criterion for radically revising their draft texts and (2) that the Council fathers take up and affirm this pastoral finality of their work in the full assembly of a General Congregation of the Council.[27]

As is well known, on November 14, 1962, the Vatican II debate began on the draft text "on the sources of revelation."[28] This came from the Preparatory Theological Commission, (1) on Tradition as a source of revealed teachings that are not attested in Scripture, (2) on biblical inspiration and interpretation, and (3) on Scripture in Church life, that is, as read by Catholics, as interpreted by Catholic exegetes, and as serving in Catholic theology as a basis of work. In the text of twenty-nine paragraphs, three places stood out that issued censures (*reprobat...damnat*) of theologians of inspiration and of scholars of the Gospels.[29]

In eighty-two speeches, the Council members evaluated the schema *De fontibus* as a whole over four days, with thirty-two speakers expressing their disapproval of the draft text and urging their fellow Council members to join them in voting it down. Of these thirty-two dissenters, eighteen appealed to Pope John's intentions for the Council, especially to *Gaudet Mater*, with which they said the schema did not conform; instead, it breathed another spirit. Suddenly, the pope's aims and intentions in convoking Vatican II became a crucial factor in the Council's development.

On the first day of this debate, Cardinals Frings and Léger said that the text lacked the "pastoral note with which the Holy Father ardently wants Council statements to be imbued" (Frings) and so it was dissonant with "the spirit of positive renewal desired by the Pope in this Council" (Léger). Cardinal Alfrink went further by citing Pope John's *Gaudet Mater Ecclesia* from October 11, namely, that the Council has not assembled to repeat settled doctrine, but to enunciate Catholic truths in a fresh way for the faithful and for dialoging with separated Christians. Bea repeated this more incisively by citing eleven lines from *Gaudet* on the Council's aim to penetrate Catholic teaching more deeply and then give it a fresh expression that would affect souls, for as the pope said, our magisterium was "pre-eminently pastoral." With this aim, *De fontibus* stood in notable dissonance. Bea added a fresh point, namely, that the Council members had already embraced the pope's pastoral aim in their "Message to All People" approved three weeks before, which was in fact a *reprise* of John XXIII's radio address on September 11, a month before Vatican II opened. At the end of the November 14 first day of debate, Bishops Manek and Soegijapranta from Indonesia said that their episcopal conference had compared the published schemas with what John XXIII said in opening the Council, and so they proposed not only a thorough rewrite of *De fontibus,* but also of the three other drafts from the Theological Commission, so that the Council might effectively attain the pastoral goal set before it by Pope John.[30]

The two Indonesian interventions made up a set with Bea's address, because when the Indonesians compared the theological schemas with *Gaudet Mater*, they were following Bea's suggestion, passed on by the Indonesians' *peritus* Pieter Smulders, SJ, who had visited Bea to collect advice. Bea recommended that the Indonesians should discuss until they reached unanimity on issues raised by the texts. Then their position and reasons should be spoken out in St. Peter's in the name of the thirty bishops and prefects apostolic. But above all, they should study Pope John's opening discourse and make appeals to it as a normative criterion.[31]

These initial interventions critical of *De fontibus* were first steps toward the vote on November 20 in which a majority of Council members (62 percent) voted to set aside the Theological Commission's draft text. Pope John XXIII confirmed this the next day by setting up a mixed commission (doctrinal and ecumenical) to revise the text thoroughly, under the copresidency of Cardinals Ottaviani and Bea.

In December 1962, in the five-day debate on *De ecclesia*, Bea argued in the same way from *Gaudet Mater* and from the members' "Message to All People," as setting a finality to which the ecclesiological draft in no way corresponded.

But by December 4, when Bea spoke against *De ecclesia*, work was well along on Pope John's directives for the "intersession" about to begin. John mandated all the commissions to reexamine their texts in light of the Council goals. To leave no doubt about the goals, which were criteria of adequate revision, the document cited no less than twenty-eight lines of *Gaudet Mater Ecclesia*. To make sure that the criteria become operative, seven cardinals, to be named, would become a new Commission of Coordination for supervising the mandated revision, which took place with considerable success in the following months in Vatican II's "second preparation," which was the extended denouement of the Council's first major drama.[32]

Cardinal Augustin Bea was very effective in this whole process, in articles and lectures on belonging to the Church, in arguing critically in the Central Preparatory commission before Vatican II opened, in his memorandum of October 16, 1962, on Council goals, and then in incisive addresses to the whole body of Council members in period 1 of 1962. He was a major protagonist of Vatican II's first great drama.

Notes

1. From the videotape of the interview, the Institut-Papst-Benedikt XVI, Regensburg, prepared the written text, which both participants approved for publication as "Der Wille der Väter. Geist und Beschlüsse des 2. Vatikanischen Konzils," in Joseph Ratzinger, *Zur Lehre des Zweiten Vatikanischen Konzils*, Joseph Ratzinger Gesammelte Schriften, vol. 7/2 (Freiburg: Herder, 2012), 1091–1105, 1234.

2. Maurice Gilbert, SJ, *The Pontifical Biblical Institute: A Century of History (1909–2009)* (Roma: Editrice Pontificio Istituto Biblico, 2009), 87. Bea published Latin texts for the students of his courses on the Pentateuch (1928, revised 1935), on biblical inspiration (1930, revised 1935), and on Daniel and other apocalyptical Old Testament books (1933, revised 1937).

3. Klaus Unterburger, ed., *Gefahren, die der Kirche drohen. Eine Denkschrift des Jesuiten Augustinus Bea aus dem Jahre 1926 über den deutschen Katholizismus* (Regensburg: Pustet, 2011). This publication, in Bea's original Latin with an annotated German translation, is a fruit of the recent opening of Vatican Archives of the pontificate of Pope Pius XI (1922–39).

4. Étienne Fouilloux, biographer of Cardinal Tisserant, the President of the Biblical Commission, says that Bea and Vosté worked together closely on the text, adding that the cardinal presented its successive drafts to Pius XII and even called it "our encyclical." *Eugène Cardinal Tisserant (1884–1972)* (Paris: Desclée de Brouwer, 2010), 265–67.

5. I follow in this section Stjepan Schmidt's early article, "Il cardinal Bea: sua preparazione alla missione ecumenica," *Archivum Historiae Pontificiae* 16 (1978): 313–36.

6. On Bea as Roman protector of the Freiburg journal in the early 1950s, see John Connelly, *From Enemy to Brother: The Revolution in Catholic Teaching on the Jews* (Cambridge, MA: Harvard University Press, 2012), 65ff, 191, and 213–19 ("Vatican Censure and Support").

7. The first issue of the *Rundbrief* opened with a message from Jacques Maritain on combating anti-Semitism. Other early issues brought out an essay by Josef A. Jungmann on the heritage of the synagogue in Catholic worship, the theses of Jules Isaac on revising Catholic presentations of Jews, and Karl Thieme's exegesis of Rom 9–11, which highlighted points that

entered Vatican II's *Nostra Aetate* 4, e.g., that Jesus, Mary, and early Christians were Jews; that the Jews remain very dear to God; that God's gifts and calls are irrevocable; that Jewish-Christian dialogue is encouraged; and that anti-Semitism has to be deplored.

8. A new collaborative volume on pre–Vatican II renewal movements in relation to Vatican II's preparation in 1960–62 gives no attention to the pioneers of a radically new Christian-Jewish relationship. Gilles Routhier, Philippe J. Roy, and Karim Schelkens, eds., *La théologie catholique entre intransigeance et renouveau: La réception des mouvements préconciliaires à Vatican II* (Louvain-la-Neuve/Leuven: College Erasme/Universiteitsbibliotheek, 2011).

9. On Jaeger's ecumenical action in the 1950s, see Wolfgang Thönissen, "Konsolidieruing und Institutionalizierung der Ökumene. Die Aktivitäten des Paderborner Erzbischofs Lorenz Jaeger in den fünfziger Jahren des 20. Jahrhunderts," in *Die Entdeckung der Ökumene. Zur Beteiligung der katholischen Kirche an der ökumenischen Bewegung*, ed. Jörg Ernesti and Wolfgang Thönissen (Paderborn/Frankfurt: BonifatiusLembeck, 2008), 158–76.

10. On the Bea-Jaeger correspondence, see Heinrich Bacht, "Kardinal Bea: Wegbereiter der Einheit," *Catholica* 35 (1981): 173–88; and Jerome-Michael Vereb, CP, *"Because He Was a German!" Cardinal Bea and the Origins of Roman Catholic Engagement in the Ecumenical Movement* (Grand Rapids: Eerdmans, 2006), 145–75.

11. The early work of the *Arbeitskreis* is mirrored in the topics of papers delivered at its meetings at which a Catholic and a Lutheran theologian treated the same subject. See the list for 1946–61, in Edmund Schlink and Hermann Volk, eds., *Pro Veritate: Ein theologischer Dialog* (Münster/Kassel: Aschendorff/Johannes Stauda, 1963), 387–95. A thorough historical and theological study of the early work of the *Arbeitskreis* is by Barbara Schwahn, *Der Ökumenische Arbeitskreis evangelischer und katholischer Theologen von 1946 bis 1975* (Göttingen: Vandenhoeck & Ruprecht, 1996), which originated in Schwahn's dissertation directed by Wolfhart Pannenberg.

12. On Höfer's influence on Bea, see Vereb, *"Because He Was a German!"* 134–39.

13. On the Catholic Conference in itself and its role at the beginning of Unity Secretariat, see Pontifical Council for Promoting Christian Unity, *Information Service*, no. 101 (1999/II–III): 62–69. Peter De Mey treated the Conference in "Johannes Willebrands and the Catholic Conference for Ecumenical Questions (1952–1963)," in *The Ecumenical Legacy of Johannes Cardinal Willebrands (1909–2006)*, ed. Adelbert Denaux and Peter De Mey (Leuven: Peeters, 2012), 49–78, and in "Précurseur du Secréteriat pour l'unité: Le travail œcuménique de la 'Conférence catholique pour les questions œcuméniques,'" in Routhier et al., *La théologue catholique entre intransigeance et renouveau*, 271–308 (quite informative on ecumenical theology in the Conference's contributions).

14. Here I follow both Stjepan Schmidt, *Augustin Bea the Cardinal of Unity* (New Rochelle, NY: New City Press, 1992), 293–96; and Vereb, *"Because He Was a German!"* 155–56.

15. Here Bea shows appropriation of a topic taken up by Willebrands's Catholic Conference for study in tandem with the World Council of Churches in 1958–59. One outcome was Yves Congar's "La seigneurie du Christ sur l'église et sur le monde," for a proposed 1959 joint discussion, which Congar published later in *Jesus-Christ, notre Mediateur, notre Seigneur* (Paris: Cerf, 1965), 187–247.

16. Klaus Wittstadt presented the early 1960 triangular interactions of Archbishop Jaeger, Pope John, and Bea his in "Die Verdienste des Paderborner Erzbischof Lorenz Jaeger um die Errichting des Einheitssekretariats," (originally 1988), in the essay collection, *Aus der Dynamik des Geistes. Aspekte der Kirchen- und Theologiegeschichte des 20. Jahrhunderts*, ed. Wolfgang Weiß (Würzburg: Echter Verlag, 2004), 308–28. Vereb related it more recently in *"Because He Was a German!"* 161–203.

17. "Cardinal Bea's Unity Secretariat: Engine of Renewal and Reform at Vatican II," *Ecumenical Trends* 41 (December 2012): 161–65, at 162–63, where I draw on Mauro Velati's marvelous presentation in *Dialogo e rinnovamento: Verbali e testi del segretariato per l'unità nella preparazione del concilio Vaticano II (1960–1962)* (Bologna: Il Mulino, 2011). I presented Velati's work more fully in "Still More Light on Vatican Council II," *Catholic Historical Review* 98 (2012): 476–502, at 477–89. I feature the Secretariat's draft text, *De Verbo Dei: Schema Decreti Pastoralis*, in "Scripture Reading Urged *vehementer* (DV, no. 25):

Background and Development," *Theological Studies* 74 (2013): 555–80, at 560–64, giving the draft in English at 573–77.

18. See Velati, *Dialogo e rinnovamento*, 104–10 (rosters) and 173–74 (members of subcommissions). I tell of the membership and subcommissions in "Still More Light," 478–81.

19. On its final days of work, June 19–20, 1962, the Central Preparatory Commission discussed the Secretariat's draft texts on religious liberty and on Catholic ecumenism, treating both in tandem with chapters of the Theological Commission's *De ecclesia*, i.e., chapter 9 on Church/state relations and chapter 11 on ecumenism. Finally, the Central Commission took up and approved for submission to the Council the Secretariat's draft texts on prayer for the unity of Christians and on the word of God.

20. Augustine Bea, "Archbishop Fisher's visit to Pope John XXIII," in *The Unity of Christians* (London: Geoffrey Chapman & The Catholic Book Club, 1963), 64–72, 66. The original Italian text, "A proposito della visita di S. G. il dott. G. Fisher," came out in *La Civiltà Cattolica* 4, no. 111 (1960): 561–68. Bea also argued that on baptism *Mediator Dei* expressed St. Paul's teaching in 1 Cor 12:13 and Gal 3:26ff.

21. Augustine Bea, "The Obstacles to Christian Unity," in *The Unity of Christians*, 38–46. Originally, "Gli ostacoli all'unione dei cristiani," *Messaggero del Sacro Cuore* 96 (1960): 577–86. Bea added as further Pauline evidence Eph 1:5ff.

22. Augustine Bea, "The Catholic Attitude towards the Problem, in *The Unity of Christians*, 38–46. Originally, "Il cattolico di fronte al problema dell'unione dei cristiani," in *La Civiltà Cattolica* 1, no. 112 (1961): 113–29.

23. Tromp's notations on Bea's position began October 1, 1960, and continued in early 1961. *Konzilstagebuch Sebastian Tromp SJ*, ed. Alexanda von Teuffenbach, vol. 1 (1960–62) (Roma: Editrice Pontificia Università Gregoriana, 2006), 85, 159, 161, 163, 175–77, and 858–62 (the February 2, 1961, memo on Bea's idea and Tromp's materials for refuting it).

24. See Emmanuel Lanne, "La contribution du cardinal Bea à la question du baptême e l'unité des chrétiens," in *Irenikon* 55 (1982): 471–99.

25. "Cardinal Bea's Unity Secretariat," 161–65, at 162–63.

26. *Acta et Documenta Concilio Oecumenico Vaticano II apparando*, series 2 (Praeparatoria), 2/1, 541–48, which is Bea's

intervention on *De fontibus,* November 10, 1961. In voting on the schema, fifty-five members indicated that Bea's points should be taken into account in revising the text.

27. *Acta Synodalia Sacrosancti Concilii Oecumenici Vaticani II,* 6 vols. in 26 parts (Vatican City: Typis Polyglottis Vaticanis, 1970–91), vol. 6, pt. 1:200–4. Cardinal Giuseppe Siri of Genoa made critical remarks on the Bea proposal in the second meeting, on October 19, but this did not stop two members of the Secretariat, Cardinals Suenens and Montini, from proposing further overall programs of the Council in subsequent meetings.

28. The text is in *Acta Synodalia,* 1, 3:14–26. The history of its genesis in the Preparatory Theological Commission has been set forth by Karim Schelkens in *Catholic Theology of Revelation on the Eve of Vatican II. A Redaction History of the Schema* De fontibus revelationis *(1960–1962)* (Leiden: Brill, 2010).

29. The text censured any effort to "extenuate" the nature of biblical inspiration (*"Ecclesia omnino reprobat"* in no. 8), certain denials of the historical truth of Gospel narratives of the deeds of Jesus (*"Synodus illos damnat errores"* in no. 21), and attributions to the evangelist or the community of the words given as from Jesus in the Gospels' texts (*"Synodus errores damnat"* in no. 22).

30. *Acta Synodalia,* 1, 3: 34 (Frings), 41 (Léger), 43–44 (Alfrink), 49 (Bea), and 55–59 (Manek and Soegijapranata, from Indonesia).

31. See my study, "Pieter Smulders and *Dei Verbum:* 2. On *De fontibus revelationis* during Vatican II's First Period, 1962," *Gregorianum* 82 (2001): 559–93, at 564–66 on Smulders's visit to gain advice from Bea.

32. I present the Vatican II drama of 1962 more amply in "Vatican II Taking Hold of Its (and Pope John's) Council Goals, September 1962-May 1963," in *Josephinum Journal of Theology* 19 (2012): 172–86 (published September 2013).

10

Dennis M. Doyle

Otto Semmelroth, SJ, and the Ecclesiology of the "Church as Sacrament" at Vatican II

Otto Semmelroth was one of several Jesuits whose work was influential in the drafting of the documents of Vatican II.[1] He attended all four sessions of the Council and kept a journal of his Council-related activities during those years.[2] In October 1963 he was appointed *peritus* for Bishop Volk of Mainz and became a member of the Council's Theological Committee. He worked on the subcommittee that drafted *Dei Verbum*. He also worked on the subcommittee on the collegiality of bishops that was connected with several documents. Later, he served on the doctrinal subcommittee for *Gaudium et Spes*.[3]

What stands as Semmelroth's most important contribution to the Council is the impact that he had on *Lumen Gentium* ("Dogmatic Constitution on the Church") through his work on the concept of the Church as a sacrament. After an initial draft of *De ecclesia* was rejected on the floor of the Council in 1962, the concept of the Church as sacrament was introduced into the 1963 draft. On September 30, 1963, Cardinal Josef Frings on the floor of the Council requested on behalf of sixty-six German and Scandinavian fathers that more explicit emphasis be given to the Church as *Ursakrament*.[4] Even more extensively than the 1963 draft, the final 1964 *Lumen Gentium* reflects the use of the concept of the Church as sacrament as a major integrating theme and structuring element.

In the background of the introduction of the concept of the Church as sacrament into the 1963 draft as well as the petition presented by Frings stood Semmelroth's famous 1953 book, *Die Kirche als Ursakrament*. A French translation of *Die Kirche als Ursakrament* appeared in 1962, as well as a Spanish translation and a third printing of the German edition in 1963.[5] Semmelroth's work on the concept of Church as sacrament was also influential on *Lumen Gentium* in other ways in addition to his book. He worked directly on various drafts of what is known as the German Schema, a text that had a direct impact on the 1963 draft, including a prototype of the opening paragraph that introduced the theme of Church as sacrament. When the American *peritus* Joseph Fenton submitted a page to the Council's doctrinal commission challenging the idea of the Church as sacrament, he directly associated the idea with Semmelroth, and it was Semmelroth who wrote the response. Finally, Semmelroth wrote a significant number of commentaries on various parts of *Lumen Gentium* as well as on the document as a whole that focused on understanding the concept of the Church as a sacrament as it developed during course of the Council.

The testimony regarding Semmelroth's impact upon *Lumen Gentium* is striking. Josef Meyer zu Schlochtern assembles an impressive cast of witnesses: Matthäus Bernards said that Semmelroth had helped to bring about a breakthrough in the thought and expression of the sacramentality of the Church; Leonardo Boff spoke of the immeasurable significance (*unermeßlichen Bedeutung*) of *Die Kirche als Ursakrament* for *Lumen Gentium*; Wolfgang Beinert called its influence considerable (*erheblich*); Heinrich Döring named Semmelroth as being among the immediate trailblazers (*unmittelbaren Wegbereitern*) of the Council.[6] Günther Wassilowsky has since written of Semmelroth's "direction-setting" (*maßgeblich*) role in the development of the Council's ecclesiology.[7] He reports that "'the Idea of the Church as (*Ur-*) *Sakrament*' helped bring about a break-through like no other."[8]

This essay will demonstrate how Semmelroth's preconciliar work on the Church as sacrament connects with several ecclesiological themes that would later be developed in *Lumen Gentium*. These themes include the importance of a lay-inclusive Church, the universal call to holiness, the relationship between Mary and the Church, a Trinitarian ecclesial spirituality, and the use of sacrament as a fundamental category for organizing and interpreting a variety of images and concepts of the Church.[9]

First will come an attempt to take the measure of Semmelroth's significant impact on *Lumen Gentium* within the context of the myriad contributions made by a large number of theologians. His first book, *Urbild der Kirche*, will then be examined for how it anticipates his later work on the Church as sacrament, particularly as connected with a conceptual quest for a lay-inclusive Church. This will be followed by a study of *Die Kirche als Ursakrament*, his work that had the most direct impact on the ecclesiology of Vatican II. Then a brief consideration of Semmelroth's later preconciliar works will show how his focus on the personal-experiential dimensions of the Church became linked with the development of a sacramental ontology.

SITUATING SEMMELROTH'S CONTRIBUTIONS AMONG A HOST OF CONTRIBUTORS

Fr. Semmelroth was known and is still remembered as a humble and somewhat quiet man with a quick wit and a pleasant temperament whose own work was widely considered to be balanced and deeply solid. Although his name was the one most associated with the concept of the Church as sacrament at the time of the Council, he had not been working alone. He was neither the inventor of the concept, nor the only one involved in introducing the concept into the document on the Church, nor the only one contributing to the development of the concept as the drafting of the document continued. In his journal of the

Council, Semmelroth does not highlight his own specific contributions. He later denied that his book or his contributions had a determinative effect on *Lumen Gentium*, and in this way he seems to have been acknowledging the truth that there were dozens of experts who made contributions to the document, among them several individuals and groups who also had very significant influence. So many voices went into the various drafts and versions that lay behind the official drafts that it can be difficult even for the people involved to claim direct influence for any one particular point or direction. Reading Catholic theological literature of this period has left me with the impression that it was generally understood that the work of the Council was to be put forth in the name of the bishops and the pope representing the Church universal with the hope that the Holy Spirit would ultimately be recognized as having had the most decisive influence on the texts.

The concept of the Church as sacrament has a complex history. Semmelroth himself cites Henri de Lubac, Karl Rahner, Heinrich Stirnimann, and Thaddäus Soiron as background sources in *Die Kirche als Ursakrament*.[10] Achim Dittrich finds the basic concept of the Church as sacrament already expressed in Carl Feckes's 1934 book, *Das Mysterium der heiligen Kirche*.[11] Feckes himself most frequently cites Matthias J. Sheeben as his source of inspiration when he speaks of the sacred humanity of Jesus as the *Ur-sacrament* of salvation and of the Church as continuing the saving presence of Christ through its sacramental organization. The sacraments, he says, give entry into the sacramental world, and the sacramental world is the world of the Church.[12] At the time of Vatican II, those most identified with the concept of the Church as sacrament were Semmelroth, his fellow Jesuit Karl Rahner, and the Dominican Edward Schillebeeckx. Also closely associated with the concept were the Jesuits de Lubac and Pieter Smulders as well as the Dominican Yves Congar.

In November 1962, after the initial draft of *De ecclesia* had been rejected, Semmelroth and Rahner collaborated on a critique, *Animadversions criticae ad Schema De ecclesia*, that recommended using the concept of the Church as sacrament as the fundamental category for understanding the Church as representing the saving will of God, extending even to non-Christians. It is hard to say who originated which idea. One might speculate, however, that in these *Animadversions,* ideas associated with the Church as sacrament of the world with regard to the salvation of non-Christians, a position that later became known as "anony-mous Christianity," stem mainly from Rahner. The basic idea that the Church as *Ursakrament* signifies God's universal saving will could be found already in Semmelroth's 1953 book, as well as the claim that *Ursakrament* provides the most fundamental category for understanding the nature of the Church.[13] Semmelroth's reference to an unpublished manuscript of Rahner that would later appear in an early volume of *Schriften der Theologie*, however, signals the possibility that Rahner's influ-ence on the 1953 book may have already been significant.[14]

The concept of the Church as sacrament was directly intro-duced into the 1963 draft of *Lumen Gentium* through the German Schema, the first paragraph of which appears in *Lumen Gentium* in an edited fashion. This German Schema was one of many documents drawn upon by the Belgian theologian Gérard Philips in putting together the 1963 draft. The Schema was itself developed over a series of four versions to which Semmelroth contributed significantly, as did Rahner as well as several other German theologians. Semmelroth and Rahner were together part of a Catholic intellectual world in which there was much cross-influence. Bishop Herman Volk of Mainz, who would soon appoint Semmelroth a *peritus,* assembled a working group of theologians that included Jesuits Johannes Baptist Hirschmann and Alois Grillmeier, as well as Joseph Ratzinger, Michael Schmaus, and Rudolf Schnackenburg.

Semmelroth thus worked as a team player in helping to develop the concept of the Church as sacrament and in intro-ducing this concept into the text of *Lumen Gentium*. His most distinctive contribution was in producing *Die Kirche als Ursakrament* as a book-length, systematic development of the concept in relation to several key ecclesiological issues of the time. When, as previously mentioned, Cardinal Frings presented the petition of the German-speaking and Scandinavian theolo-gians requesting that more stress be placed upon the Church as

Ursakrament in the text of *Lumen Gentium*, the work of Otto Semmelroth stood recognizably in the background. Yves Congar, recounting this event in his journal of the Council, noted that "O. Semmelroth had first highlighted this expression in order to describe the Church."[15]

URBILD DER KIRCHE (1950)

Although Semmelroth does not explicitly call the Church a sacrament in this first book, *Urbild der Kirche: Organischer Aufbau des Mariengeheimnisses*,[16] he comes within a hair's breadth, clearly expressing the underlying theology. In an early passage, Semmelroth connects the ideas of type, symbol, and mystery with the sacramental life of the Church.[17] Yet both Mary's role as archetype and the Church as sacrament operate in support of what comes through as a yet more urgent theme. Read with hindsight against the background of the body of his later work, Semmelroth's first book appears to have as its main purpose the development of a fully lay-inclusive ecclesiology, emphasizing the importance of every Christian's reception of and response to God's gracious offer of salvation.[18] A lay-inclusive ecclesiology affirms the crucial importance of the hierarchy, but tends to stress its service to the laity's living out the faith in the context of the world. Other purposes of the book, in my judgment, function as secondary and in support of this main purpose.

In the immediate background of *Urbild der Kirche* stands Pius XII's pending 1950 declaration of the bodily assumption of Mary.[19] In order for a doctrine to be eligible to be formally declared in an infallible manner, it must be something taught, as the phrase goes, for the sake of our salvation. Semmelroth forcefully made the case for this connection. He argued that the deepest, most fundamental point in Mariology is that Mary is Archetype of the Church and that all other points of Marian doctrine and devotion, including her assumption, find their grounding in this point. What makes Mary the Archetype of the Church is her active role in the saving mystery of Christ and how her role parallels the call of every Christian to actively cooperate in their own salvation. For this reason, the doctrine of the assumption can be said to be taught for the sake of our salvation.

Semmelroth contrasts his own position with that of Carl Feckes, who held that the mother/bridal character of Mary, rather than Mary as *Urbild* of the Church, should be recognized as the most theologically grounding Marian concept. Feckes in this 1934 book had already claimed that Mary is the *Urbild* of the Church; that Christ is the sacrament of God and the Church the continuing presence of Christ; that a focus on the hierarchy should not obscure the Church as the bride, which includes all of the laity, and that a focus on individual salvation should complement rather than overshadow a focus on living out the sacramental life in this world.[20] Semmelroth argued that the various images of Mary, as the Second Eve, as the Mother of God, as the Bride who says yes, all take on their full meaning in connection with the doctrine of salvation as they are interrelated within the deeper category of Mary as Archetype of the Church. If, as Feckes held, Mary's bridal character is what is most fundamental, then it becomes hard to justify the doctrine of the assumption as being taught for the sake of our salvation. Mary as Archetype, in contrast, holds together various images and roles of Mary as integral to each other. Only by operating within such a framework can one make a case for an integral connection between the doctrine of the assumption and what is taught for the sake of our salvation. This use of Archetype as a meta-category that stands above and organizes other categories anticipates Semmelroth's later use of the concept of the Church as a sacrament.

For Semmelroth, the Church of which Mary is the Archetype is the Church of the laity. He highlights the distinction within the body of Christ between those who represent the head and those who represent the members. Mary is the Archetype of the Church of the members, of those who respond to the offer of God's grace. Mary exemplifies the Church as the bride of Christ, as the representative type of what it means for the Church to cooperate with the saving, sacramental work of Christ.

Semmelroth refers to the Church with its sacraments as a continuation of the sacramental event of Christ:

Since the Church lives within a world extended in time and space, Christ's work must be taken up in time and space. His sacrifice is one only....This one sacrifice must unfold within a Church growing in time and space into multiple single acts from the one sacramental event. The sacraments raise Christ's work from its historical and temporal setting to a supra-temporal level of mystery. At the same time they extend the work within the space-time confines of our own earthly existence.[21]

Semmelroth's main purpose here in applying sacramental theology to the Church is to emphasize the theme of receptive cooperation in the response of Mary as well as that of all Christians to God's offer of salvation. Just as sacraments require that the one who receives has a proper disposition and the intention of living in accordance with the grace received, so does one's fundamental participation in the life of the Church pose the same requirement.

For Semmelroth, being a Christian is something that should carry over into how one lives one's life in the world. Traditional Catholic sacramental theology already combined a strong affirmation of the objective reality of the grace being offered with significant attention to the disposition required of the subject receiving it. Semmelroth finds that Mary exemplifies the proper disposition to the point that she is the model of receptive cooperation:

The Church, the Bride of Christ, must confront Him as a personal figure and seize hold of the work fully accomplished by Him alone. Here Mary's function enters. She gives her consent to the approaching *Logos* because, redeemed and endowed with grace, she is able to do so. Because she gives her affirmation for the coming of the *Logos* and for Christ's Sacrifice, she has taken on the work of Christ and made its fruits of grace her own. These gifts are ours "through Christ's death alone." But Mary's cooperation with her own redemption is performed by her for herself, and through her as representative of the humanity which is to become the Church—"in the place of the entire human race." Mary, that is to say the Church, has become "disposed" for the reception of the Arch-sacrament, the Incarnate God and His sacrifice on the Cross. Because of this receptivity, or rather through it, "the fullness of all blessings has been deposited in her," that is to say, the *pleroma* that fills the Church.[22]

Semmelroth suggests that in his emphasis on reception and cooperation he is building upon *Mystici Corporis Christi*, a document that he refers to frequently. He pays special attention to the claim in no. 12 that "through the Church every man performs a work of collaboration with Christ in dispensing the graces of Redemption." Semmelroth adds, "Therefore they are 'co-redeemers.'"[23] Semmelroth will drop the controversial term *co-redeemers* in his later work. The underlying meaning of the free response of human beings to the offer of God's grace and their continuing cooperation, however, will remain a key theme in Semmelroth's theology of the laity and of the Church as sacrament. In *Urbild der Kirche*, Semmelroth used sacramental theology to stress that redemption has two phases, the pure gift accomplished and given by Christ, and the human embrace and working out of that gift. In *Die Kirche als Ursakrament*, this twofold characteristic will be applied directly and explicitly to Christ and the Church in their sacramental natures.

DIE KIRCHE ALS URSAKRAMENT (1953)

The title of Semmelroth's *Die Kirche als Ursakrament* announces clearly that he will no longer hesitate to call the Church itself a sacrament. He retains from his first book both the theme of Mary as Archetype of the Church and the theme of the sacramental nature of the Church, but the leading and supporting roles are reversed. Here the theme of the Church as sacrament takes front stage. Semmelroth tells his readers in a foreword that he had previously connected the parallel living realities of the consciousness of the Church (*Kirchenbe-wusstsein*) with Marian thought in order to bring both together in the concept of Mary as the Archetype of the Church. He finds, however, that the awareness of the mystery of the Church in his time is so tightly connected with the objective practice of the liturgy and the sacraments that he will here put forth a study of the sacramental being of the Church. He will show, however, that the Marian as well as the sacramental approaches, along with the consciousness of the Church, represent together key points of religious interest of the then-present decade, and that these three things are intrinsically connected.[24]

In other words, Semmelroth finds that the concept of the Church as sacrament adds to his previous work an explicit way of bringing together the objective and the subjective. He takes care to note that the concept underlying the Church as sacrament, though not the label, can be found in *Mystici Corporis Christi*,[25] and that an emphasis on the sacramental dimensions will guard against any naturalistic or mystical misinterpretations. A naturalistic misinterpretation is one that focuses exclusively on the visible elements of the Church, a mystical misinterpretation on the invisible elements. Semmelroth notes that each of these errors make ecumenical efforts appear to be unimportant. In other words, if the Church is only visible, then ecumenism is merely the return of schismatics and heretics to the Catholic fold. If the Church is only invisible, then all belong already to the mystical body of Christ. In response to these potential errors, Semmelroth draws upon a developing theological view that sees in Christ the sacrament of God and in the Church the sacrament of Christ. The concept of the Church as sacrament brings together the invisible and the visible elements. The Church as the mystical body of Christ is not to be understood in a purely mystical way, but rather in a way that the invisible, mystical dimensions are expressed and made present and effective in and through the visible, social dimensions. The human organization of the social body of the Church simultaneously signifies and contains the mystical body of Christ.

As in *Urbild der Kirche*, a central, perhaps *the* central, goal of *Die Kirche als Ursakrament* is establishing the theological priority of a lay-inclusive Church. Semmelroth works toward this goal in a way that anticipates what *Lumen Gentium* will label "the universal call to holiness."[26] He laments that the word *Church* seems most often to be used to refer to the Church of offices in a way that implies that the laity do not fully belong:

> From a very fundamental standpoint the community is the most important element among the complex collective elements of the "Church." For the conse-crated offices are created for the sake of the commu-nity. The Church has its significance in this, that it is the visibly unfolding saving will, God's economy of salvation for human beings. For this reason every ele-ment in this human community connected with sal-vation and with the Church as led to Christ by the pure virgin stands in the forefront. That, however, is the community to the extent that it is objectively becoming Christian as it stands in a polar relation-ship with those in the offices. For this reason, in fact, when one says "Church," it should elicit in the con-sciousness of the speaker much more the community as bride, whereas today for most people it is the reverse: they mean, when they say "Church," first always the official Church to which they themselves do not belong. For this reason, then, it happens that to them the Church has become a strange, perhaps downright uncomfortable quantity, not, however, that reality in which they themselves are bound up with their own salvation. (170)

When Semmelroth speaks of the Church as "bride," he means the Church of the laity, the people of God. In 1953, Semmelroth did not use the image of the people of God in a way that included both the hierarchy and the laity. His position is in its own way very progressive, though, in that he identified the laity, understood as the people of God, as the more important element in the Church with the hierarchy in their service. He used a different concept, that of the total Christ, to put forth a representation of the Church that includes all members, both lay and clerical. He quoted St. Augustine: "The total Christ is the head and the body: The head, the only-begotten Son of God, his body, the Church: Bridegroom and Bride, two in one flesh."[27]

Semmelroth saw a sacramental polarity in the way that the hierarchy stands in the place of Christ, the head and the Bridegroom, whereas the laity represents the body and the bride, as typified in Mary (181).[28] He used this polarity as a way of emphasizing simultaneously the objective and subjective dimensions of the Church as sacrament. He drew upon a line in Pius XII's *Mediator Dei* to explain how the distinctive role of the hierarchy helps to guarantee that one who participates in the sacramental life of the Church will truly come into contact, in an objective manner, with the saving work of Christ on the cross (175–76). In contrast with *Lumen Gentium*, he applied the threefold designation of Christ's ministry as priest, prophet, and king only to the hierarchy, not to the entire people of God (196). Through his application of the concept of sacrament, however, he expressed other positions that do directly anticipate *Lumen Gentium*.

The sacramental polarity between the hierarchy and the laity opened up the possibility for Semmelroth to explore more fully the lay side of the equation. He stressed how the role of the hierarchy and the role of the laity are both essential in the living out of the sacrament that is the Church. He referred to the laity as belonging to a community grounded in baptism and confirmation (172) and as having a mission that flows from their baptism and confirmation (234). He described the real offering that the laity makes in the consecration of the Eucharist (196). He spoke of Catholic Action and of how the laity, in connection with the hierarchy, shares in the apostolic mission of the Church (224). And he explained how the laity live out their mission in the Church in the various spheres of family, business, culture, and politics in ways that are not directly mediated through the Church's offices (233).

Semmelroth thus developed many progressive positions while operating with this strong distinction between, on the one hand, the Church of hierarchical offices, and, on the other hand, this Church of the laity, also known as the people of God and as the Church typified in Mary. Although the hierarchy stands as the guarantee of the objective reality of God's gift of grace, Semmelroth stressed even more that grace is not an object and that the encounter with God's revelation is personal. This personalist-experiential theme concerning revelation as encounter will later surface in a significant way not only in *Lumen Gentium* but also in *Dei Verbum*, the "Constitution on Divine Revelation" (for which Semmelroth served on the composing subcommission).[29] Semmelroth argued that grace is Christ himself insofar as he has brought human beings into his living community. Receiving grace is thus being and living in Christ. In this regard, the Church as the community of the saved is the community living with Christ in the unity of his mystical body. The entire Church is the forward living of Christ (199).

Yet one more important way in which Semmelroth built off the sacramental polarity of the hierarchy and the laity is in his extensive exploration of the Church as proceeding from the planning and execution of the Trinity as well as being itself the image of the Trinity. Semmelroth drew upon the Last Supper discourse in John's Gospel to recall God's sending of the Son: "As the Father has sent me, so I send you" (John 20:21). The Holy Spirit is the love between the Father and the Son. Semmelroth first applied this threefold dynamic to marriage, in which the love between the man and the woman make as it were a third person expressing the unity between them (212–14; 221). The laity is sent into the world in a way that reflects how the Son is sent into the world. In addition to the two elements in polar tension, there is furthermore the relationship of love between them (221).[30] Semmelroth also discussed a Marian form of the reception of one's mission based on Mary's response to Gabriel that has its own immediacy (230–31). This reception of mission stands alongside the form given to the apostles, and can be applied to the manner in which the laity live out their mission in the world.

This trinitarian approach to the Church maintains the strong personalist-experiential stress on divine revelation. There is a focus on how Christians become adopted children of God (207) who, like the Son, carry out a mission to transform the world (233). This approach thereby connects the sign element of the Church as sacrament with participation in the life of the Trinity and the instrumental element with the moral living out of the sign in the world. This secular world itself belongs to God and possesses a kind of autonomy. It is a place in which Christians, empowered by their baptism and confirmation, can encounter God in ways that are not directly mediated through the official Church. Invisible grace receives visible embodiment in the manner in which Christians live their lives in the world.

Semmelroth ended this book with a reflection on a Marian passage near the end of *Mystici Corporis Christi*. It is almost as though he were saying that, after all, *Die Kirche als Ursakrament* is but a theological meditation that reflects upon the teachings already contained in the encyclical. And, indeed, *Mystici Corporis Christi* did promote an ecclesiological personalism over against a juridical reductionism. It did itself present the Church as the total Christ (67) and spoke of all Church members sharing in the Church's mission, along with a special mention of Catholic Action (98). It explicitly named and addressed the errors of naturalism (along with rationalism) and mysticism (9). Without applying the term *sacrament* directly to Christ or the Church, it did express the way in which the Church as the body of Christ and the Church as a social institution are elements of one complex reality (64–65). The final passages presented Mary as a type of the Church and stress her role in the plan of salvation (110–11).

For Semmelroth, naming the Church a sacrament enabled him to acknowledge the objective reality of God's gift of grace while giving serious emphasis to the free human embrace of this grace and the need for ongoing cooperation. He granted primary ecclesial status to the sacramental nature of Christian life lived out in the world as an encounter with the God who reveals and saves. The laity does not represent a theological afterthought to be appended to a Church that is centered in the hierarchy. In Semmelroth's vision, the Church itself should be recognized as fully lay inclusive. It is a Marian Church, the people of God, a Church that gives birth to hierarchical offices and is served by them.

In the chart that follows, some of the visible/invisible sacramental relationships may seem repetitious. The differences can be subtle, but I think they are important for capturing the implications of specific points made by Semmelroth.

Die Kirche als Ursakrament 1953	
INVISIBLE	**VISIBLE**
Mystical body of Christ	Church as a social body
Clergy as head of mystical body (representing Christ the head)	Laity as other members of the mystical body
Christ as Bridegroom	Mary/Church as bride
Clergy as Bridegroom	Laity as bride
Christ as sent by Father	Laity as sent by clergy (as sacramental representatives of Christ)
Mary saying yes to God/ incarnation	Laity saying yes to God
God to be encountered in the world	Laity as those who have been empowered through baptism and confirmation

BETWEEN *URSAKRAMENT* AND VATICAN II

Semmelroth wrote many books and articles between the time of *Die Kirche als Ursakrament* and Vatican II. They all contribute in some way to his mission to awaken a lay-inclusive Church to discern and take up its call to live out the gospel in the world of the twentieth century. One book explored the false dichotomy found in the choice between devotion to Christ or devotion to Mary by explaining how correct Marian devotion is always connected with the mystery of salvation through Christ.[31] Another book focused on the existential encounter with God while bringing the discussion around to Christ, the Church, and the sacraments.[32] Yet another book considered the meaning of the offices in the Church, their connections with word and sacrament, their crucial role in the Church, their existential dimensions, and finally their connections with apostolic succession.[33] The following book offered an extensive theological and pastoral reflection on the Church in its many dimensions.[34] Yet another book spent the second half discussing the meaning of each of the seven sacraments after spending the first half explaining the meaning of the Church as sacrament and the saving work of the Church through word and sacrament.[35] Still another book countered the impersonalism of the modern world with an exploration of how the natural world takes on its meaning and purpose when understood as God's creation in which the human person receives a call, ultimately from Christ.[36] These books all continued Semmelroth's interest in developing a lay-inclusive ecclesiology focused on the Church as sacrament and including the personal experience of and encounter with God.

In a 1959 article, Semmelroth summed up well his overall approach to the Church as sacrament, drawing upon three basic images of the Church: *people of God; body of Christ; bride of Christ*.[37] He spoke about the category of the Church as *Ursakrament* in a way that hearkened back to what he had earlier claimed about the category of Mary as Archetype of the Church. The Church as *Ursakrament* is not just one concept of the Church among others, but rather consciousness of the supernatural ontology that expresses itself through the most commonly used predications about the Church in revelation. All images and concepts of the Church convey in some way that what is invisible is expressed through what is visible, bringing together the Church's "meta-empirical-divine interior" with its "social-human-outward realization."

Grasping the reality of the Church as *Ursakrament* gives one a framework for (1) addressing an issue that cannot be resolved with the use of a particular image and (2) reconciling images that could otherwise appear incompatible. As an example of the problem of irresolvable issues, Semmelroth discussed how the mystical body of Christ is identical with the visible

Catholic Church to which it is necessary to belong in order to be saved, and yet it is also true that there are righteous people outside of the visible Church. He suggested that the mystical body of Christ cannot in itself resolve this difficulty, and that a more appropriate image should be used in this case. What justifies this approach is an understanding that, since the Church is *Ursakrament*, no one image can fully express or exhaust its mystery. If one image creates irresolvable difficulties on the literal level, other images can be used in its place.

As an example of hard-to-reconcile images, Semmelroth points to the difficulty of thinking of the *people of God* and the *mystical body of Christ* as expressing the same reality. How can the same thing be both a *people* and a *body*? Semmelroth again uses the concept of the Church as *Ursakrament* as the solution, but in a very specific way. In the realization of a sacrament there are three elements: the visible sign, the saving power of the sign, and the human disposition. All three images being discussed—*people of God, body of Christ, bride of Christ*—in themselves entail the expression of divine mystery through visible signs, but each one has extra value in relation to one of the elements of a sacrament. Semmelroth explains that *people of God* is best suited for focusing on the visible sign; the *body of Christ* is best suited for focusing on the saving power of the sign; and the *bride of Christ* is best suited for focusing on the element of human disposition.[38] These images are compatible insofar as they are all express important aspects of the sacramental nature of the Church, yet none of them offers anything like full comprehension of what remains an inexhaustible mystery.

What finally holds these images together is not just another image or concept, but a type of consciousness, a consciousness of a supernatural ontology. It is a consciousness of how the mystery of the invisible, transcendent God is made manifest sacramentally through visible things in this world, primarily through the saving work of Christ. The personalist-experiential dimensions of the Church as *Ursakrament* had now come fully to the fore.

CONCLUSION

Two areas remain to be explored further. First, the concept of the Church as sacrament was opposed at the Council by a group of traditionalists. Another group accepted the Church as sacrament but wanted it to play a secondary, supporting role to the leading concept of the Church as a communion. How did the Church as sacrament fare in the midst of its opponents and its moderators? Second, the Church as sacrament was developed much further in *Lumen Gentium* between the drafts of 1963 and 1964. Semmelroth was involved in the drafting, in some ways as a contributor but even more so as a learner and later as a commentator. How did the Church as sacrament fare as the Council progressed? These areas will be the subject of further essays.

This essay has focused on the preconciliar work of Semmelroth on the Church as sacrament that made such a significant impact on the ecclesiology of Vatican II, especially in the transition from the first draft of *De ecclesia* to the 1963 draft of what came to be called *Lumen Gentium*. The Church as sacrament was introduced in the very first passage of the 1963 draft such that it was linked with the concept of the Church as a mystery. The people of God as linked with the laity became a chapter, as did the universal call to holiness. Among several important contributors, including especially Karl Rahner, when it came to the introduction of the Church as sacrament to the 1963 draft as well as to the decision to place yet more emphasis upon the concept during the final year of drafting, it was Otto Semmelroth, SJ, who stood the tallest.

Notes

1. I am grateful to the *Deutscher Akademischer Austausch Dienst* for its generous funding of six months of teaching and study in 2012–13 at the University of Augsburg, where I completed the bulk of the research for this essay.
2. "Otto Semmelroth, SJ, *Tagebuch des II: Vatikanischen Konzil*" is being prepared for publication. I accessed a photocopy of the *Tagebuch* in the Vatican II Archive at KU Leuven. Hereinafter, referred to as TBOS. My thanks to Peter De Mey and

Dries Bosschaert for their help with my archival work. In addition to TBOS, see also Santiago Madrigal Terrazas, "El Vaticano II en el Diario Conciliar de Otto Semmelroth," *Estudios Eclesiásticos* 87 (2012): 105–64.

3. Semmelroth's participation in working groups at the Council can be traced through using the indices of the *History of Vatican II*, ed. Giuseppe Alberigo, trans. Joseph A. Komonchak, 5 vols. (Maryknoll, NY: 1995–2005). Günther Wassilowsky traces through Semelroth's contributions specifically in relation to *Lumen Gentium*. See *Universales Heilssakrament Kirche: Karl Rahner's Beitrag zur Ekklesiologie des II. Vatikanums* (Innsbruck: Tyrolia-Verlag, 2001).

4. See also Alberigo and Komonchak, *History of Vatican II*, 3:44.

5. *L'église, sacrement de la redemption*, trans. Germain Varin (Paris: Éditions Saint-Paul, 1962); *La Iglesia como sacramento original*, vol. 79 of *Colección Prisma*, trans. Victor Bazterrica (San Sebastian: Dinor, 1963).

6. The following four references are found in Josef Meyer zu Schloctern, *Sakrament Kirche: Wirken Gottes im Handeln der Menschen* (Freiburg: Herder, 1992), 121; Matthäus Bernards, "Zur Lehre von der Kirche als Sakrament," in *Münchner Theologische Zeitschrift* 20 (1969): 29–54, at 35; Leonardo Boff, *Die Kirche als Sakrament im Horizont der Welterfahrung: Versuch einer struktur-funktionalistischen Grundlegen der Kirche in Anschluß an das II. Vatikanische Konzil* (Paderborn: Bonifacius Druckerei, 1972), 344; Wolfgang Beinert, "Die Sakramentalität der Kirche im Theologische Gespräch," in *Theologische Berichte 9*, ed. Josef Pfammater and Franz Furger (Zürich: Einsiedeln, 1980), 13–66, at 27; Heinrich Döring, *Grundriß der Ekklesiologie: Zentrale Aspekte des katholischen Selbstverständnisses und ihre ökumenische Relevanz* (Darmstadt: Wissenschaftliche Buchgesellschaft, 1986), 103.

7. Wassilowsky, *Universales Heilssakrament*, 170.

8. Günther Wassilowsky, "Otto Semmelroth," in *Personenlexikon zum Zweiten Vatikanischen Konzil*, ed. Michael Quisinsky and Peter Walter (Freiburg: Herder, 2012), 250–51.

9. This essay is the first part of a larger study that connects the work of Semmelroth on the Church as sacrament with Vatican II. I intend to write a second article focusing on understanding the Church as sacrament in tension both with anti-

modernists and with those who favor a dominant focus on the Church as a communion. I plan yet a third article focusing on Semmelroth's experience and interpretation of how the Church as sacrament developed further between the 1963 draft and the final document, *Lumen Gentium*.

10. Semmelroth cites de Lubac, Rahner, Stirnimann, and Soiron respectively on pp. 38, 43, 45, and 45. See Henri de Lubac, *Meditation sur L'Eglise* (Paris: Seuil, 1953), 157; Heinrich Stirnimann, "Die Kirche und der Geist Christi," *Divus Thomas* (1953): 16; Karl Rahner, *Sacramentum radicale: De paenitentia tractatus historico-dogmaticus* (Innsbruck 1952) as a manuscript; Thaddäus Soiron, *Der Sakramental Mensch* (Freiburg: Herder Verlag, 1946), 4ff. De Lubac had discussed the Church as sacrament in *Catholicisme: Les aspects sociaux du dogme* (Paris, Cerf, 1938). Semmelroth also cites a line from Augustine: "There is no other sacrament of God except Christ" [my translation], cited in *Ursakrament*, 102; 239n81 (Ep. 187, n. 34–ML 38, 835).

11. Achim Dittrich, *Mater Ecclesiae: Geschichte und Bedeutung eines umstrittenen Marientitels* (Würzburg: Echter Verlag, 2009), 745.

12. Carl Feckes, *Das Mysterium der heiligen Kirche* (Paderborn: Ferdinand Schöningh, 1934), 93–102.

13. As quoted earlier: "The Church has its significance in this, that it is the visibly unfolding saving will, God's economy of salvation for human beings." Semmelroth, *Ursakrament*, 170.

14. Semmelroth cites Rahner's use of the term *root-sacrament (Wurzelsakrament)* in *Die Kirche als Ursakrament*, 45n35 (p. 46 in the 1953 edition).The note itself on p. 238 reads, "Sacramentum radicale. K. Rahner S.J., De paenitentia tractatus historico-dogmaticus. Innsbruck 1952 (als Manuskript vervielfältigt). 411."

15. Yves Congar, *My Journal of the Council*, trans. Mary John Ronayne and Mary Cecily Boulding (Collegeville, MN: Liturgical Press, 2012 [French orig. 2002]), 322n4.

16. Otto Semmelroth, *Urbild der Kirche: Organischer Aufbau des Mariengeheimnisses* (Würzburg: Echter-Verlag, 1950). English: *Mary: Archetype of the Church* (New York: Sheed & Ward, 1963). Meyer zu Schloctern's *Sakrament Kirche* devotes an entire and quite helpful chapter to Semmelroth, but he begins with the 1953 *Die Kirche als Ursakrament* and does not include Semmelroth's Mariology. That *Urbild der Kirche* anticipates some

of the positions in *Die Kirche als Ursakrament* might be simply an interesting side point if it were not for the important connections between Mariology and the Church as sacrament found in the text of *Lumen Gentium* as well as in the commentaries by Semmelroth.

17. Semmelroth, *Urbild der Kirche*, 24. In the 1963 English translation, Semmelroth inserts here an explanatory note to his 1953 *Die Kirche als Ursakrament* (see p. 31 of *Mary: Archetype*), thus confirming my claim that the theme if not the explicit phrase is already present in the 1950 book. This is one of only two substantive changes I have found between the German and the English editions, the other being referred to in the note to *Munificentissimus Deus* below.

18. Many theologians of the time were stressing some type of lay-inclusive ecclesiology, including Romano Guardini, who staunchly defended the mystical body of Christ as the reigning image of the Church, and Feckes, Grosche, and Koster, who challenged it. On Guardini, see Robert Krieg, *Romano Guardini: A Precursor of Vatican II* (Notre Dame, IN: University of Notre Dame Press, 1997). Yves Congar's 1950 *Vraie et fausse réforme dans l'Église*, appearing the same year as *Urbild*, also promotes a lay-inclusive approach.

19. Pius XII, *Munificentissimus Deus*, November 1, 1950. In the original 1950 *Urbild der Kirche*, 105, Semmelroth speaks of the doctrine as not yet being defined as dogma. He refers to the papal definition in the 1963 *Mary: Archetype*, 161.

20. Feckes, *Das Mysterium*. These thematic points are made throughout the text.

21. Semmelroth, *Mary: Archetype*, 84 (*Urbild der Kirche*, 57).

22. Ibid., 85 (57–58).

23. Ibid., 82 (56). The English translation mistakenly includes the word *co-redeemers* as part of the quote from *Mystici Corporis*. In the original German Semmelroth adds *Miterlöser* (co-redeemers) as an explanatory term not to be taken as quoted from the text.

24. Semmelroth, *Ursakrament*, 7–8 (same in 1963 edition.)

25. Ibid., 29 (p. 30 in 1963 edition).

26. The theme of the universal call to holiness goes hand in hand with the theme of the lay-inclusive Church, and in varying terminologies and with different nuances was promoted by many theologians, including Guardini, Feckes, Grosche, Koster,

and Congar. See Robert Grosche, *Pilgernde Kirche* (Freiburg im Breisgau: Herder, 1938); also M. D. Koster, *Ekklesiologie im Werden* (Paderborn: Verlag der Bonifacius Druckerei, Mainz, 1940).

27. Semmelroth, *Ursakrament*, 205. Semmelroth's citation of Augustine reads, *Contra Donat. Ep.*, cap. 4, n. 7–ML 43, 395. This concept of the "total Christ" is not unique to Semmelroth, and is today associated with the preconciliar work of Congar.

28. Semmelroth is still stressing Mary's connection with the plan of redemption, though now without his naming of Mary analogously as coredeemer and as comediator. He was probably influenced by the well-known essay of Karl Rahner in which he argued against the naming of Mary as coredeemer, though Semmelroth did not cite it. See Rahner, "Probleme Heutiger Mariologie," in *Aus der Theologie der Zeit: Herausgeben im Auftrag der Theologischen Fakultät München von Gottlieb Söhngen* (Regensburg: Gregorius-Verlag, 1948), 85–113.

29. Alberigo and Komonchak, *History of Vatican II*, 3:374. Richard R. Gaillardetz brings out the personalist connection between *Lumen Gentium* and *Dei Verbum* in *By What Authority: A Primer on Scripture, the Magisterium, and the Sense of the Faithful* (Collegeville, MN: Liturgical Press, 2003), 43–45; see also *Teaching with Authority: A Theology of the Magisterium of the Church* (Collegeville, MN: Liturgical Press, 1997), 69–76.

30. In one regard, the hierarchy is to the laity as the bridegroom is to the bride. In another regard, the laity is sent into the world as the Son has been sent by the Father.

31. Otto Semmelroth, *Maria oder Christus* (Frankfurt: Josef Knecht, 1954).

32. Otto Semmelroth, *Gott und Mensch in Begegnung* (Frankfurt: Josef Knecht, 1956).

33. Otto Semmelroth, *Das Geistliche Amt* (Frankfurt: Josef Knecht, 1957).

34. Otto Semmelroth, *Ich Glaube an der Kirche* (Dusseldorf: Patmos-Verlag, 1959).

35. Otto Semmelroth, *Vom Sinn der Sakramente* (Frankfurt: Josef Knecht, 1960).

36. Otto Semmelroth, *Die Welt als Schöpfung* (Frankfurt: Josef Knecht, 1962).

37. Otto Semmelroth, "Um die Einheit des Kirchenbegriffs," 319–35, in *Fragen der Theologie Heute*, eds. Johannes Feiner et al. (Einsiedeln: Benziger Verlag, 1959).

38. Semmelroth, "Um die Einheit," 328–34.

11

Susan K. Wood, SCL

Henri de Lubac and the Church-World Relationship in *Gaudium et Spes*

The problem of the Church-world relationship is at the very center of the conciliar document *Gaudium et Spes.* Known in the English-speaking world as "The Pastoral Constitution on the Church in the Modern World," the original Latin title is actually *Constitutio pastoralis de ecclesia in mundo huius temporis,* that is, the "Pastoral constitution on the church in the world of this time" or as Norman Tanner translates it, "the church in the world of today."[1] Thus the focus is not a treatise on the Church in relation to modernity as such or a document on the general or universal nature of the Church abstracted from the world, but rather a pastoral response to the contemporary situation of the Church in a particular time and place. The preposition *in* emphasizes the existential contextualization of both the document and the Church. The Church is *in* the world. The document is really the Council addressing the whole of humanity about how it understands the presence and function of the Church in the world of today (*GS* 2).

This essay examines the contributions, interpretations, and response of one Jesuit theologian, Henri de Lubac, to the Church-world relationship as it was developed and finally promulgated in the pastoral constitution. However, since the Council did not

set out to explicate this relationship theologically or systemati-
cally, it is helpful first to indicate the circuitous and serpentine
route that ultimately led to the text we have today. Then the
essay will identify de Lubac's contribution to the process and
indicate his response to *Gaudium et Spes* through three themes:
the christological center of the text, the anthropology developed
in the text, and the relationship between the Church and the
world. The Church-world relationship in de Lubac's thought is
analogous to his anthropology, and his anthropology, in turn, is
dependent upon his Christology. Finally, his response to the
Church-world relationship will be clarified through his
response to Edward Schillebeeckx's description of the Church as
sacramentum mundi, "sacrament of the world."

De Lubac's interpretation of *Gaudium et Spes* is found in
comments in his journals of the Council,[2] his 1968 book,
Athéisme et sens de l'homme,[3] his reflections on his publications
in *At the Service of the Church*,[4] and in the interview recorded
in *Henri de Lubac: A Theologian Speaks*.[5] His response to Edward
Schillebeeckx is in an appendix in *A Brief Catechesis on Nature
and Grace*.[6] *Athéisme et sens de l'homme* was developed from a
report he had given at an international theological congress in
Chicago in 1966. The clear connection de Lubac makes between
his own work on the supernatural and themes developed in
Gaudium et Spes is evident in his description of *Athéisme et sens
de l'homme* as

> a kind of follow-up to *Drame de l'humanisme athée*
> as well as an adaptation of my writings on the super-
> natural to the present problem of the relation between
> the earthly future and eternal salvation, in the per-
> spective of *Gaudium et Spes* and the Teilhardian
> vision.[7]

THE GENESIS OF *GAUDIUM ET SPES*

The *History of Vatican II*, edited by Giuseppe Alberigo and
Joseph Komonchak, states,

None of the sixteen texts promulgated by Vatican II went through as slow, as long, and as complex a development as the schema that, last on the list on the CC's [Coordinating Commission] agenda in January 1963, was therefore called schema XVII....No other conciliar text was so lacking in coherent preparatory work, and no other conciliar commission was so late in becoming aware of the extent of the problems handed to it.[8]

The Document's Origins

The document originated from Cardinal Suenens's ideas on the *Ecclesia ad extra*; Pope John XXIII's message of September 11, 1962; Suenen's statement to the Council on December 4, 1962; and discussion in the Commission for the Lay Apostolate in December 1962 and January 1963.[9] Cardinal Suenens had suggested to John XXIII the distinction between the *Ecclesia ad intra*, that is, the Church's internal affairs, and *Ecclesia ad extra*, the Church in the world. The pope's speech on September 11, 1962 mentions this distinction. Two dominant themes in John XXIII's hopes for the Council were unity among all peoples and openness to the world. In his opening address to the Council, John XXIII signaled a departure from a catastrophic reading of the relationship between the Church and the world by those he called "prophets of gloom," a departure from fear and suspicion that encourages isolation and a defensive posture of the Church. He did not advocate a restoration of a golden age of Catholicism, but engagement with the present, with the new conditions and new forms of life introduced into the modern world.[10] The Commission for the Lay Apostolate had plans for a section on the effective presence of the Church in the social order and in the community of peoples. Cardinal Suenens, in his speech on December 4, 1962, proposed that the schemata be grouped around the two poles, *ad intra, ad extra*. This speech became the immediate impetus for the document, giving it the distinction of being the only major document to have originated directly from the floor of the Council.[11] The Council fathers approved, and the Coordinating Commission arranged the schemata around the phrase *Ecclesia Christi, Lumen Gentium,* "The Church of Christ, light of the nations."[12] The last two words eventually became the introductory words of the "Dogmatic Constitution on the Church." This links *Gaudium et Spes,* the "Pastoral Constitution on the Church in the Modern World," to *Lumen Gentium,* the "Dogmatic Constitution on the Church." *Gaudium et Spes* represents the Church *ad extra,* and *Lumen Gentium,* the Church *ad intra.*

Three schemas with social themes had been developed in the preparatory theological Commission. To put this into perspective, one must note that a total of seventy schemata were composed, amounting to over two thousand printed pages.[13] The social schemata included Schema III, a dogmatic constitution on the moral order, and Schema IV, a dogmatic constitution on chastity, marriage, the family, and virginity. These had originated with the theological commission over which Cardinal Alfredo Ottaviani presided and of which Father Sebastian Tromp, SJ, was the secretary.[14] The drafts reflected Roman neo-Scholastic theology and tended to be negative and defensive in tone.

Thus there were converging themes for what would become the "Pastoral Constitution of the Church in the Modern World," although the potential topics were so diverse as to lead some to remark that "Schema 13 was the Noah's Ark into which all the themes for which there was no place elsewhere were put for the time being."[15] The plan was to draw up a joint schema that included the social documents of Ottaviani's Commission and the fourth part of the schema on the lay apostolate.[16] The group charged with producing a schema was a mixed commission from the very beginning, with members from both the Doctrinal Commission and the Commission for the Lay Apostolate, about sixty members in all. At the meeting of the Coordinating Commission in January 1963, Cardinal Suenens proposed that the document be comprised of these six chapters:

1. On the admirable vocation of man according to God
2. On the human person in society
3. On matrimony, the family, and demographic problems
4. On human culture

5. On the economic order and social justice
6. On the community of nations and peace

The plan was to divide the combined schema into two parts, a more theoretical section, which would present principles, and a more pastoral section with a few concrete applications on various topics.[17]

The first text prepared by the Mixed Commission originated in the period from February to March 1963. Jean Daniélou, one of the principal authors, undoubtedly contributed to its biblical and patristic perspective: the creation of human beings in the image of God, the restoration of all people in Christ, human glorification, and the expectation of the resurrection and of the kingdom.[18] This first text was only a beginning; there were finally six texts in all developed from 1963 to 1965...and most of those with multiple versions! Many of them were developed under the pressure of the uncertainty concerning the duration of the Council, whether it would end after the third session or whether there would be a fourth session.

The encyclical of John XXIII, *Pacem in Terris* (April 11, 1963), raised the questions of methodology. Should descriptions of concrete situations be used as a starting point rather than purely biblical and theological language? The development of the text swung along a pendulum of a number of polarities: a predominantly theological approach versus a more sociological approach; optimism regarding the world versus an account of the effects of sin; a more static and essentialist approach versus an approach incorporating historical consciousness; a more deductive approach starting with principles or an inductive approach beginning with "signs of the times"; naturalism versus a supernatural emphasis on eternal destiny, a sense of the divine, and the transcendence of our supernatural vocation.[19] De Lubac would be sensitive to these dualisms and, as we shall see, interpreted their resolution in conformance with his work on nature and grace.

It was not clear at the beginning to whom the text was addressed and by whom. It was finally determined that the Church as the people of God addressed this text to all people.

Christians spoke to the world rather than the text addressing Christians about the world.[20]

Initially the text consisted of a more theological section followed by a number of appendices on concrete issues. The status of these appendices varied. These were incorporated into the amended text after the conciliar debates in the fall of 1964, at which time each subcommission was instructed to revise the text according to three parts: description of facts, theological principles, and applications.[21] Overall, these texts had been more stable throughout the revisions than the first part, the dogmatic section, even though the two most contested topics were atheism and marriage.

Charles Moeller cites these themes as appearing in all versions: (1) Christian anthropology with the theme of humans made in the image of God, (2) the autonomy of secular activities in their own sphere, (3) the Church that "civilizes by evangelizing," (4) the ambivalence and paradox of the term *world* as applying either to human society or human action.[22] Casualties of the revisions, that is, themes that were dropped along the way included the following: (1) the Holy Spirit acting in history and recreating and renewing human life; (2) the liturgy as transformative of the world; (3) the human values within the Sermon on the Mount as the "charter of the kingdom of God"; and (4) Christian cosmology as a view of history and the universe in the perspective of the plan of salvation.[23] Moeller comments that these themes are all closely related to Eastern theology and that their absence contributes to the Western bias of the text.

The final vote on the text was taken December 7, 1965. Out of 2391 votes, 2309 approved the text, 75 did not approve, and 7 were invalid. The "Pastoral Constitution on the Church in the Modern World" was promulgated by Pope Paul VI on December 8, 1965.

HENRI DE LUBAC

Henri de Lubac spent at least parts of six years in Rome, first as a member of the Preparatory Commission, which was under the direction of Cardinal Ottaviani and numbered several theologians from the curia, and later as a *peritus* (expert) for the Council. These appointments constituted a sort of rehabilitation for him, as they did also for Yves Congar, both theologians having been under suspicion and silenced in the early years of the 1950s. In their journals both speak of a certain coolness if not hostility toward them, particularly at the beginning of the Council. Both complain that the French bishops did not make use of the French theologians. De Lubac had the impression that his appointment was purely "symbolic" and that he had the impression of both being a "hostage" and "accused." The requirement of confidentiality precluded any public statements on the work of the Commission, thus imposing an obligation to silence. Since the Commission was dependent upon the Holy Office, a number of the theologians involved were the very people who played a role in his censure a decade previously.

During the Council, he regularly participated in meetings of the Theological Commission, which worked on the editing of dogmatic texts. As Jean-Pierre Wagner observes, it is difficult to discern de Lubac's exact role at the Council because de Lubac did not speak publicly of his interventions and remarks in the Theological Commission. Moreover, de Lubac was convinced that the contributions of individual theologians were so reworked by the Commission and then taken up by the bishops that it became difficult to attribute the result to particular individuals.

De Lubac states that he was involved in the elaboration of the text only in its final stages.[24] His influence on the text tended to be primarily indirect through his conversations with members of the Mixed Commission. He struck up a friendship with Karol Wojtyla, who would become the future Pope John Paul II, and worked side by side with him on Schema 13, which later became *Gaudium et Spes*. Although Wojtyla was a member of the Commission on the Apostolate of the Laity and de Lubac was a *peritus* on the Theological Commission, members of the two groups formed a Mixed Commission, which worked on Schema 13. De Lubac and Wojtyla were of a common mind concerning the problems encountered in the redaction of the Constitution. Wojtyla was the editor of chapter 4 of the first part of the constitution, "The Role of the Church in the Modern World," considered by some to be one of the most important texts of the Council.[25] Both tended to be critical of an overly optimistic characterization of the world and of a tendency to grant it a certain autonomy vis-à-vis the supernatural, although in an interview published in 1985, de Lubac comments that the document "is not so naïvely 'optimistic' as one had accused it," noting that the first words are "joy and hope, grief and anguish," and that the Commission had at first chosen the opening words to be "joy and grief, hope and anguish."[26]

With respect to the chapter on culture, de Lubac complained that one spoke of a "Christian concept," but very little of "Christian faith." He thought "they confused *aggiornamento*, which liberates us from our outmoded things, our narrowness, our lack of culture, clerical egoism, with that which would liberate us from evangelical vigor, which on the contrary we must reclaim."[27]

ANTHROPOLOGY IN THE LIGHT OF CHRIST

De Lubac served on the subcommission working on the human person.[28] The three themes that concerned de Lubac the most in the first section of *Gaudium et Spes* were the christological center of the text, the anthropology developed in the text, and the relationship between the Church and the world. He was convinced that anthropology is inseparable from Christology. In his notebooks he approvingly cites the observations of Bishop Hermann Volk that the draft of the text lacked a developed Christology since Jesus Christ only appeared in an extrinsic fashion as an argument and as a model. The text did not present him as the head and foundation of the world.[29] On another occasion he cites Wojtyla's objection that the text lacked any mention of Christ as Redeemer and Judge and seemed too content to simply affirm the world as it is.[30]

The final key text of *Gaudium et Spes* in this regard is no. 22, which solidly placed Christology at the center of anthropology:

In reality it is only in the mystery of the Word made flesh that the mystery of humanity truly becomes clear. For Adam, the first man, was a type of him who was to come, Christ the Lord. Christ the new Adam, in the very revelation of the mystery of the Father and of his love, fully reveals humanity to itself and brings to light its very high calling. It is no wonder, then, that all the truths mentioned so far should find in him their source and their most perfect embodiment. (*GS* 22)[31]

This text of *GS* 22 reiterates the theme of vocation and underscores that the human person is incomprehensible apart from Christ. It also relates all the truths of the person mentioned so far in the text—such as women and men being created "in the image of God," the social character of men and women, the unity of body and soul and the value of bodily life, human intellect, which gently draws the human mind to look for and to love what is true and good and to be led through visible realities to those that are invisible, and the dignity of moral conscience—to their perfect fulfillment in Christ. Furthermore, what holds true for Christians also applies to all people of good will in whose hearts grace is active invisibly: "For since Christ died for everyone, and since all are in fact called to one and the same destiny, which is divine, we must hold that the holy Spirit offers to all the possibility of being made partners, in a way known to God, in the paschal mystery" (*GS* 22).

THE HUMAN VOCATION

For de Lubac, anthropology cannot be understood apart from a human person's final destiny. The notion of "vocation," evident in the very title of part 1 of the constitution, "The Church and the Human Vocation," correlates with de Lubac's theology of nature and grace. I would argue that the notion of "vocation" is a much more dynamic concept than the simply the expressions *supernatural destiny* or *supernatural finality* and possibly avoids some of the pitfalls in which the nature/grace controversy has been embroiled. The notion of vocation clearly signals divine initiative and freedom, evoking a human response also given in freedom. Since a person's supernatural vocation is only known through revelation,[32] vocation sidesteps the problem of exigencies of nature, although when de Lubac speaks of "divine exigency," he understands it to be on the part of God, according to Augustine's expression in Sermon 15: *Totum exigit te, qui fecit te* ("He requires everything of you, who made you").[33] Exigency is not something required by nature, but something required by God, similar to how a vocation is addressed to a person by God. In the theological controversy this exigency was understood as an exigency on the part of the human person, which became a right the person claimed from God. The notion of vocation prevents this kind of misunderstanding and casts the relationship in personalistic rather than metaphysical terms. In this way the anthropology in *Gaudium et Spes* can be read as another stage in the nature and grace debate.

De Lubac interpreted the human vocation as also a divine vocation. He explains,

> In the expression of "vocation of man," inscribed in the title of the first part of *Gaudium et Spes*, there is, in effect, as we have said, at the same time "a Christian vocation of man" and "a human vocation of the Christian"; double vocation with mixed and interdependent aspects; of time and of eternity: of "earth" and of "heaven." And the second part of the Constitution explains to us, by such examples chosen for their importance and their contemporary relevance, at the same time how the eternal vocation resounds in the temporal, and how temporal action, in return, resounds in eternity.[34]

This is reinforced by the following comment:

> She [the Church] affirms or rather she constantly supposes a certain relation between the goodness of things in the natural order (and by this we mean as

well the things of culture and of civilization), the goodness of human and terrestrial realities—and the final end, supernatural, to which each man [sic] is called in the Mystery of Christ.[35]

Created in the image of God, the human person is *called* to eternal life. Each of the four chapters in part 1 of *Gaudium et Spes* culminates in a reference to the return of the Lord and the kingdom to come.[36] Part 2 of the Constitution, which treats of specific questions of the temporal order, follows directly from part 1 insofar as temporal problems can only be addressed adequately in the light of human destiny. This avoids an extrinsicism where the world is autonomous and dealt with apart from its supernatural destiny. Similarly, the supernatural vocation of human beings is lived out in the midst of temporal realities.

NATURE AND THE SUPERNATURAL IN *GAUDIUM ET SPES*

That de Lubac viewed *Gaudium et Spes* through the lens of his work on nature and the supernatural is uncontestable.[37] In his journal he writes of a meeting with the French bishops where he spoke to them about "nature and the supernatural with regard to Schema 13."[38] He thought that this classic formulation of the problem, however, could sound too abstract and removed from human concerns and that the same relationship could be described by other terms such as "earthly activity" and the "eschatological kingdom,"[39] or framed in terms of the relation between human nature and the covenant or the mystery of Christ,[40] or even between the worldly concerns of daily life and the inner realties of faith.[41]

In de Lubac's opinion, one of the achievements of *Gaudium et Spes* was to reject the extreme dualism implied by the language of "two orders," nature and the supernatural. He cites M. Jean Mouroux, who observed, "There are in the universe different levels of analysis (creation, sin, redemption), there are not two different orders, but only one, that of the Covenant for which creation is the first moment and for which Christ is the Alpha and the Omega, the center, and the end; and this order is supernatural."[42] Although De Lubac at first feared that the autonomy the Constitution granted to the secular order could raise specters of extrinsicism, in an interview in 1985, de Lubac asserted, "Without any exaggeration, one can say that the Council broke away from extrinsicism which (was) the illness of modern Catholicism 'which had misunderstood the full character of the desire of nature' (Congar) purposefully avoiding the vocabulary of two 'orders.' It took an extremely important position (Mouroux)."[43]

De Lubac feared both the danger of immanentism and that of extrinsicism. Immanentism collapses God into nature. Pierre Teilhard de Chardin was accused of this error by many of his critics, and de Lubac wrote five books and spent much energy while in Rome during the Council to exonerate him from the charge. Another kind of immanentism, a "historical immanentism," envisages the end of historical development as a "universal reconciliation" that would exclude everything supernatural or that would develop a dialectic of transcendence within the human being.[44] Extrinsicism, on the other hand, grants absolute autonomy to nature, and God acts like the deist clockmaker God, who has no connection to the natural laws set in motion at the creation of the world. The first results in pantheism; the second in total secularization. De Lubac observes,

> While wishing to protect the supernatural from any contamination, people had in fact exiled it altogether—both from intellectual and from social life—leaving the field free to be taken over by secularism. Today that secularism, following its course, is beginning to enter the minds even of Christians. They too seek to find a harmony with all things based upon an idea of nature which might be acceptable to a deist or an atheist: everything that should lead to him [God], is pushed so far into the background as to look like it is disappearing for good. The last word in Christian progress and the entry into adulthood would then

appear to consist in a total secularization which would expel God not merely from the life of society, but from culture and even from personal relationships."[45]

The danger of separating the two orders, the natural and the supernatural, was that in seeking to protect the supernatural from all contamination, the supernatural had become isolated apart from social life leaving a vacuum to be filled by secularity, what de Lubac calls *laïcisme*. De Lubac found this secularity to be often atheistic and a threat to the very conscience of Christians.[46] While *Gaudium et Spes* exhorts Christians in faithfulness to conscience to be "united with all other people in the search for truth and in finding true solutions to the many moral problems which arise in the lives of individuals and in society" (*GS* 16), de Lubac feared that the "opening to the world" would be sought within an idea of human nature that could suit everyone and that would be adopted by the Christian as well as by the deist or atheist. He feared that everything that comes from Christ, everything that must lead to him, and everything that recalls that the human person is made for God would be relegated to the shadows and would risk disappearing for good. He thought that "the last word of progress and entrance into adulthood would seem to consist of a total 'secularization' which would expel God not only from social life, but from culture and even the relationships of private life."[47] If a religious dimension of life were not necessary for human fullness and had nothing to do with the conduct of life, then an atheistic attitude would be entirely legitimate. The Church would then have nothing to say regarding the things of this world because these things would not have any light to receive from the Gospel.[48]

Gaudium et Spes, however, did not follow this path. It declares that

Christ, who died and was raised for everyone, offers to the human race through his Spirit the light and strength to respond to its highest calling; and that no other name under heaven is given to people for them to be saved. It [the Church] likewise believes that the key and the focus and culmination of all human history are to be found in its Lord and master....It is accordingly in the light of Christ, who is the image of the invisible God and first-born of all creation, that the council proposes to elucidate the mystery of humankind and, in addressing all people to contribute to discovering a solution to the outstanding questions of our day. (*GS* 10)

So how, then, is the autonomy of the natural order to be understood? It does not mean independence from the Creator and a systematic absence of any reference to the ultimate end of the human person. It is legitimate, however, to affirm that human activities have structures, rules, and norms that people can determine by relying on the resources of a properly human rationality.[49] To affirm the supernatural destiny of human history does not imply a theocracy or even an inappropriate overreaching of the institutional Church into secular affairs. Nevertheless, the goal and culmination of history and culture is the same as that for an individual, namely a final destiny in Christ. Anthropology and the grace/world relationship have essentially the same structure as nature, with a supernatural graced destiny best described as a divine vocation. Thus de Lubac's third theme, an evaluation of the world, is likewise inseparable from the supernatural vocation revealed in Jesus Christ.

DE LUBAC'S EVALUATION OF "WORLD" IN *GAUDIUM ET SPES*

The relationship between nature and the supernatural necessitates certain conclusions concerning the relationship between the Church and the world. A major problem in the development of *Gaudium et Spes*, however, was the ambivalence of the word *world*. De Lubac was convinced that it is necessary to define the word *world* according to Scripture and not to make an abstraction of the mystery of evil working in the world. From the introduction of the document, he thought that it must be clear that the world is both wounded and it must be consecrated. Parting ways with Teilhard, whom he thought too optimistic with respect to the world, de Lubac said, "This earth will never be paradise."[50] The presence of sin, suffering, and evil in the world needed to balance a sometimes overly optimistic view of the world.

De Lubac, along with Wojtyla, feared that the commission would be content to simply affirm the world as it is,[51] resulting in an overly profane and humanistic document. While Christians were to participate in human culture, the text did not state that they should Christianize it.[52] This amounted to a sort of abdication since it is a question of the active presence of the Church in the world.[53]

Furthermore, as Gerard Philips expressed it, there were two perspectives. One addressed the role of the Church in the temporal order; the other addressed *de Ecclesia in mundo hujus temporis* (the Church in the world of this time), the expression that later became the name of *Gaudium et Spes*.[54] The first amounts to an essentialist perspective; the second to an existential perspective. The confusion between the two perspectives contributed to the confusion in the editing of the schema and in the interventions, although this was not well understood.

Once again wishing to avoid the problem of extrinsicism, de Lubac noted that although it is necessary to distinguish between human hope (*espoir*) from the perspective of the natural order, and Christian hope (*espérence*) from the perspective of the supernatural order, if this distinction or even dualism were to become an absolute dichotomy, this would amount to a radical negation of Schema 13 since "in reality, it is by virtue of its supernatural mission that the Church has something to say to people even for this world, and can help the world with its 'natural' or 'temporal' problems."[55] For hope for eternal life to remain simply within the depths of our being and not be active in the world amounts to a corruption of Christian hope.

DE LUBAC'S CRITIQUE OF SCHILLEBEECKX

Indicative of de Lubac's attitude toward "world" in *Gaudium et Spes* is his response to Edward Schillebeeckx's claim that the Church is a "sacrament of the world." In appendix B to his book, *A Brief Catechesis on Nature and Grace*, de Lubac cites a text of Schillebeeckx:

> The Church manifests, as in a sacrament, what grace the *ehevh asher eheveh* is already accomplishing everywhere in human-existence-in-the-world.
>
> In this context it is fitting to quote one of the most felicitous passages in the Constitution *Lumen Gentium*: "in Christ, the Church is as it were the sacrament, i.e., the sign and instrument, of intimate union and of the unity of the entire human race" (Introduction, no. 1). The Church is the "sacrament of the world." Personally, I consider this declaration as one of the most charismatic that have come from Vatican II. It stands out all the more since it is found again—as though all its consequences had been felt spontaneously in advance—in the Pastoral Constitution on the Church and the world (pt. I, chap. 4, no 4).
>
> The Church, the form in which the progressive sanctification of the world shows itself explicitly (as a profane reality) by the law of the living God, is at the same time an intrinsic aspect of the history of this world sanctified by God's unconditional "Yes."...
>
> The deepest secret of what grace is accomplishing in the profane world, in virtue of the unknown and hence unexpressed name of God, is *named* and proclaimed by the "Church of Christ" and practically heralded in the witness afforded by her works. This is why belonging to the Church should be accompanied by an active will, full of hope, to change the face of the world through love for men.[56]

241

THE LEGACY OF VATICAN II

De Lubac criticizes this text primarily because the term *sacrament of the world* does not exist in the conciliar documents and because it describes the Church as the manifestation of the "progressive sanctification of the world," a sanctification that seems to occur apart from the Church. This seems to imply that the order of creation is equated with the order of redemption such that creation and covenant come from one divine structure.[57] When the order of grace is so identified with the world, the conclusion is that the world is Christian. Schillebeeckx does speak of the world as an "implicit Christianity."[58] This makes the referent of the sacramental symbol immanent rather than transcendent and leads de Lubac to question whether Schillebeeckx adequately distinguishes between the sanctification of the world and the technical construction of a new sociopolitical world. De Lubac asserts that there is a real discontinuity between the objective construction of a new society and "the secret flowering of the Kingdom."[59]

Other problems associated with Schillebeeckx's position are that (1) Christ becomes an archetype of a creation that has no real need of him since grace is already given, (2) when grace is considered to be a structure of creation, it loses its character as a historical event, and (3) it compromises the gratuity of grace, since structures cannot be free. Finally, without the freedom of grace, there is no possibility of sin or conversion.[60]

Where Schillebeeckx sees the Church as a sacrament of grace already present in the world, de Lubac considers the Church to be an efficacious sign of a unity between humanity and God effected through the Eucharist.[61] For de Lubac, unity between humanity and God is not prior to the Church, but always exists through the Church.

To sum up de Lubac on the Church-world relationship in *Gaudium et Spes,* we find that he responds to the dialectical tension between Church and world within the framework of an analogous tension between the dialectical pairs of nature and the supernatural, the order of creation and the order of redemption, and immanence and transcendence. These tensions are not resolved, but are maintained according to the hermeneutical principle of paradox so central to de Lubac's thought.[62] Although his thought is not without ambiguity, the very fact that he insists on the use of the adjective *supernatural* rather than the substantive *supernature* is indicative of his efforts to avoid a dualism even as he maintains a distinction. Even though the pair *nature-supernatural* must be thought of as a relationship of opposition, of spiritual otherness, and of infinite distance, it resolves itself finally into an association of intimate union.[63] In the closest union, however, there is distinction that maintains both the absolute transcendence of God and grace and the deep realism of the quality of "children of God." The alternative to extrinsicism is not immanentism, but transformation, incorporation, and adoption, where the supernatural remains totally other, not identified with nature, but where nature becomes a "new creation," qualitatively different. Likewise, the order of creation and the order of redemption are united, but not identical.[64] If this distinction is not retained, redemption is equated with the perfection of creation and world progress becomes world salvation. De Lubac distances himself from what he perceives to be Schillebeeckx's error when he insists that we must take care not to confuse the "progress of this world" with the "new creation." The new creation, the object of our hope, presupposes a transformation by the cross.[65] He says, "Every notion which tends to bring down the supernatural order to the level of nature tends, by that very fact, to mistake the Church for the world, to conceive of her after the model of human societies."[66] The Church is neither an extension of the world or a sacrament of the world, or, on the other hand, a supernatural entity in a separate realm from the world. It is a complex human-divine reality (*LG* 8), a sacrament of the intimate union of God and humanity (*LG* 1), which participates in the transformation of the world into the new creation, the realization of its supernatural vocation.

Notes

1. Norman P. Tanner, SJ, ed., *Decrees of the Ecumenical Councils*, vol. 2 (Washington, DC: Georgetown University Press, 1990), 1069.

2. Henri de Lubac, *Carnets du Concile*, vol. 1–2 (Paris: Cerf, 2007).

3. Henri de Lubac, *Athéisme et sens de l'homme*, in *Œuvres completes* 4 (Paris: Cerf, 2006).

4. Henri de Lubac, *At the Service of the Church: Henri de Lubac Reflects on the Circumstances That Occasioned his Writing*, trans. Anne Elizabeth Englund (San Francisco: Ignatius Press, 1993).

5. Henri de Lubac and Angelo Scola, *De Lubac: A Theologian Speaks*, trans. Stephen Maddux (Los Angeles: Twin Circles Publishing, 1985). The English is a translation from the original Italian publication of the interview in *30 Giorni*, July 18, 1985. The French version, *Entretien autour de Vatican II: Souvenirs et reflections* (Paris: Cerf, 1985), is a slightly expanded version of the original Italian publication.

6. Henri de Lubac, *A Brief Catechesis on Nature and Grace*, trans. Richard Arnandy, FSC (San Francisco: Ignatius Press, 1984). Original: *Petite catéchèse sur nature et grace* (Paris: Fayard, 1980).

7. De Lubac, *At the Service*, 121.

8. Giuseppe Alberigo, ed. *History of Vatican II*, trans. Joseph A. Komonchak, 5 vols. (Maryknoll, NY: Orbis, 1997), 2:412–13. The schema on the Church in the world was identified as Schema 17 until a new numeration and arrangement of the schemata in July 1964 turned it into Schema 13. It was also identified as a "Pastoral Constitution," although its name was a topic of dispute throughout its many revisions.

9. Alberigo and Komonchak, *History of Vatican II*, 2:413.

10. John XXIII, *Gaudet Mater Ecclesia* (October 11, 1962). Available in *The Documents of Vatican II*, ed. Walter M. Abbott, SJ (New York: America Press, 1966), 710–19.

11. Donald R. Champion, SJ, "The Church Today," in Abbott, *The Documents of Vatican II*, 183.

12. Charles Moeller, "History of the Constitution," in *Commentary on the Documents of Vatican II*, vol. 5: *Pastoral Constitution on the Church in the Modern World*, ed. Herbert Vorgrimler (New York: Herder and Herder, 1969), 12.

13. Alberigo and Komonchak, *History of Vatican II*, 2:411.

14. Ibid., 415.

15. Moeller, "History of the Constitution," 38.

16. Alberigo and Komonchak, *History of Vatican II*, 2:413.

17. Moeller, "History of the Constitution," 13.
18. Ibid., 13–14.
19. For a history of the Schema 13 and the various tensions at play in its development, see Alberigo and Komonchak, *History of Vatican II,* 5:122–77.
20. Moeller, "History of the Constitution," 48.
21. Ibid., 45.
22. Ibid., 71–72.
23. Ibid., 72.
24. Henri de Lubac, *Entretien autour de Vatican II* (Paris: Cerf, 1985), 45.
25. Ibid., 47; Antonio Russo, *Henri de Lubac* (Paris: Brepols, 1997), 211.
26. De Lubac, *Entretien,* 48.
27. De Lubac, *Carnets du Concile,* vol. 2 (Paris: Cerf, 2007), 374.
28. De Lubac, *Entretien,* 412.
29. De Lubac, *Carnets du Concile,* 414.
30. Ibid., 364.
31. John Paul II, who worked on this text at the Council, stated on several occasions that the organic relation between theo-[Christo]centrism and anthropocentrism is the most fundamental principle taught at Vatican II. See *Dives in Misericordia,* no. 1; cf. *Redemptor Hominis,* 1–12. Cf. also John Paul II's *Crossing the Threshold of Hope* (New York: Alfred Knopf, 1994), 48–49; and Cardinal Wojtyla's *Sources of Renewal* (San Francisco: Harper & Row, 1980), 75. Cited by David L. Schindler, "Introduction," in Henri de Lubac, *The Mystery of the Supernatural* (New York: Crossroads/Herder & Herder, 1998), xxvii. See also David L. Schindler, "Christology and the *Imago Dei:* Interpreting *Gaudium et Spes,*" *Communio: International Catholic Review* 23 (Spring 1996): 156–84.
32. De Lubac, *Athéisme et sens de l'homme,* 474.
33. De Lubac, *Entretien,* 31.
34. De Lubac, *Athéisme et sens de l'homme,* 487.
35. Ibid., 493.
36. Ibid., 472.
37. Critics of de Lubac are divided on the significance of de Lubac's theology of the supernatural for an interpretation of *Gaudium et Spes.* David Schindler, who wrote the introduction for the new edition of the English translation of *The Mystery of*

the Supernatural, along with many of the authors associated the journal *Communio,* sees a positive link between the two. On the other hand, Stephen Duffy and Peter Ryan, SJ, think that de Lubac's theology of the supernatural undercuts the proper autonomy of the temporal realities affirmed by *Gaudium et Spes.* See Stephen Duffy, *The Graced Horizon: Nature and Grace in Modern Catholic Thought* (Collegeville, MN: Liturgical Press, 1992) and Peter F. Ryan, SJ, "Moral Action and the Ultimate End of Man: The Significance of the Debate between Henri de Lubac and His Critics" (PhD diss., Pontificia Universitas Gregoriana, 1996). See Robert F. Gotcher's account of these views in "Henri de Lubac and *Communio:* The Significance of his Theology of the Supernatural for an Interpretation of *Gaudium et Spes,"* (PhD diss., Marquette University, 2002), chapter 5.

38. De Lubac, *Carnets du Concile,* 271.
39. De Lubac, *Athéisme et sens de l'homme,* 488.
40. De Lubac, *At the Service of the Church,* 198–99.
41. See Schindler, "Introduction," xvi.
42. Cited in *Athéisme et sens de l'homme,* 478.
43. De Lubac, *Entretien,* 28. "On peut dire sans excès que le Concile a rompu avec 'l'extrinsécisme qui (était) la maladie du catholicisme moderne' en la matière et qui avait 'fait longtemps méconnaître le plein caractère du voeu de la nature' (Congar): 'en évitant à dessein le vocabulaire des deux 'ordres.' Il a réalisé une prise de position extrêmement importante' (Mouroux)."
44. De Lubac, *The Mystery of the Supernatural,* xxxv.
45. Ibid.
46. Ibid., 478–79.
47. Ibid., 479. De Lubac thought that if the authors of *Gaudium et Spes* had been more familiar with the thought of Pierre Teilhard de Chardin, they could have drawn more solid distinctions to better clarify the debate posed in the polarities "liberation of man" and "salvation in Jesus Christ." See de Lubac, *At the Service of the Church,* 121.
48. De Lubac, *The Mystery of the Supernatural,* 481.
49. Ibid., 482.
50. De Lubac, *Carnets du Concile,* 243.
51. Ibid., 364.
52. Ibid., 375.
53. Ibid.
54. Ibid., 365.

55. Ibid., 421. De Lubac identified human hope (*espoir*) with Marxism.

56. This translation of Schillebeeckx's text is the English translation of the French translation in *A Brief Catechesis on Nature and Grace*, trans. Richard Arnandez (San Francisco: Ignatius Press, 1984), 191–92. Although de Lubac criticizes Schillebeeckx for leaving out *cum Deo* in citing *LG* 1, this was an error in the French translation he was using. The Dutch original reads, "In Christus is de Kerk als het sacrament dat is: teken en instrument, van de innige vereniging *met God* en van de eenheid van heel het menselijk geslacht" (emphasis added). *Wereld en Kerk*, Theologische Peilingen Deel III (Bilthoven: H. Nelissen, 1966), 124. Schillebeeckx does not envision human solidarity apart from union with Christ: "Expressed in more modern terms, this means that the source of the grace of Christ is not human solidarity itself, but human solidarity with Christ who has, however, disappeared from our empirical horizon since his death, but who wishes to remain present among us post-paschally by virtue of the Spirit of God, in his body, the Church." Edward Schillebeeckx, *World and Church*, trans. N. D. Smith, *Theological Soundings*, vol. 4 (New York: Sheed & Ward, 1971), 124.

57. De Lubac, *A Brief Catechesis on Nature and Grace*, 55.

58. Ibid., 199.

59. Ibid., 223.

60. Susan K. Wood, *Spiritual Exegesis and the Church in the Theology of Henri de Lubac* (Grand Rapids: Eerdmans, 1998), 112.

61. See Henri de Lubac, *Corpus Mysticum*, trans. Gemma Simmons (London: SCM, 2006).

62. See Henri de Lubac, *The Church: Paradox and Mystery*, trans. James R. Dunne (New York: Alba House, 1969); Henri de Lubac, *Further Paradoxes*, trans. Ernest Beaumont (Westminster, MD: The Newman Press, 1958); Henri de Lubac, *Paradoxes of Faith* (San Francisco, CA: Ignatius Press, 1986.)

63. De Lubac, *A Brief Catechesis on Nature and Grace*, 101.

64. Ibid., 118.

65. De Lubac, *Athéisme et sens de l'homme*, 499.

66. De Lubac, *A Brief Catechesis on Nature and Grace*, 109–10.

12

David Hollenbach, SJ

Religious Freedom in Global Context Today

SOME CONTRIBUTIONS BY VATICAN II AND JOHN COURTNEY MURRAY

There are several good reasons why it was most appropriate that Boston College marked the one hundred and fiftieth anniversary of its founding by also commemorating the fiftieth anniversary of the Second Vatican Council and, in particular, the contributions of the Jesuit John Courtney Murray to the Council. First, Murray was one of the most significant theological voices at the Council. He was also an alumnus of Boston College, receiving a BA in 1926 from Weston College, one of the institutions that has become B.C.'s School of Theology and Ministry that sponsored our conference, and also received an MA in philosophy from Boston College in 1927.[1] Murray's major influence at the Council was through his crucial contribution to the drafting of the Council's "Declaration on Religious Freedom," *Dignitatis Humanae*. Through his contribution to the creation of this Declaration, Murray was without doubt the single most influential U.S. theologian at the Council. Second, Murray's work on religious freedom enabled the U.S. Catholic Church to make its most important contribution to Vatican II by helping the Roman Catholic community throughout the world come to see

248

the crucial connection between Christian faith and freedom in civil society and politics, especially the connection between Christian faith and the civil right to religious freedom. When *Time* magazine put Murray on the cover of its issue of December 12, 1960, it somewhat impishly described the way Murray brought the American and Catholic traditions into dialogue with each other as "Loyola meets Tom Paine."[2] Third, it is appropriate that we celebrate the anniversaries of both Vatican II and Boston College by highlighting the contribution of a theologian to the Council. It is a remarkable coincidence that the year of Murray's birth was also the birth year of three other great theologians who made crucial contributions to the Council. Murray was born in 1904, and so were Yves Congar, Bernard Lonergan, and Karl Rahner. As we commemorate the anniversaries of both the Council and of Boston College, these four great theologians can lead us to ask how theology, this School of Theology, and this university can contribute to both Church and society in ways that seek to follow their examples.

My approach to Murray's role at the Council will, of course, focus on his contribution to the drafting of *Dignitatis Humanae*. I propose to take an approach to his contribution that has particular importance today by considering the continuing relevance of religious freedom to peace and justice within nations and among them. In very recent decades, religion has been playing an increasing public role in world affairs.[3] The interaction of religion and politics sometimes leads to injustice toward religious minorities and, too often, to conflict and even war. The shape of the issues today would be of great concern to Murray because his work on religious liberty arose from his strong interest in the public role of religion, and also because of his theological and ethical engagement with the ethics of war and peace.[4] Vatican II, in its "Pastoral Constitution on the Church in the Modern World," *Gaudium et Spes*, also devoted major attention both to the public role of the Church and to the Church's possible contribution to justice and world peace. The issues of religious freedom, justice for minorities, and interreligious conflict are increasingly intertwined today. This essay will therefore draw on the thought of both Murray and the Council concerning religious freedom to suggest how the Church and other faith communities can help build a more just and peaceful world.

Elsewhere I have discussed the implications of the treatment of religious freedom by Murray and the Council for a recent controversy between the U.S. Catholic bishops and the Obama administration.[5] The bishops see the administration's mandate that health care insurance at Catholic institutions cover the provision of contraception to its female employees as a demand that these institutions violate some aspects of Catholic moral teaching. The bishops see this as an infringement of their religious freedom and of the religious freedom of some Catholic institutions and of individual employers who for religious reasons hold that contraception is morally unacceptable. I have argued earlier, however, that a compromise could be worked out between the bishops and the administration that is fully compatible with Catholic doctrine and traditional principles of Catholic moral theology on cooperation in the actions of others that are judged to be immoral. Such compromise is the route taken by the Catholic Health Association in both 2012 and most recently in July 2013.[6] Because my view of this controversy has not changed, I will not repeat the analysis I have previously published, though a fuller development of this analysis would surely be possible in light of the way the controversy has unfolded.

The practical focus of this essay is due to the fact that religious communities have been playing an increasingly influential role in public life in the past few decades. Thus the need to consider the significance of religious freedom from the social standpoint, including that of international peace and justice, is itself a recent development. This essay will join the discussion of this need from the distinctive standpoint of the approach to religious freedom taken by Murray and Vatican II.

It is well known that Murray's contribution to the Council had a distinctively American accent. At the same time, Murray was not afraid to propose strong criticisms of some aspects of the culture prevailing in the United States in his day. Murray feared that despite the great wisdom embodied in the institutions by which the United States was governed, including First Amendment protections of religious freedom, there was a real danger that the United States culture was losing its appreciation of this wisdom. Indeed, he suggested that the United States was threatened by the weakening of the bonds that link citizens in the common project of building civil society together through shared argument and debate. He feared, in other words, that the United States was losing cultural and institutional commitment to the common good that Cicero and Augustine knew was essential to the flourishing of a republic.[7]

The absence of the shared conversation and argument that link citizens from diverse traditions together in a civil community is evident in many approaches to religious freedom in today's postmodern context. In the United States it is not uncommon to hear religion called a strictly private matter. Seeing religion, and indeed all value commitments, as private affairs is one of the results of the individualism that is such an important current in United States culture. This individualistic approach to religion can highlight the intimate relation between one's religious belief and one's deepest identity as a person and thus its high importance. Seeing religion as a purely private affair, however, can also reduce religion to an insignificant level that verges on triviality. In addition, when a strictly private view of religion prevails, it will be easy to overlook the importance of the public, institutional dimensions of religious freedom and the influence of faith communities on the public realities of peace and justice. Or if the role being played by religion in public life cannot be ignored due to religious conflict or threats to social justice, many Americans will likely call for the faith communities involved to go back to the private sphere where they belong.[8] Religious freedom can thus become identified with the privatization of religion.

Neither Murray nor Vatican II saw religion as a private reality. Both certainly saw the deeply personal aspects of faith and wanted to preserve the crucial role religious freedom plays in enabling individual persons to shape who they themselves are. But both Murray and the Council also saw freedom, including religious freedom, as achieved only in society and in public life. Religious freedom has important public dimensions that depend on the political and juridical institutions that shape both society and its members. Strictly private or individualist understandings of religious freedom do not have the tools needed to help faith communities envision their roles in public society in ways that help build up the common good of individual countries and of the larger international society. This essay, therefore, will explore how Murray and Vatican II saw religious freedom not only as an essential protection for the personal act of faith, but also as a social, public reality with important political implications. It will draw upon both Murray and the Council to help clarify how religious freedom is particularly important today because of its essential contributions to global peace and justice.

RELIGIOUS FREEDOM AS A PERSONAL REALITY

Stressing the importance of the connection between religious freedom and matters of global peace and social justice, of course, should not lead us to overlook the fact that religious freedom is a personal reality that reaches into the heart of each individual. Before considering how religious freedom is important for the promotion of peace and justice, therefore, we will make a few comments on how both Murray and the Council saw religious freedom as a deeply personal reality. A person's religious belief or nonbelief shapes her identity in paramount ways. Thus the protection or violation of religious belief has effects that could hardly be more personal.

The Council's *Dignitatis Humanae* argues for the human and civil right to religious freedom by noting several ways the protection of this freedom is important to the innermost identity of persons.

First, the Council appeals to the longstanding Catholic conviction concerning the high importance of freedom of conscience. It is a basic affirmation in Catholic tradition that every person has an obligation to follow the dictates of his or her conscience. This obligation binds not only in the moral sphere but religiously as well. As *Dignitatis Humanae* put it,

> The human person sees and recognizes the demands
> of divine law through conscience. All are bound to fol-
> low their conscience faithfully in every sphere of
> activity so that they may come to God, who is their
> last end. Therefore the individual must not be forced
> to act against conscience nor be prevented from act-
> ing in accord with conscience, especially in matters
> religious. (*Dignitatis Humanae* 3)[9]

Freedom of conscience in the domain of religion thus implies
the existence of a personal right to religious freedom. The exercise of conscience is a profoundly personal activity. This was
made clear by the Council's *Gaudium et Spes*, when it wrote
that "conscience is people's most secret core, and their sanctuary.
There they are alone with God whose voice echoes in their
depths" (16).[10] The Council sees conscience, and thus religious
freedom, as exercised in the intimacy of each person's heart
where they encounter God. The language could hardly be more
personalist. We will see below, however, that despite the tone of
this statement, the Council did not hold that religious belief is a
private reality nor that religious freedom will be protected by
keeping religion in the private sphere.

Second, the Council stresses religious freedom's personal
dimensions when it argues that the right to this freedom is based
on the fact that a person can come to a conviction that a belief
is true only through personal deliberation conducted in freedom.
Some of the more conservative bishops at the Council, such as
the head of the Holy Office, Cardinal Alfredo Ottaviani, feared
that the affirmation to religious freedom rested on an indifference to truth. This suspicion had led to the effective silencing of
Murray on the issue of religious freedom just a few years before
the Council.[11] To counter this concern, *Dignitatis Humanae* 2
unambiguously affirmed that its understanding of religious
freedom presumed that all persons have a duty to affirm the
truth: "All persons should be at once impelled by nature and
bound by a moral obligation to seek the truth, especially religious truth. They are also bound to adhere to the truth once they
come to know it, and to direct their whole lives in accordance

with the demands of truth (2)."[12] This duty, however, can be followed only in freedom. Human beings can seek and come to hold the truth about God and the human condition in relation to God only through free deliberation and freely given personal assent. The Declaration thus affirms that all persons should be free from coercive interference with their duty to fulfill this obligation, and therefore have a right to religious freedom.

Third, the Council grounds religious freedom on that fact that the act of faith must itself be free if it is to be a genuine act of faith. As *Dignitatis Humanae* put it, "The act of faith or its very nature is a free act. The human person...can assent to God's self-revelation only by being drawn by the Father and through submitting to God with a faith that is reasonable and free" (10).[13] Because of this essential connection between authentic faith and freedom, the civil protection of personal religious freedom is closely associated with the advancement of freedom more generally understood. Securing religious freedom is thus closely linked with the institutions of democracy that protect freedom more broadly conceived.

Murray synthesized these personal dimensions of religious freedom by arguing that they are all expressions of the essential connection between the freedom of faith and fundamental dignity of the human person. In one of his final writings on the Declaration, Murray eloquently explained the Council's understanding of human dignity as the ontological foundation of the right to religious freedom. This freedom is not only the freedom of choice by which persons decide among various options that appear on a kind of menu of specific religious alternatives. The religious freedom that is a deep expression of human dignity is the freedom of the person to decide who she is and what she will become. It is a decision about the ultimate meaning of one's life. It is the kind of freedom through which a person puts at risk her whole existence. In Murray's words,

> The primordial demand of dignity, then, is that man acts by his own counsel and purpose, using and enjoying his freedom, moved, not by external coercion, but internally by the risk of his whole existence....Human

dignity consists formally in the person's responsibility for himself and, what is more, for his world. So great is his dignity that not even God can take it away.[14]

Human dignity, therefore, comes to expression in human freedom, and the deepest meaning of one's dignity as a person is shaped by the use of one's religious freedom.

The Council, therefore, makes a philosophical claim about the nature of the human person as free and self-determining when it argues for the right to religious freedom. It also goes on to make a theological claim when it affirms that freedom— including religious freedom—is one of the key characteristics that constitute human beings as created in the image of God. Through these theological and philosophical arguments, the Council sets forth why the right to religious freedom is of such high personal importance to every human being. These arguments are the basis of the Council's affirmation that religious freedom is an essential expression of personal dignity "as known through the revealed word of God and by reason itself" (*Dignitatis Humanae* 2).[15]

Murray and Vatican II had clear secular philosophical warrants for their affirmation that the protection of religious freedom is essential to treating humans as what they are, in other words, as free, self-determining beings. They also had strong Christian theological warrants for affirming this right. Both kinds of warrants set Murray and the Council at odds with those currents in modern and postmodern thought that affirm the importance of religious freedom because of skepticism about religious or even secular philosophical truth claims about what it is to be human. At the same time, the Council did not hesitate to affirm that those who rejected its reasons were nonetheless still entitled to respect for their religious freedom. Indeed, though the Council argued that religious freedom is grounded in the truth about the human person, it also maintained that this freedom must be respected "even in those who do not live up to their obligation of seeking the truth and adhering to it" (*Dignitatis Humanae* 2).[16]

Thus the Council's strongly personalist understanding of the importance of religious freedom did not lead it to hold that religion should be kept private, as do some other modern and postmodern understandings of religious liberty. Far from it. The Council argued that the right to religious freedom means not only that individual persons ought not to be forced to act against their convictions, but also that they should be free to act in accord with those convictions "in private or in public, alone or in association with others" (*Dignitatis Humanae* 2).[17] Indeed, the right to free exercise of religion, to borrow the U.S. constitutional term, includes the right of religious communities to form social organizations that aim to influence public life by "demonstrating the special value of their teaching for the organization of society" (*Dignitatis Humanae* 4).[18]

Murray and the Council, therefore, were strongly committed to the importance and legitimacy of public activity by the Church for justice and peace. The Council and, even more so, Murray were aware, however, that in a pluralistic society, public religious action can lead to considerable tension. Indeed, in our day the public action of religious communities has sometimes led to significant conflict in global politics. At the same time, the impact of faith communities in public life has also often been very positive, with religious leaders and believers at large making significant contributions to justice and peace nationally. To set the stage for a consideration of dimensions of religious freedom that go beyond the protection of individual freedoms, we now turn to a description of several examples of both negative and positive social influences of religion in public life. This will enable us better to clarify how Murray and the Council understood the relation between religious freedom and the promotion of peace and justice in society.

PUBLIC RELIGION, CONFLICT, AND PEACE: SOME EXAMPLES

Vatican II holds that the liberty to exercise religion in public includes the freedom of a faith community to seek to shape public policy and otherwise influence public affairs. A quick overview of the recent historical record shows that such a public role of religion can have both negative and positive effects. It can generate conflict and lead to the violation of the requirements of justice for some members of the communities affected. Or this public role of religion can be a source of enhanced social unity, reconciliation, peace, and justice. One need only contrast the roles played by Osama bin Laden and by Archbishop Desmond Tutu of South Africa to see that the effects of public religion can be quite diverse. The multiple kinds of influence of religion in the affairs of the larger society have led Scott Appleby to speak of the "ambivalence of the sacred."[19] Before turning to the way Murray and the Council propose that faith communities, including the Catholic Church, should seek to influence the institutions of public life, it will be useful to note some recent examples of both the negative and positive influences of religious communities in public life. This will help show that religious freedom is not simply a personal reality, much less a strictly private affair, but that it has important public, institutional dimensions.

On the negative side of the ledger, Brian J. Grim and Roger Finke have noted several regrettable twentieth-century cases in which religious communities have denied religious freedom to people of other faiths, leading to grave injustice and conflict.[20] In the early 1900s, for example, there were more than three million Christians in Turkey, about 20 percent of the population. Today there are but three hundred thousand, or about 2 percent. Most of the difference is due to the large number of Armenians who perished in what can appropriately be called genocide. Better known is the Shoah in which anti-Judaism and anti-Semitism led to the genocide of the Jewish people at the hands of the National Socialist regime in Germany, taking the lives of about two-thirds of all the Jews living in Europe when the Nazis came to power. During the cultural revolution in China in the 1960s and '70s, religion was a particular focus of state persecution; all religious practice was banned and many religious leaders faced prison and even death.

The record in the first years of the twenty-first century is also deeply distressing. Drawing upon data gathered by the U.S. State Department, by the Pew Forum on Religion and Public Life, and by several other sources, Grim and Finke have concluded that 86 percent of the 143 counties with populations of more than two million have experienced at least some cases of people being abused or displaced from their homes because of their religion. Religious persecution is today so widespread in much of the Middle East and South Asia that Grim and Finke conclude it has become the norm in those regions and that the injustice of such persecution is one of the principle causes of the conflict and bloodshed in the region.[21] There are severe cases of religious persecution and conflict in Africa as well. In Sudan, for example, the long civil war between south and north had religion as one of its driving forces, with Christians and adherents of traditional African religion in the south resisting efforts by the north to Islamize the whole of Sudan. This conflict took over two million lives and created over five million displaced persons.[22] Since the Comprehensive Peace Agreement of 2005 and the independence of South Sudan in 2011, Christians in the north, including the 300,000 living in the capital Khartoum, face arrest, detention, and deportation.[23] Though religion is not the sole source of conflict in Sudan or some of these other regions, it has played a significant role in generating and sustaining conflict.

Persecution because of religion is less present in Europe and the United States but it is certainly not absent. Martha Nussbaum has made a strong appeal to resist what she calls the "new religious intolerance" directed at Muslims in Europe and, to a lesser degree, in the United States. Nussbaum cites European legislation banning Muslim women from wearing head scarves in certain public settings and the U.S. controversy over the proposal to construct a mosque near the "ground zero" of the September 11 attacks on the World Trade Center in New York.[24] A particularly vivid illustration of the rise of "Islamophobia" in the West is the recent case of remarks made by Marine Le Pen, head of the National Front in France and member of the European Parliament. Madame Le Pen compared the public presence of veiled women and of Muslims praying in public because of insufficient space in mosques to the Nazi occupation of France during World War II. Le Pen and the National Front are significant political actors in France. Although the European

Parliament has rejected Le Pen's views, the fact that she received 17.9 percent of the vote in the first round of the French presidential election in 2012 indicates she cannot be ignored.[25]

Failure to respect those who are religiously different has also led to violent conflicts. For example, the commitment of the ruling family of Saudi Arabia to exclusive state support for the Wahhabi school of Islam has led to resistance by other schools of Islam. It has helped generate jihadist movements, including al-Qa'ida. The resulting conflicts in Afghanistan and Iraq have been grave. Buddhist control of the government in Sri Lanka was the cause of resistance by the minority Hindu community that generated a bloody civil war. In India, the Hindu nationalist convictions of the Bharatiya Janata Party was one of the sources of the rise of Lashkar-e-Taiba, a Muslim group with ties to Pakistan that in 2008 carried out terror attacks in Mumbai, killing many.

The role of religion in the civil wars of recent decades is similarly discouraging and has been rising. 19 percent of the civil wars begun in the 1940s were fought at least in part over religious issues. This percentage rose to 41 percent in the 1980s, to 45 percent in the 1990s, and to 50 percent of the 16 civil wars underway in 2010. Such religiously linked civil wars are not only of concern to the countries in which they occur but internationally as well. Intrastate wars almost always produce serious effects on neighboring regions, through the disruption of economic activity, the displacement of refugees, and through their possible effects on the balance of power and ideological alignments. When civil wars are religiously based, such international consequences are likely to be magnified because religious identity is almost always tied to membership in a community that reaches across national borders. Thus when conflicts have religious dimensions they easily flow over into the affairs of other countries.[26]

These are examples of the negative effects religious communities can have if they pursue their public roles without attending sufficiently to the rights of other religious communities, including their rights to religious freedom. Vatican II was well aware of the ways that faith communities, including

Catholicism, have engaged in behavior that has led some to see religion as a threat to human well-being, including the peace and justice needed to sustain such well-being, thus presenting a distorted picture of religion and indeed of God.[27] The attaining of peace and justice calls for protecting society from such social misuse of religion.

Fortunately, public activity by religious communities also often has very positive results. Religious leaders such as Mohandas Gandhi, Martin Luther King Jr., the Dalai Lama, Pope John Paul II, and Archbishop Desmond Tutu have played significant roles in the pursuit of social justice, peace, and reconciliation. Gandhi's nonviolent campaign for the independence of India from British rule was grounded in his Hindu beliefs, interpreted with the help of his reading of Christian authors such as Tolstoy. His nonviolence has inspired movements for justice and peace among Christians, such as Martin Luther King Jr.'s campaign for racial justice in the United States and Anglican Archbishop Tutu's participation in the anti-apartheid movement that led to the nonracial democracy that elected Nelson Mandela its first president in 1994. Pope John Paul II was deeply involved in Poland's struggle for freedom from control and domination by the Soviet Union. The pope's support for the Solidarity movement in Poland contributed in very important ways to tearing down the Berlin Wall in 1989 and to the collapse of the Soviet Union and its empire in 1991. The Dalai Lama has been a powerful Buddhist voice raised on behalf of the people of Tibet in the face of their oppression by the People's Republic of China. His voice, like that of many other religious people engaged in campaigns for justice, has appealed for significant change through nonviolent means. One of the most notable developments of recent international affairs has been the significant rise of nonviolent movements for political change, and many of these movements have been religiously inspired. Despite the conviction of many political realists that nonviolence is an ineffective political strategy, many of these movements have been successful.[28] The commitment to respect those who are different, including those who are religiously different, has enabled these movements to seek greater justice in public life in vigorous ways while remaining committed to the use of peaceful means.

The efforts of religious communities to contribute to greater justice in society by promoting democratic political processes and institutions have also been very visible in recent years. Particularly notable among these efforts have been the contributions made by the Catholic community to the process of democratization. The late Samuel Huntington concluded that the post–Vatican II Catholic Church has become one of the strongest worldwide forces for human dignity, human rights, and democracy. He saw the modern rise of democracy occurring in three waves. The first wave was the U.S. and French revolutions in the eighteenth centuries, the second was the democratization of the former Axis Powers of Germany, Italy, and Japan following the Second World War, and the third wave has been underway since the early 1970s. This third wave included the coming of democracy to Spain and Portugal, the decline of military and authoritarian rule in Latin America, South Korea, and the Philippines, and the end of communism in the Warsaw Pact nations. From his analysis of the data, Huntington concluded that "in its first fifteen years, the third wave was overwhelmingly Catholic....Roughly three-quarters of the countries that transited to democracy between 1974 and 1989 were Catholic."[29]

Toft, Philpott, and Shah have reinforced Huntington's conclusion about this dramatic contribution of the Catholic community by reviewing existing data on the spread of democracy between the years 1972 and 2009. During this period they conclude that seventy-eight countries in the world experienced substantial democratization. Religious communities played a role in advancing democracy in forty-eight of these countries, and religious communities took the leading role in advancing democracy in thirty of these countries and a supporting role in eighteen of them. In nations such as India, Indonesia, and Kuwait, Islam was a leader in support of democracy. Hinduism was a leader in India, Orthodoxy in Serbia, and Protestantism played a leading role in several African countries, as well as in South Korea and Romania. Catholicism showed notably stronger leadership than these other faith communities. Toft et al. conclude that between 1972 and 2009 the Catholic community played a role in promoting democracy in thirty-six of the seventy-eight countries that experienced substantial advances for democracy, and that the Catholic community had a leadership position in the democratization of twenty-two of these countries.[30]

This move of Catholicism from its more traditional alignment with authoritarian modes of political organization to support for democracy was certainly dramatic, even revolutionary. There seems little doubt that the shift of the Catholic political stance from a tendency to support authoritarian government to a quite unambiguous commitment to democracy can be attributed to the innovations of the Second Vatican Council, and especially to Vatican II's strong support for human rights, including the right to religious freedom. This shift was brought about by recognition of the dangers of authoritarian regimes such as Nazism and Stalinism in the several decades before the Council. These dangers threatened the Church's own freedom. The deep Catholic tradition of strong commitment to the freedom of the Church in these circumstances helped Murray persuade the bishops at Vatican II that endorsement of the right to religious freedom was in continuity with important dimensions of the larger Catholic tradition.[31] At the same time, the broad range of the violations of human dignity by Hitler and Stalin showed that more than the Church's own well-being and freedom was at stake. The experience of the multiple kinds of abuse by authoritarian rule led John XXIII to strong support of the full range of human rights in his encyclical *Pacem in Terris*, which was issued during the Council. This broader human rights agenda had been earlier developed with the drafting of the United Nations' *Universal Declaration of Human Rights* immediately following World War II.[32] When Vatican II followed the lead of *Pacem in Terris* in its endorsement of the full range of human rights articulated by the United Nations, the Council moved the Church to the forefront of the struggle for human rights and democracy. Furthermore, both the *Universal Declaration* and *Pacem in Terris* explicitly see respect for human rights as essential to the protection of peace.[33] In a similar way, Vatican

II's commitment to human rights and religious freedom supports the Council's strong encouragement of the Church's mission for peace. A credible case can be made, therefore, that Murray's thinking on religious freedom and its adoption by Vatican II played key roles in leading the postconciliar Church to important new initiatives not only for democracy but also for a broader agenda of human rights, social justice, and peace.

POSITIVE PUBLIC CONTRIBUTIONS BY RELIGION: INSTITUTIONAL CONDITIONS

If it is correct that these consequences for the Church's engagement with issues of human rights, social justice, and peace were stimulated by the Council's affirmation of the right to religious freedom, it should be clear that this right has implications that reach well beyond a private zone of personal faith. Support for religious liberty is not simply a matter of individual freedom but has important effects for social and political institutions both within nations and globally. Clarifying how Murray and Vatican II understood the institutional requirements of religious liberty will help show why their support for religious freedom had significant consequences for the Church's broader engagement with matters of social justice and global peace.

Drafts one and two of the Council's Declaration sought to base the right to religious freedom on the personal foundations of persons' duty to follow the dictates of their consciences and on the fact that the act of faith must be free if it is to be authentic faith. In Murray's view, however, these personalist arguments were insufficient to show that there is a right to free exercise of religion in the midst of society, especially in cases where a cogent argument can be made that the religious beliefs being exercised have morally objectionable public consequences. The existence of a right necessarily implies a correlative duty that others should respect this right. This raises the question of whether others in society have a duty to respect my conscience when it is in error. To be sure, they have a negative duty not to coerce me to act in a way that would violate my convictions. But do they have a positive duty to permit me to act on my convictions if acting upon those convictions can be reasonably judged to be harmful to others, perhaps in serious ways. Murray maintained that the arguments of those who answer this question negatively "are not negligible....Another's error of conscience can create no duties in me, nor can it guarantee for me the rightness of his action."[34] Thus Murray argued that the Council needed to go beyond appealing to freedom of conscience in order to develop an adequate understanding of the public dimensions of the right to religious freedom and how respect for freedom should be expressed politically and legally. This is a matter of clarifying the way political and legal institutions should deal with religion when it exercises public influence.

The limits of the appeal to freedom of conscience and the need for a consideration of the roles of political and juridical institutions in protecting religious liberty can be illustrated by a South African case that arose well after the Council. The apartheid regime, which legally required that different races and ethnic groups live apart from one another, had been developed by some Afrikaner Dutch Reformed Christians on the basis of their interpretation of parts of the Bible, particularly the story of the Tower of Babel (Gen 11). They understood the story's description of God "scattering" people of diverse languages to different parts of the earth as indicating that separation of diverse peoples is the will of God. Most people today, both outside and within South Africa, are convinced that apartheid is an immoral system and that it was rightly abolished in 1994. However, after 1994 some Afrikaners continued to hold on conscientious religious grounds that racial separation was their religious duty. They sought legal approval of their right to act on this conviction by being permitted to exclude blacks from their towns and businesses and to create a new white "homeland" within South Africa based on racial/ethnic separation. Those who are convinced that such Afrikaner beliefs are simply false will need a theory of religious freedom that goes beyond appealing to respect conscience if they are to affirm *both* the right to religious freedom *and* the new South African constitution's refusal to grant these Afrikaners the freedom to continue racial separation.

This South African example comes from a time after Murray's death. But it shows why Murray maintained that the Council needed grounds other than freedom of conscience if it were to present an adequate understanding to the right to exercise religious freedom in public life. He made his case in a significant argument with several progressive, Francophone, proreligious freedom theologians who were advising the bishops at the Council.[35] Murray's argument appears in imperfect form in the later drafts of what became *Dignitatis Humanae*. He introduced into the Conciliar declaration that idea that religious freedom depends on an understanding of the institutional relationship between the state and other bodies in civil society and on the limited power of legal or juridical institutions to implement the fullness of the common good. Murray's key argument, in other words, was political—it concerned the power of the state and the laws implemented by the state.[36]

The state is essentially limited in power, especially in relation to religious faith and the Church. The argument for the limited power of the state has theological grounds. It goes back to the apostles' statement that "we must obey God rather than any human authority" (Acts 5:29), and to the medieval investiture controversy in which the popes defended the freedom of the Church by resisting attempts by princes to appoint bishops. Both of these arguments presuppose that the spirit of the human person transcends politics. This transcendence, which Murray following Jacques Maritain called "the primacy of the spiritual,"[37] means there is more to human beings than can be encompassed by politics and the state. This sets definite limits to the exercise of state power.

The relevance of this theological argument for the political realm comes from the fact that protection of the religious transcendence of the person and of the freedom of the Church have as a direct consequence the freedom of society from any form of absolutist control by the government. Society and state are distinct from one another. Just as there is more to the person than can be controlled by the state, so there is greater richness to life

265

in society than politics can encompass. A misguided effort to bring the totality of society under state control is the very definition of totalitarianism, and it should be opposed both in the name of the right to religious freedom and of human rights more generally. Citizens should be free from state control in their religious belief, which grounds the civil right to religious freedom. Analogously, citizens should also be free in other, broader ranges of their social life. Murray thus argued that religious freedom is linked with the full range of civil and political rights that are guaranteed by constitutional democracy and democratic self-government. In political life the person "is fully citizen, that is, not merely subject to, but also participant in, the processes of government."[38] The Catholic community's engagement in struggles for human rights and democracy in the decades since the Council has been an effort to live out this insight.

The approach to religious freedom taken by Murray and the Council had important implications for the relation between juridical and legal institutions and the broader domain of the ethical or moral. Because the state is limited, its reach does not extend to the promotion of the full moral reality of the common good that should be achieved in society, but only to the most basic moral requirements of social life that Murray and the Council called public order. Public order includes genuinely moral values, including public peace, justice, and those standards of public morality on which consensus exists in society.[39] These minimal moral standards are the concern of the government. But working for the attainment of the fullness of virtue and the totality of the common good is the vocation of the Church, of families, and of the many educational and cultural bodies that form civil society. The state's moral role is more limited: the protection of the basic requirements of peace, justice, and human rights that make life in society possible at all. This is the basis on which the Council affirmed that, when public order is at stake, law may legitimately limit human freedom, including religious freedom.[40]

This specification of when legal restraint is called for shows why the Afrikaners mentioned in the example above may be legally prevented from continuing with their racially separatist practices despite the fact that they claim these practices are required by their religious beliefs. Religious freedoms, like all human freedoms, are fundamental values, but they are not absolute. They are to be restricted only when and in so far as is strictly necessary to secure peace and justice. Murray called this the principle of the "free society," which affirms that each human person "must be accorded as much freedom as possible, and that this freedom is not to be restricted unless and insofar as necessary." Through his influence, this principle was enshrined in the *Declaration on Religious Freedom*. In words that Murray himself surely wrote, the Council declared, "The usages of society are to be the usages of freedom in their full range. These require that the freedom of the human person be respected as far as possible, and curtailed only when and insofar as necessary."[41]

Both the Council and Murray were thus very much aware of the link of the right to religious freedom with the full range of other freedoms. It was certainly not an accident, therefore, that the development of Church teaching on religious freedom that occurred at the Council stimulated new engagement by the Church on the broader global agenda of social justice, including the promotion of democracy. Recent experience has also shown that the promotion of freedom for religious communities removes that sense of oppression that often leads religious groups to feel that resorting to armed struggle is the only way to protect themselves and to bring their vision of society to the public realm. Protection of religious freedom is thus often a precondition for greater peace in society, both within countries and among them.[42] Thus in addition to helping move the Catholic community to greater engagement with issues of social justice and democratization, the Council's commitment to religious freedom also helped deepen the Church's engagement in the promotion of peace. The Catholic Church's strong engagement in the promotion of these broader issues of justice, democracy, and peace in the decades since Vatican II, of course, was not brought about solely by this new commitment to religious freedom. Additional factors surely include the Council's encouragement of deeper pastoral engagement with poverty in the developing world, its suggestion that the dangers posed by nuclear weapons require "a completely fresh appraisal of war,"[43] and its new support for interreligious dialogue and cooperation.

Nevertheless, the development of the Church's understanding of religious freedom brought about at the Council with Murray's help surely set the Catholic Church on a course that enabled it to make important contributions to justice and peace in society. My hope is that the movement along this course will see renewed vigor in the years ahead. The world is in great need of such a contribution to religious freedom, and to the justice and peace that is often linked with this freedom. By continuing on the path blazed by Murray and the Council, we can help respond to that need in our time as they did in theirs.

Notes

1. Donald Pelotte, *John Courtney Murray: Theologian in Conflict* (New York: Paulist Press, 1976), 3.

2 "City of God and Man," *Time*, cover story, December 12, 1960, 64.

3. See, for example, José Casanova, *Public Religions in the Modern World* (Chicago: University of Chicago Press, 1994).

4. For Murray's most influential discussion of the ethics of war and peace, see his "Remarks on the Moral Problem of War," *Theological Studies* 20 (March 1959): 40–61, reprinted in slightly revised form as chap. 11 of Murray's *We Hold These Truths: Catholic Reflections on the American Proposition* (New York: Sheed & Ward, 1960), 249–73.

5. See my "Religious Freedom, Morality, and Law: John Courtney Murray Today," *Journal of Moral Theology*, inaugural issue, 1, no. 1 (2012): 69–91. Online at: www.msmary.edu/jmt. See also my article written with Thomas A. Shannon, "A Balancing Act: Catholic Teaching on the Church's Rights—and the Rights of All," *America* 206, no. 7 (March 5, 2012): 23–26.

6. For the July 3, 2013, statement of the president of the U.S. Conference of Catholic Bishops on the final ruling issued by the U.S. Department of Health and Human Services on the provision of contraception coverage in health insurance, see "HHS Final Rule Still Requires Action in Congress, By Courts, Says Cardinal Dolan," online at the bishops conference website, at http://www.

usccb.org/news/2013/13-137.cfm. For the June 28, 2013, position of the Catholic Health Association, see "Overview of Final Rules on Contraceptive Coverage for Religious Employers and Other Religious Organizations," online at CHA website, at http://www.chausa.org/newsroom/women%27s-preventive-health-services-final-rule.

7. *We Hold These Truths*, introduction, esp. 9–15.

8. Since 1991 there has been a significant increase in the percentage of Americans who hold that religious leaders should not seek to influence government decisions or the way people vote. The belief that religion is "too political" is particularly strong among young Americans. See Robert D. Putnam and David E. Campbell, *American Grace: How Religion Divides and Unites Us* (New York: Simon & Schuster, 2010), 121.

9. Vatican Council II, "Declaration on Religious Liberty," in *Vatican Council II: Constitutions, Decrees, Declarations*, ed. Austin Flannery, revised translation (Northport, NY: Costello Publishing, 1996).

10. Vatican Council II, "Pastoral Constitution on the Church in the Modern World," in Flannery, *Vatican Council II*.

11. See Joseph A. Komonchak, "The Silencing of John Courtney Murray," *Cristianesimo nella storia: Saggi in onore di Giuseppe Alberigo* (Bologna: Il Mulino, 1996), 657–702; and Komonchak, "Catholic Principle and American Experiment: The Silencing of John Courtney Murray," *U.S. Catholic Historian* 17, no. 1 (1999): 28–44.

12. Vatican Council II, "Declaration on Religious Liberty."

13. Ibid.

14. Murray, "The Arguments for the Human Right to Religious Freedom," in *Religious Liberty: Catholic Struggles with Pluralism*, ed. J. Leon Hooper (Louisville, KY: Westminster John Knox Press, 1993), 238.

15. Vatican Council II, "Declaration on Religious Liberty."

16. Ibid.

17. Ibid.

18. Ibid.

19. See R. Scott Appleby, *The Ambivalence of the Sacred: Religion, Violence, and Reconciliation* (Lanham, MD: Rowman & Littlefield, 2000).

20. See Brian J. Grim and Roger Finke, *The Price of Freedom Denied: Religious Persecution and Conflict in the Twenty-First Century* (Cambridge: Cambridge University Press, 2011), xi–xii.

21. Ibid., 19.

22. See Francis M. Deng, "Sudan—Civil War and Genocide," *Middle East Quarterly* 8, no. 1 (Winter 2001): 13–21.

23. See Fredrick Nzwili, "Christians in Sudan Face Increased Hostility," from Religion News Service, July 16, 2013, online at *Washington Post* On Faith site, at http://www.washingtonpost.com/national/on-faith/christians-in-sudan-face-increased-hostility/2013/07/16/7c9ad0a4-ee4b-11e2-bb32-725c8351a69e_story.html.

24 Martha Nussbaum, *The New Religious Intolerance: Overcoming the Politics of Fear in an Anxious Age* (Cambridge: Belknap Press of Harvard University Press, 2012), esp. chaps. 1 and 6.

25. "France's Marine Le Pen Loses Immunity as MEP," *BBC News*, July 2, 2013, online at http://www.bbc.co.uk/news/world-europe-23142984. This report indicates that Le Pen's immunity from prosecution for the crime of inciting hatred because of her membership in the European Parliament was withdrawn by the Parliament on June 25, 2013. See the report from the Parliament's Committee on Legal Affairs online at http://www. europarl.europa.eu/sides/getDoc.do?type=REPORT&mode=XML&reference=A7-2013-236&language=EN.

26. Monica Duffy Toft, Daniel Philpott, and Timothy Samuel Shah, *God's Century: Resurgent Religion and Global Politics* (New York: W. W. Norton, 2011), 152.

27. Vatican Council II, "Pastoral Constitution on the Church in the Modern World" 19.

28. For a valuable set of studies of such nonviolent movements in recent politics, see Adam Roberts and Timothy Garton Ash, eds., *Civil Resistance and Power Politics: The Experience of Non-violent Action from Gandhi to the Present* (New York: Oxford University Press, 2009).

29. See Samuel Huntington, "Religion and the Third Wave," *National Interest* 24 (Summer, 1991): 29–42.

30. Toft, Philpott, and Shah, *God's Century*, chap. 4, esp. tables 4.1, 4.2, 4.3, and 4.4.

31. See Murray, *The Problem of Religious Freedom* (Westminster, MD: Newman Press, 1965), chap. 2, "The Tradition," esp. its treatment of the "freedom of the church" at pp. 47–64.

32. *Pacem in Terris* 8–27 affirms most of the human rights set forth in the *Universal Declaration on Human Rights. Pacem in Terris* is available on the Holy See's website, at http://www.vatican.va/holy_father/john_xxiii/encyclicals/documents/hf_j-xxiii_enc_11041963_pacem_en.html.

33. See *Universal Declaration of Human Rights*, Preamble, online at http://www.un.org/en/documents/udhr, and *Pacem in Terris* 1 and 8–9.

34. Murray, "The Declaration on Religious Freedom: A Moment in Its Legislative History," in *Religious Liberty: An End and a Beginning* (New York: Macmillan, 1966), 25.

35. For a discussion of this debate between Murray and those progressive, largely Francophone, theologians who wanted to affirm religious freedom strictly on the basis of freedom of conscience, see Richard J. Regan, *Conflict and Consensus: Religious Freedom and the Second Vatican Council* (New York: Macmillan, 1967).

36. Murray, "The Declaration on Religious Freedom," 31–32.

37. See Jacques Maritain, *Primauté du spiritual* (Paris: Plon, 1927).

38. Murray, "The Declaration on Religious Freedom," in *War, Poverty, Freedom: The Christian Response, Concilium* 15 (New York: Paulist Press, 1966), 13.

39. Vatican Council II, "Declaration on Religious Freedom" 7. See Murray's comment on this passage in footnote 20 of the Declaration in *The Documents of Vatican II*, ed. Walter M. Abbott and Joseph Gallagher (New York: America Press, 1966), 686.

40. Vatican Council II, "Declaration on Religious Freedom" 2.

41. Murray's statement of the "free society" principle is in his "Arguments for the Human Right to Religious Freedom," in *Religious Liberty*, ed. J. Leon Hooper, 239. The parallel sentence from the Council is from *Dignitatis Humanae* 7, as translated in Abbot and Gallagher, *The Documents of Vatican II.*

42. For an argument that advancement of religious freedom is today very often linked with similar advancement of other freedoms, rights, and peace, see Grim and Finke, *The Price of Freedom Denied*, chap. 7, "Do Religious Freedoms Really Matter?" For a particularly strong case on the link between religious

freedom and peace, see The Task Force on International Religious Freedom of the Witherspoon Institute, Timothy Shah, principle author, *Religious Freedom: Why Now? Defending an Embattled Human Right* (Princeton, NJ: The Witherspoon Institute, 2012), esp. part 2.

43. Vatican Council II, "Pastoral Constitution on the Church in the Modern World" 80.

Andrea Vicini, SJ

Conclusion
A RENEWED HOPE

Vatican II inaugurated a season of hope both in the history of the Church and of humankind. It is not, however, a naïve, generic, superficial, and vague hope. On the contrary, it is biblically inspired, theologically provoking, influenced by the historical context, and in dialogue with contemporary interlocutors. It is a hope expressing and embodying a vision of the Church and of its relation *ad intra* and *ad extra* that is prophetically transformative. With their expertise and love for the Church, the twelve prestigious scholars gathered in this volume helped us to uncover, define, and appreciate this hope. They guided our reflection first orally, at the occasion of the conference "The Legacy of Vatican II" at Boston College in September 2013, then in their expanded essays offered here.

Without aiming at an encyclopedic completeness,[1] I briefly point to the threefold concreteness and timeliness of hope generated by Vatican II that is discovered anew in this volume. First, this hope can be found in the selected theological and ecclesial *themes* that the Council addressed. John O'Malley vividly highlighted reconciliation, both as the Council's task and as its goal—an agenda that is still unfinished and badly needed. He also pointed out how even the Council's style—its demonstrative rhetoric—fostered reconciliation. Christoph Theobald stressed

273

the novelty of the Council's pastoral approach—its "pastorality" —which is centered on a new attention to the historical and cultural roots of the gospel's recipients and to how, in their diverse locations and situations, God is discovered already present and acting. Hence, the Council's call to reinterpret continually the whole revelation according to the experiences of those to whom the gospel is announced and transmitted. Peter Hünermann further shows how the epochal changes that were occurring in society and in culture at the time of the Council influenced the Council's renewed understanding of Christian faith. The Council's new hermeneutic approach keeps together how the believers express their faith and what they believe.[2] O'Malley, Theobald, and Hünermann show how the Council defines a specific style of Christian life that expresses faith in transformative praxes.

By focusing on these themes, Vatican II situated itself both in continuity with the whole Christian tradition and, at the same time, renewed this tradition in light of novel theological insights and style, and because of the Council's attention to human experience and to its contemporary challenges. Change had been prepared by the theological renewal preceding the Council and was stimulated by the engaged and open dialogue with the contemporary culture and society.

Leslie Woodcock Tentler, however, invites us to remember what the Council did not address (e.g., contraception) and how this absence challenged the hope generated by the Council. She shows how influential were the commitments of key players (in particular, Fr. John Ford, SJ). By briefly commenting on the debates concerning some provisions of the 2010 U.S. Affordable Care Act concerning contraception, David Hollenbach indicates how these unresolved issues loom for long in the history of the Church and of its relation with civil society. They shade and shake our hope.

Second, the realism of hope is further explored by examining the Council's *engagements* with civil society. Richard Gaillardetz convincingly highlights the Council's theological and practical willingness to embody humility as a constitutive way of being and of acting. Humility should continue to inform the ecclesial dynamics within the Church and with the world. John Baldovin traces the progressive implementation of the conciliar liturgical reform by focusing on three funerals involving the Kennedy family between 1963 and 2009. The choice of reflecting on the universal (even eschatological and cosmological) scope of the liturgy by examining it in the particular context of these three U.S. public events reveals how the liturgical reform addresses the relation (or, for some, tension) between the universal and the particular—between the universal and eternal celebration of our faith and the particularity of the historical contexts and social situations in which our faith is lived liturgically.

Lisa Sowle Cahill critically discusses the conciliar openness to the world and its overly optimist bias in envisioning the ecclesial interaction with civil society. Moreover, she highlights how the Council's focus on a certain interpretation of natural law and on the gospel, as well as the underlying personalism of the Council as foundations of Christian life and ethos, lead to unsettling dynamics within the public arena, which often are marked by conflicts and by tensions. These theological foundations are then expressed and articulated in diverse ways of living one's faith in today's world. Insightfully, for Cahill these ways can be summed up as neo-Augustinian, neo-Thomist, and neo-Franciscan in light of three major influences in Christian history and in today's practice. Finally, she remarks how the Council generated a profound hope in a greater involvement of the laity at all levels of ecclesial life. In the last fifty years, numerous positive examples and achievements actualize this conciliar hope. At the same time, however, Cahill notes how the empowerment of the laity is still an ongoing challenge.[3]

Lay Catholic communities contributing to promote grass-roots democracy constitute one of the success stories of the post-conciliar years—as Bradford Hinze carefully describes by focusing mostly on U.S. examples. The readers who are not familiar with the influence of these communities will be inspired, and their hope in an expanded and renewed Catholic role in fostering grassroots democracy will be strengthened.

In reflecting on engagements, the contributions of these four scholars sketch a portrait of the Council that is dominated by change and renewal more than by continuity. Moreover, the unfinished current state of this portrait makes it quite attractive—at least to hopeful people. The Council's hope continues to call for creative and ongoing implementations. In other words, the conciliar hope generates hope anew. This renewed hope asks us to be imaginative in keeping up reforming the Church's ecclesial, liturgical, and ethical dynamics as well as its ways of proceeding—at the institutional, communal, and social levels.

Third, the personalist approach that animated the Council is also highlighted by studying a selected group of *figures* who contributed to prepare the theological climate leading to the Council (i.e., Otto Semmelroth and Henri de Lubac) or who were "players" both in the years preceding the Council and during the conciliar works (i.e., Augustin Bea and John Courtney Murray). The Jesuit bias is evident and intentional. Without aiming at examining the overall Jesuit contribution to the Council, such a preference is not motivated by blindness to the outstanding influence of other relevant figures—lay or belonging to other religious orders. Instead, the focus on these four Jesuits is a further example of how particularity matters and demands inquisitive attention. The narratives and critical reflections provided by Jared Wicks (on Bea), Dennis Doyle (on Semmelroth), Susan Wood (on de Lubac), and David Hollenbach (on Courtney Murray) shed light on these four inspiring figures who, with their theological competence, passion for the Church, and creative genius contributed to the Council's success. These four Jesuits continue to illuminate our way of articulating theological reflection and to live our discipleship in today's Church and world. Their achievements give a concrete face to our hope and stimulate our endeavors.

In this volume, the twelve contributing authors remind us that our hope is rooted in the *past*. With them, we turned back to Vatican II, to study it in renewed ways. These authors helped us to appreciate the Council's theological richness, its novel language, and its vision. Nourished by this reappropriation of our past, hope is experienced and enjoyed in the *present*, by all those who constitute today's Church—laypeople, ministers, religious, clergy, and members of the Catholic hierarchy. On the latter,

O'Malley, Gaillardetz, Baldovin, Cahill, and even Faggioli in his introduction emphasize the renewal that the pontificate of Pope Francis is promoting. They highlight how Pope Francis's theological approach, style, and praxis generate hope of ecclesial transformation by making the Catholic Church more visibly a living embodiment of the gospel and of God's reconciling justice.

Finally, hope animates God's people to envision the *future* and to contribute in shaping it. Vatican II continues to tell us that tomorrow's Church will be the result of a collaborative and reconciling engagement, characterized by a privileged care for the poor, animated by the pursuit of religious freedom, strengthened by a reformed liturgy, in dialogue with other religions and with secular society, and fostered by grassroots communities.

Vatican II nourishes a hope that is *thematic, engaged,* and *personalist*—and that is shaped by remarkable figures and communities. Since the closure of the Council, these last fifty years have seen both major steps forward and disappointing setbacks in living out the Council's hope. As contemporary believers and readers, and with the help of the twelve scholars gathered in this volume, we receive the Council's heritage and witness. With renewed hope, and with the commitment that hope inspires, we will contribute to fulfill and even to expand the Council's way of being and of becoming Jesus' disciples in today's world and in history.

Notes

1. For remarkable essays studying Vatican II, see seven recent issues of *Theological Studies* (September 2012–March 2014, for a total of twenty-six articles) and one issue of *Recherches de Science Religieuse*, "Le concile Vatican II en débat" (1/2012).

2. To echo Theobald and Hünermann, Alain Thomasset, SJ, relies on "pastorality" and on a hermeneutic approach (inspired by Paul Ricoeur) to reflect on the heritage of Vatican II in theological ethics. See Alain Thomasset, "Dans la fidélité au Concile Vatican II: La dimension herméneutique de la théologie morale," *Revue d'Éthique et de Théologie Morale* 263 (March 2011): 51–61; Alain Thomasset, "Dans la fidélité au Concile

Vatican II: La dimension herméneutique de la théologie morale (suite et fin)," *Revue d'Éthique et de Théologie Morale* 264 (June 2011): 9–27.

3. For a further historical assessment of Vatican II and for an overview of the relevant contributions in theological ethics that the Council generated during the last fifty years, see James F. Keenan, SJ, "Vatican II and Theological Ethics," *Theological Studies* 74, no. 1 (2013): 162–90.

Contributors

John Baldovin, SJ, is Professor of Historical and Liturgical Theology at Boston College School of Theology and Ministry. He has taught at the Jesuit School of Theology at Berkeley and Fordham University. His latest book is *Reforming the Liturgy: A Response to the Critics* (Liturgical, 2008).

Lisa Sowle Cahill is J. Donald Monan, SJ, Professor of Theology at Boston College. She is a past president of the Catholic Theological Society of America (1992–93) and the Society of Christian Ethics (1997–98). She is a fellow of the American Academy of Arts and Sciences. In 2008 she received the John Courtney Murray Award, a professional achievement award, from the Catholic Theological Society of America, and is the recipient of eleven honorary degrees. Some of Cahill's books are *Global Justice, Christology and Christian Ethics* (Cambridge, 2013); *Theological Bioethics: Participation, Justice and Change* (Georgetown, 2005); *Bioethics and the Common Good* (Marquette, 2004); *Sex, Gender and Christian Ethics* (Cambridge, 1996); and *Love Your Enemies: Discipleship, Pacifism and Just War Theory* (Augsburg Fortress, 1994), which is being revised for a new edition.

Dennis M. Doyle is a Catholic theologian at the University of Dayton who specializes in ecclesiology. He earned his doctorate in religious studies from the Catholic University of America. He is the author of numerous articles and two books, *The Church Emerging from Vatican II* (Bayard, updated 2002) and *Communion Ecclesiology: Vision and Versions* (Orbis, 2000). He recently coedited *Ecclesiology and Exclusion: Boundaries of Being and Belonging in Postmodern Times* (Orbis, 2012). He spent the 2012–13 academic year as a guest professor at the University of Augsburg.

Massimo Faggioli is an associate professor of theology and director of the Institute for Catholicism and Citizenship at the University of St. Thomas in St. Paul (Minnesota). He is the author, among other books, of *Vatican II: The Battle for Meaning* (Paulist Press, 2012), *True Reform: Liturgy and Ecclesiology in "Sacrosanctum Concilium"* (Liturgical, 2012), *Sorting Out Catholicism: A Brief History of the New Ecclesial Movements* (Liturgical, 2014), and *Pope Francis: Tradition in Transition* (Paulist Press, 2015).

Richard R. Gaillardetz is the Joseph Professor of Catholic Systematic Theology at Boston College. He received his PhD in systematic theology from the University of Notre Dame and has since published numerous pastoral and academic articles while authoring or editing ten books, including *Keys to the Council: Unlocking the Teaching of Vatican II* (coauthored with Catherine Clifford; Liturgical, 2012) and *Ecclesiology for a Global Church: A People Called and Sent* (Orbis, 2008). In 2013–14 he served as the president of the Catholic Theological Society of America. He is currently the director of graduate studies in the Boston College Theology Department.

Bradford E. Hinze is professor and the Karl Rahner, SJ, Memorial Chair in Theology at Fordham University, New York. His publications include *Practices of Dialogue in the Roman Catholic Church: Aims and Obstacles, Lessons and Laments* (Bloomsbury, 2006); "The Prophetic Mission of the Local Church: Community Organizing as a School for the Social Imaginary," in *Ecclesiology and Exclusion: Boundaries of Being and Belonging in Postmodern Times* (Orbis, 2012); and "Talking Back, Acting Up: Wrestling with Spirits in Social Bodies," in *Interdisciplinary and Religio-Cultural Discourses on a Spirit-Filled World: Loosing the Spirits* (Palgrave, 2013).

David Hollenbach, SJ, holds the University Chair in Human Rights and International Justice at Boston College, where he teaches Christian social ethics. His research interests are in human rights, religion in political life, and issues facing refugees. He recently published *Driven from Home* (Georgetown, 2010) and *The Global Face of Public Faith* (Georgetown, 2003). He has regularly been visiting professor at Hekima College in Kenya. He assisted the National Conference of Catholic Bishops in drafting their 1986 pastoral letter *Economic Justice for All.* He received the John Courtney Murray Award for distinguished achievement in theology from the Catholic Theological Society of America.

Peter Hünermann taught dogmatic theology in Münster until 1982, when he accepted the appointment as professor of dogmatic theology in the Catholic theological faculty of Tübingen. Since 1997, he has been professor emeritus. Hünermann was past president of the Catholic Academic Exchange Service (KAAD) and founding president of the European Society for Catholic Theology. His main publications include *Jesus Christus: Gottes Wort in der Zeit. Eine systematische Christologie* (Aschendorff, 1997); *Dogmatische Prinzipienlehre: Glaube, Uberlieferung, Theologie als Sprach, und Wahrheitsgeschehen* (Aschendorff, 2003); *Herders Theologischer Kommentar zum Zweiten Vatikanischen Konzil* (with Bernd Jochen Hilberath, eds., Herder, 2004–5). He is editor of *Enchiridion Symbolorum: Definitionum et Declarationum der Rebus Fidei et Morum* by Heinrich Denzinger, 44th edition (Herder, 2014).

Mark S. Massa, SJ, is Dean of the School of Theology and Ministry at Boston College and Professor of Church History. A student of the American Catholic experience, his books include *Catholics and American Culture: Fulton Sheen, Dorothy Day, and the Notre Dame Football Team* (Crossroad, 1999, which won the Alpha Sigma Nu Award for best work in theology for 1999–2001) and his most recent monograph, *The American Catholic Revolution: How the Sixties Changed the Church Forever* (Oxford, 2010).

John W. O'Malley, SJ, University Professor at Georgetown University, is a historian of religious culture. His best-known book is *The First Jesuits* (Harvard, 1993) translated into ten languages. He has written extensively on Vatican II, including his monograph *What Happened at Vatican II* (Harvard, 2008). His two most recent books are *Trent: What Happened at the Council* (Harvard, 2013) and *The Jesuits: A History from Ignatius to the Present* (Rowman & Littlefield, 2014). In 1995 he was elected to the American Academy of Arts and Sciences and in 1997 to the American Philosophical Society.

Leslie Woodcock Tentler is Emerita Professor of History at the Catholic University of America, where she specialized in the history of American Catholicism. Her most recent book is *Catholics and Contraception: An American History* (Cornell, 2004). She is also the editor of *The Church Confronts Modernity: Catholicism since 1950 in the United States, Ireland, and Québec* (The Catholic University of America Press, 2007). Her current research concerns the reception of Vatican II reforms in the United States, particularly in the context of tensions over race.

Christoph Theobald, SJ, is professor of fundamental and dogmatic theology at the Facultés Jésuites de Paris–Centre Sèvres. He teaches in the history of exegesis; the history of dogmas, systematic theology, and spiritual theology; aesthetics; and practical theology. He is the chief editor of *Recherches de Science Religieuse* and of the authorized critical edition of the works of Karl Rahner. He serves as director of the *Unam Sanctam* collection and is a member of the scientific committee of the Istituto per le scienze religiose—Fondazione Giovanni XXIII in Bologna. Among his ten volumes are *Le christianisme comme style: Une manière de faire de la théologie en postmodernité* (Cerf, 2007); *"Dans les traces" de la constitution "Dei Verbum" du concile Vatican II* (Cerf, 2009); *La réception du concile Vatican II. 1: Accéder à la source* (vol. I, Cerf, 2009).

Andrea Vicini, SJ, MD, received his PhD in theological ethics from Boston College and the STD from the Faculty of Theology of Southern Italy. He is associate professor of moral theology at the Boston College School of Theology and Ministry, member of the Planning Committee of Catholic Theological Ethics in the World Church, coeditor of the *Moral Traditions Series* (Georgetown), and editorial consultant of *Theological Studies*. Among his publications are *Genetica umana e bene comune* (San Paolo, 2008; Portuguese translation, 2011); "Bioethics: Basic Questions and Extraordinary Developments," in *Theological Studies* (2012); "La loi morale naturelle: Perspectives internationales pour la réflexion bioéthique contemporaine," in *Transversalités* (2012); and "Le neuroscienze e la bioetica," in *La Civiltà Cattolica* (2014).

Jared Wicks, SJ, gained his ThD in the Faculty of Catholic Theology of the University of Münster with a dissertation on Luther and then taught at the Jesuit School of Theology in Chicago 1967–79. He moved to the Gregorian University in Rome for teaching from 1979 to 2004, with service as Dean of the Theology Faculty 1991–97. He served on world-level Lutheran-Catholic dialogues on ecclesiology, and after moving to John Carroll University in 2004, he worked on the U.S. Lutheran-Catholic dialogue on *The Hope of Eternal Life* (2011). Fr. Wicks is now scholar-in-residence at the Pontifical College Josephinum, Columbus, Ohio, where he prepares reports for ongoing Lutheran-Catholic dialogues and researches Vatican II for articles and reviews in *Gregorianum, Catholic Historical Review, Theological Studies,* and *Ecumenical Trends*.

Susan K. Wood, SCL, a Sister of Charity of Leavenworth, Kansas, is professor and chair of the Department of Theology at Marquette University. Very active in ecumenical work, she serves on the U.S. Lutheran-Catholic dialogue (1994–present), the North American Roman Catholic-Orthodox Theological Consultation (2005–present), the conversation between the Roman Catholic Church and the Baptist World Alliance (2006–10), and the International Lutheran-Catholic Dialogue (2008–present). She is an associate editor of *Pro Ecclesia* and serves on the editorial advisory board of the journal *Ecclesiology*. Some of Wood's books are *Spiritual Exegesis and the Church in the Theology of Henri de Lubac* (Wipf and Stock, 2010), *Sacramental Orders* (Liturgical, 2000, also translated into Spanish), and *One Baptism: Ecumenical Dimensions of the Doctrine of Baptism* (Glazier, 2009). She is currently president-elect of the Catholic Theological Society of America.

Index

Catholic Health Association, 250

Catholicism: anti-Semitism and, 10–11; Church history and, xiii, 12–13; Church-world relationship and, 15–16; community organizing and, 152–53; conservative Catholics and, 142–43; current trend in, 143–44; ecumenism and, 9–10; grassroots democracy and, 153–56, 262; Hispanic influx in United States and, 142; *Human Vitae* as litmus test for loyalty to, 78; identity of, 137–39, 275; liturgical reform and, 122; multiculturalism and, 8–9; openness to modern world and, 130–33, 145n1, 228, 275; positive public contributions of, 263–68; post–Vatican II, 261; promotion of peace and, 267–68; shift in political stance of, 262; social movements and, 152; Tradition of Church and, 15; Vatican II and modern, xi, xiv. *See also* Church

Catholicism and Democracy (Perreau-Saussine), 154, 177n4

Center for Applied Research of the Apostolate (CARA) of Catholic University, 132, 143–44

Central Preparatory Commission, 194–95, 197

Chambers, Ed, 164, 174–75

Change, 10–11, 13–16, 26–27, 35, 38–39, 94, 131. *See also* Epochal transition of faith; *specific type*

Charity, 101–2, 136–38, 193

Chauvet, Louis-Marie, 134–35, 147n27

Chenu, Marie Dominique, 155

Chomsky, Noam, 36n3

Christ: as Alpha and Omega, 237; anthropology in light of, 233–34; Church and, 95–96, 98–100, 104–6, 190–91, 210, 213–14, 218–19; *Dei Verbum* and, 98–99; Eucharist and, 55, 94, 117; *Gaudium et Spes* and, 238–39; grace of, 99–100, 247n56; living with, 215; Mariology and, 208–11; membership in body of, 192–93; mystery of, 31, 47–48, 236; sacrament of, 212, 216; Schillebeeckx and, 242, 247n56; sin and, 134; total, 213–14, 216; way of, 33–34. *See also* Christology

Christian community, formation of, 31. *See also* Faith-based communities

Christian Family Movement, 160, 166

Christian lifestyle, 50, 135

Public religious expression,
256–63

Quintilian, 17

Rahner, Karl, 49, 60n36, 117,
126n21, 138, 206–7, 222n14,
224n28
Ratio fidei, 46, 48–50, 56
Ratzinger, Joseph Cardinal,
116, 125n6, 185–86
Reason and faith, 45–46, 56
Reasoning, importance of, 33
Reconciliation, 4–7, 9, 11, 15–17,
20–23, 103, 237, 273
Reformation, 6
Relativization, 29–30
Religious conflict, 259
Religious freedom:
conservative Catholics and,
142–43; contraception and,
250; democracy and, 12;
denial of, 257–59; *Dignitatis
Humanae* and, 96, 252–53,
263; discussions about, 12;
faith and, 249–52, 254, 256,
263; Murray and, 248–49,
251–52, 262–63, 265–68; as
personal reality, 252–56;
public religious expression
and, 256–63; question of, 12;
Unitatis Redintegratio and,
96; in United States, 250–51;
Vatican II and, 252–56,
262–63, 264–68. *See also
Dignitatis Humanae*
Religious persecution, 257–58
Religious pluralism, 9–11, 35

Rerum Novarum, 11–12
Res et sacramentum, 117
Ressourcement, 152, 192
Reuss, Josef Maria Bishop, 70
Reveille for Radicals (Alinsky),
163–64, 167–68
Revelation, 28–29, 42, 45,
47–49, 53, 56, 98–101, 103, 195,
215, 234–35, 274
Rhetoric, 17–21
Ricci, Matthew, 8
Rock, John, 65, 80n7
Roman Missal, new, 112–13,
119–20
Rush, Ormond, 99, 108n24

Sacrament, 13, 47, 55, 135, 194.
See also Church; *specific
type*
Sacramental polarity, 214–15
Sacramental theology,
135, 210
Sacrosanctum Concilium
("On the Sacred Liturgy"):
Austin and, 116–17; change
and, 14; discontinuity
between Vatican II and
Church Tradition and, 55;
Gaudium et Spes and, 117;
humility of the Church
and, 93–94; multiculturalism and, 8–9; mystery and,
47; need for reform and,
93–97; ordination and,
116–17; pastorality and, 18;
pilgrim Church and, 95;
resistance to, 116, 118; timing
of approval of, 109; voice of

God and, 32–33. *See also*
Liturgical reform
Salvation, 45, 47, 55–56, 90, 99,
105, 140, 206–10, 213, 216–17,
227, 231, 243
Same-sex marriage, 120–21,
142
Satter, Beryl, 164, 179n28
Schillebeeckx, Edward, 206,
227, 241–43, 247n56
Schooyans, Michel, 154, 176n1
Science and faith, 45
Scientific Revolution, 7
Scotus, John Duns, 44, 49,
58n21
Searle, John R., 52
Seckler, Max, 53
Second revolution, 26
Second Vatican Council. *See*
Vatican II
Secretariat for Christian
Unity, 5
Secularization, 237–38
Self-abasement, 88
Self-assessment, 88, 90–97
Self-celebration, 88
Self-knowledge, 88
Semmelroth, Otto: being
Christian and, 210–11;
Church as bride and,
213–14, 219; Church as
sacrament and, 211–12,
216–20, 222n16, 223n17;
co-redeemers and, 211;
context of contributions of,
205–8; *De ecclesia* and,
206–7; *Die Kirche als
Ursakrament* and, 204–7,

211–17; *Gaudium et Spes*
and, 203; grace and, 209–11,
215–16; lay-inclusive
ecclesiology and, 208,
212–13, 223n18; *Lumen
Gentium* and, 204–8;
Mariology and, 208–11, 216,
218, 224n28; Rahner and,
206–7; sacramental polarity
and, 214–15; time between
Die Kirche als Ursakrament
and Vatican II and, 217–20;
trinitarian approach to
Church and, 215–16; *Urbild
der Kirche* and, 205, 208–11;
Vatican II and, 203–5, 220,
221n3
Shah, Timothy Samuel, 261,
270n26
Sheeben, Matthias J., 206
Sheil, Bernard J., 163–64
Shifts provoking authority
crisis, political and social,
11–13
Shoah, 257
Signs of the times, reading, xi,
32, 129–30
Sin, 13–15, 21, 47–48, 73, 75, 95,
108n20, 117, 130, 134, 240
Skorka, Rabbi Abraham, 22
Smulders, Pieter, 196–97, 206
Sobrino, Jon, 139
Social equality, 136–37
Social ethics, 131–33, 134–39.
See also Moral theology
and ethics
Social movements and
Catholicism, 152